ON A
DATE

A GUIDE TO
ROMANCE

JOHN GRAY, Ph.D.

Vermilion

This edition published in 2003 by Vermilion,
an imprint of Ebury Publishing
A Random House Group company

First published in the United States in 1997 by Harper Collins
First published in the United Kingdom in 1997 by Vermilion

The Random House Group Limited Reg. No. 954009

Addresses for companies within the Random House Group can be found
at www.randomhouse.co.uk

A CIP catalogue record for this book
is available from the British Library

Penguin Random House is committed to a sustainable future for
our business, our readers and our planet. This book is made from
Forest Stewardship Council® certified paper.

MIX
Paper from
responsible sources
FSC® C018179

Printed and bound in Great Britain by Clays Ltd, St Ives plc

ISBN 978-0-09-188767-4

To buy books by your favourite authors and register for offers visit
www.randomhouse.co.uk

Contents

Acknowledgments

I thank my wife, Bonnie, for once again sharing the journey of developing a new book. Parts of this book are directly inspired by the beginning of our relationship when we moved through the five stages of dating.

I thank our three daughters, Shannon, Juliet, and Lauren, for their continued love and for their insight and brilliant feedback regarding many of the ideas in this book. A special thanks to Shannon for managing my office while I wrote this book.

I thank the following family members and friends for their suggestions and valuable feedback to the ideas in this book: my mother, Virginia Gray; my brothers David, William, Robert, and Tom Gray; my sister, Virginia Gray; Robert and Karen Josephson; Susan and Michael Najarian; Renee Swisko; Ian and Elley Coren; Trudy Green; Martin and Josie Brown; Stan Sinberg; JoAnne LaMarca; Bart and Merril Berens; Reggie and Andrea Henkart; Rami El Batrawi; Sandra Weinstein; Bill Sy; Robert Beaudry; Jim and Anna Kennedy; Alan and Barbara Garber; and Clifford McGuire.

I thank my agent, Patti Breitman, who has always been there at every step of this book, and I thank my international agent, Linda Michaels, for getting my books published around the world in over forty languages.

I thank my editor, Diane Reverand, for her expert feedback, direction, and advice. I also thank Laura Leonard, Meaghan Dowling, David Flora, and the other incredible staff members at HarperCollins for their responsiveness to my needs. I could not ask for a better publisher.

I thank the thousands of individuals and couples who have

taken the time to share with me their insights and stories about being single and getting married.

I thank Bonnie Solow, Robert Geller, and Daryn Roven for their assistance in producing the audio version of the book as well as Anne Gaudinier and the other staff members of HarperAudio.

Introduction

In past generations, the challenge of dating was different. Men and woman wanted a partner who could fulfill their basic needs for security and survival. Women looked for a strong man who would be a good provider; men searched for a nurturing woman to make a home. This courting dynamic, which has been in place for thousands of years, has suddenly changed.

The new challenge of dating is to find a partner who not only will be supportive of our physical needs for survival and security but will support our emotional, mental, and spiritual needs as well. Today we want more from our relationships. Millions of men and women around the world are searching for a soul mate to experience lasting love, happiness, and romance.

It is no longer enough to just find someone who is willing to marry us, we want partners who will love us more as they get to know us: we want to live happily ever after. To find and recognize partners who can fulfill our new needs for increased intimacy, good communication, and a great love life, we need to update our dating skills.

Even if by good fortune you find a soul mate, without the right dating skills, you may not recognize him or her and get married. Eighteen years ago I was lucky enough to meet my soul mate but not skilled enough to make the relationship work. Bonnie and I dated for about a year and half. Although we loved each other very much, we didn't get married.

We broke up and went our separate ways. Four years later, we got back together. This time, because we dated differently, we eventually got married and have lived happily ever after. By creating the right conditions for love to grow, our hearts opened, and we experienced a "soul love," which "loves no matter what." Discovering this un*conditional* love was the result of first creating the right *conditions* for love to grow.

The first time we dated, we eventually knew we loved each other, but not enough to get married. We hadn't yet felt the inner knowing that comes when the right conditions are satisfied. Without an updated approach to dating and relationships, we mistakenly concluded that we were not right for each other.

The second time we dated, with a new understanding of how men and women are different, we were able to make our relationship work. As we grew together in love, our hearts opened. It was then that we were able to experience unconditional love for each other. We were soul mates. With this confidence I proposed marriage and she was able to accept.

As a relationship counselor, I began sharing these new insights in counseling sessions and in my seminars. The results were dramatic and immediate. With this new understanding of how men and women think and feel differently, couples were able to improve communication and start getting what they wanted in their relationships. With renewed hope, they were able to find a deeper love in their hearts, heal and release the old resentments that may have closed their hearts, and rekindle the fires of romance and passion.

Encouraged by these practical benefits in my own marriage and in the lives of my clients and seminar participants, I went on to write *Men Are from Mars, Women Are from Venus*, which has now sold more than ten million copies worldwide. A bestseller in more than forty languages, it has helped men and women around the world.

My office continues to receive more than three hundred calls and letters a day from people who have greatly benefited from the book and workshops. Besides the seminars that I personally teach each month, hundreds more Mars/Venus workshops are being given around the world by trained Mars/Venus facilitators. While this simple message has been helpful to so many couples, something was still missing for singles.

Repeatedly, singles and dating couples have raised questions that were not directly answered or dealt with in *Men Are from Mars, Women Are from Venus*. In the process of finding practical answers to their questions over the last twelve years, the ideas, principles, and insights of *Mars and Venus on a Date* were formulated. This book is directly written for singles and dating couples who are interested in finding true and lasting love.

Yet married couples will also find these principles and insights invaluable. Couples who are happily married can enjoy these ideas from the perspective of how they can add to the playfulness and romance in their relationship. No matter how good a relationship is, there is always room for growth. Even the best athletes still listen to their coaches for feedback and direction.

Married couples who are experiencing difficulty in their marriage may discover what is missing in their relationship. Quite often couples skipped one or two stages of dating, and this affects their marriage adversely. By going back and going through the dating stages, many couples have reunited in love.

Married couples who want to rekindle the romance of dating will benefit greatly from this practical guide. By reviewing the elements of a great date and putting them into practice, they can once again experience the passion and romance they felt in the beginning. By applying these simple insights, they will not only rekindle the fire of passion but learn how to keep it burning.

The insights contained in *Mars and Venus on a Date* provide practical answers for the most common frustrations singles and dating couples experience. So often in our dating relationships we misunderstand and misinterpret our partner's actions and reactions. With a correct understanding of our different ways of thinking and feeling, dating can be a source of joy, support, pleasure, and fulfillment, instead of a potential source of frustration, discouragement, worry, and embarrassment.

With this new approach, the clouds of confusion associated with dating begin to clear away. As you read *Mars and Venus on a Date* and begin to experience the practical benefits of this shift in your dating approach, you will begin to discover that you already know a lot more than you thought. When a few missing pieces of the puzzle are found, suddenly everything can fall into place.

Supported by this new approach, you will find the motivation, skill, and confidence necessary to find the right person for you while you enjoy the dating process. As you read though this book, the feelings that you have deep in your soul will be validated. This commonsense approach explains all of the most frustrating moments of dating and provides a clear plan for success.

No book can tell you if a person is right for you, but a book can point you in the right direction and assist you in creating the right conditions so that you can know. When the principles and insights of *Mars and Venus on a Date* are put into practice, you will be prepared to meet and recognize your soul mate.

This book has many suggestions that may not be right for

everyone. They are only suggestions. More than anything, this book will provide you with the information to assess a situation and to make the right decisions for you.

As with my other books, there are many generalizations about men and women. This does not imply that all men are one way or all women are another way. It just means that many men and many women are that way. If you don't perfectly fit the generalizations, it doesn't mean something is wrong with you. When you meet someone whose behavior is different from yours, pull out your copy of *Mars and Venus on a Date* and use it as a guide to help make sense of that.

Some people may be tempted to keep this book a secret. It definitely gives you an edge in knowing how to win over the opposite sex. But there is an even greater benefit in letting your date know that you have read it. If you both agree with many of the principles and values, you will be able to trust each other more right from the beginning.

Discussing the ideas in *Mars and Venus on a Date* is a great way to get to know someone. Many dating couples have done this with *Men Are from Mars*. Reading *Mars and Venus on a Date* together during the various stages of dating will be even more useful.

Sometimes it is difficult to discuss your wants and needs in a relationship. If this book fairly represents what you want, then it will assist you in communicating that to your partner. One of the greatest values of these insights is that they are expressed in language that is fair and supportive to both sexes. You can talk about the differences between Martians and Venusians without stepping on each other's toes.

If the values in this book resonate with who you are but they don't resonate at all with a potential partner, it may be a clear sign that that person is not right for you. This is not always the case, though. Someone may just not like my style of writing about dating, love, and relationships. Even if he or she is closed to reading a book about relationships, it doesn't mean this is not the right person for you.

The real test is going through the stages and seeing if you can get your needs met. Even if your partner doesn't read *Mars and Venus on a Date*, you will gain the power to bring out the best in him or her when you read it. Then you will know if this is the right person for you.

Women commonly make the mistake of quoting authorities to change a man's behavior. Even if a man likes my books it is a good idea not to quote from them. Particularly with men, a request for change is best heard when it is personal and based on what you feel is right for you and not what a book says is right.

For years women have asked me how to get a man to read *Men Are from Mars, Women Are from Venus*. The answer is the same with this book. A woman should ask a man what he thinks about some of the ideas that describe men. By asking him to read that section to answer her questions, she is not implying that he needs this, but that he is the expert about men and that his expertise could help her. Men love to be experts and they like to be helpful. As he reads the text, he may find that it is very interesting and helpful for him as well. After all, if he is from Mars, how is he supposed to understand Venusians?

When *Men Are from Mars, Women Are from Venus* was first published, mainly women bought it. As more men heard about it, this trend changed dramatically. Now, after it has been a bestseller for four years, men buy it just as much as women. Men are also interested in having better relationships; they simply needed to discover that it was a "male friendly" book.

Another approach to motivate a man to read this book is

simply to ask him to do it as a favor to you. You should not imply that he needs it, but that you would love to discuss it with him and that it would help you. When approached the right way, many men are happy to read it. Some men just don't read. If that's the case, lend him a copy of the book on tape or watch the videos together for fun. These same suggestions could also apply when a man wants a woman to read the book.

As you read *Mars and Venus on a Date*, lightbulbs will go on in your mind. Suddenly things that never made sense will start to make sense. This shift will help prepare you to find and meet your soul mate. When you can clearly understand your past mistakes in this new light, you will not have to repeat them. With this new understanding, you will be released from past patterns and be free to create the relationship of your dreams. You will quickly discover that you do have the ability to find the right person for you.

It is a great pleasure for me to share *Mars and Venus on a Date*. It is the culmination of twelve successful years of assisting millions of people like you to improve communication with the opposite sex. By successfully understanding and meeting the challenges of each of the five stages of dating, you too will find true and lasting love.

April 4, 1997
Mill Valley, California

This book is dedicated with deepest love and affection to my soul mate and wife, Bonnie Gray. Her radiant love continues to bring out the best in me.

1

Mars and Venus on a Date

During my relationship seminars, single women often come up to me and describe in great detail what they thought was a wonderful date. The question that follows is almost always the same. Every one of these women says, "I can't understand why it didn't work out." If everything went so well, each wonders, why didn't he want to pursue the relationship? To most women, men are still a mystery. Their questions often reveal a complete misunderstanding and misinterpretation of men.

Women ask:

- How do I attract the right guy for me?
- Why do men talk so much about themselves?
- Why don't men call back?
- Why don't men commit?
- How do you get a man to open up?

- Why do I have to do everything to make this relationship work?
- Everything is great, but my partner doesn't want to get married and I do. What can I do?
- Why do I keep getting involved with the same kind of guy?

A woman's questions tend to revolve around one issue: How do I secure a loving, lasting relationship? Women want to make sure they can get what they need in a relationship. Men, on the other hand, have different questions. Their questions focus on making sure they are successful in their relationships but also reveal a misunderstanding and misinterpretation of women.

Men ask:

- How do I know what a woman wants?
- Why are women so indirect about things?
- Why do we start arguing about the littlest things?
- Why can't a women just say what she means?
- How do I know if she is the one?
- Why does she always want to talk about the relationship?
- Things are fine now, so why rock the boat and get married?
- Why do women ask so many questions?

Although men's and women's questions reflect different orientations toward dating, they do have two things in common: Men and women want their relationships to be loving, and they definitely don't understand each other. We feel powerless at times to get what we want in our relationships. It might seem hopeless, but it is not. Once men and women learn how they approach dating and relationships differently, then we have the necessary information and insight to begin finding the answers to our questions. Without a deeper understanding of our differences, it is inevitable that we will continue to misinterpret our dating partners and create unnecessary problems.

HOW WE UNKNOWINGLY SABOTAGE RELATIONSHIPS

When we misinterpret each other, it can cause us to sabotage our relationships unknowingly. A woman may mistakenly conclude her date is "just another man incapable of making a commitment" and give up. A man may think his date is another woman whose needs may smother him and take away his freedom. As a result, he loses interest.

No matter how sincere you are, if your partner is misinterpreting your innocent and automatic reactions and responses, your attempts to create a relationship may be unsuccessful. It is not enough merely to be authentic in sharing yourself; to succeed in dating you need to consider how you will be interpreted as well. For this reason there are times when we cannot just "be ourselves." Instead, we must hold back our initial gut reactions and measure our responses in ways that will communicate where we are coming from.

> It is not enough to merely be authentic in sharing yourself; to succeed in dating you need to consider how you will be interpreted as well.

Making sense of the opposite sex frees us to make decisions and choices conducive to getting what we want, but in a way that works. To do this, it is essential that we have a deeper understanding of the different worlds we come from. While I have explored many of these differences in my previous book *Men Are from Mars, Women Are from Venus*, there are many issues specifically relevant to being single that were not covered.

A deeper understanding of single men and women can be immensely helpful in navigating through the five different stages of dating: attraction, uncertainty, commitment, intimacy, and engagement. With this new insight, it will be easier to interpret each other's behavior correctly and act accordingly.

THE FIVE STAGES OF DATING

Stage One: Attraction

In stage one of dating, we experience our initial attraction to a potential partner. The challenge in this first stage is to make sure you get the opportunity to express that attraction and get to know a potential partner. With a clear understanding of how men and women approach dating differently, you will be able to put your best foot forward.

Stage Two: Uncertainty

In stage two, we experience a shift from feeling attraction to feeling uncertain that our partner is right for us. The challenge in this stage is to recognize this uncertainty as normal and not be swayed by it. To become uncertain doesn't mean that someone is not right for you. When you are dating someone who seems really special to you, it is quite normal suddenly to wonder whether you wish to continue dating that person. Without an understanding of this stage, it is too easy for a man to drift from one partner to another and for a woman to make the mistake of pursuing a man more than he is pursuing her.

Stage Three: Exclusivity

In stage three we feel a desire to date a person exclusively. We want the opportunity to give and receive love in a special relationship without competition. We want to relax and have more time to share with our partner. All of the energy that went into looking for the right person can now go into creating a mutually loving and romantic relationship. The danger in this stage is that we become too comfortable and stop doing the little things that make our partners feel special.

Stage Four: Intimacy

In stage four we begin to experience real intimacy. We feel relaxed enough to let down our guard and share ourselves more deeply than before. The opportunity of this stage is to experience the best in ourselves and our partner, while the challenge to deal with our less-than-best sides. Without an understanding of how men and women react differently to intimacy, it is easy to conclude mistakenly that we are just too different to proceed.

Stage Five: Engagement

In stage five, with the certainty that we are with the person we want to marry, we become engaged. In this stage we have the opportunity to celebrate our love. This is the time to experience our relationship joyfully, happily, peacefully, and lovingly. This is a time of great excitement and promise.

Many couples make the mistake of rushing into getting married. They do not understand that this is a vital time to gather positive experiences of sharing together and resolving disagreements and disappointments before the bigger challenges of being married, moving in together, and having a family. This stage provides a strong foundation for experiencing a lifetime of love and romance.

Throughout *Mars and Venus on a Date,* we will explore in great detail the five stages of dating and the various questions that come up in each stage. Each chapter will provide you with fundamental insights about how men and women approach dating differently so that you can correctly interpret your partner and then choose to respond in ways that will not be misunderstood. In this way you will make use of every opportunity to create the relationship of your dreams.

DATING CAN BE MUCH EASIER

Whether you are starting over, just starting to date, or have been dating for years, one thing doesn't seem to change: Dating is awkward and has definite moments of pain and discomfort. For some people, one of the primary motivations for getting married is to avoid dating. Yet dating doesn't have to be so dreary or difficult, nor does it have to seem endless. As a matter of fact, if you are looking for that special someone, the fastest way of finding him or her—and being found—is to create positive dating experiences.

The fastest way of finding a special partner or being found by someone is to create positive dating experiences.

Knowing what to expect in each of the five stages of dating makes it incredibly easier. For example, in the first stage—attraction—when a woman understands why a man doesn't call back the next day, even when he is attracted and interested, it frees her from worrying unnecessarily. By learning a new approach for calling him that doesn't minimize her position with him, it frees her even more to enjoy the dating process: no more sitting by the phone wondering when he will call.

In a similar way, this understanding of our differences makes the whole process of dating much easier for a man. For example, when a man understands exactly what women need and what he needs to do to satisfy those needs, then it gives him the confidence that he can succeed in winning over the woman he wants and loves. Quite often, what he would want is not necessarily what she wants. By learning these differences, he can understand what to do at each of the five stages.

THE POWER OF PREPARATION

When we are prepared for what is to come, we are not thrown off guard, nor do we have to doubt ourselves. When our relationships make sense to us, we don't make as many mistakes; we are also able to learn from mistakes and are thus released from making the same mistakes again and again. With this understanding of differences, we can be released from repeating negative patterns.

> Learning from mistakes helps prevent
> the repetition of negative patterns.

Understanding that men are from Mars and women are from Venus will not necessarily make any date a lasting relationship, but it will make the process of dating more fun, more comfortable, and more rewarding. Sometimes it will help you to realize sooner that you are with the wrong person. This clarity will make it easier for you to move on to finding the right person. The sooner you discover that a person is not right for you, the sooner you can move on and find the right person.

Through understanding the five stages of dating, you will clearly know where you are and where you want to go. When you are stuck in a pattern, you will be able to realize how to break free and move on. Without a doubt, when you are ready to fall in love with your soul mate, someone you connect with from your soul, your mate will be there. Through taking the risk of following your heart and exploring relationships with the intent to find the right person for you, you are preparing yourself to find true and lasting love.

2

Finding the Right Person for You

Finding the right person for you is like hitting the center of a target in archery. To aim and hit the center takes a lot of practice. Some people may hit the center right away, but most do not. In a similar way, most people date several people before finding the right one. Some people take much longer than necessary because something is missing in their approach. By exploring this metaphor from archery, we can clearly see what may be lacking.

Imagine that you aim for the target and you miss. Your shot is too far to the left. By simply acknowledging that you went too far to the left, your mind will automatically self-correct, and next time you will shoot more to the right. Through a series of attempts, your mind will continue to self-correct and you will eventually hit the target.

It is the same in relationships. Each time you go out and discover that this is the wrong person for you, your mind

9

will self-correct, and next time you will feel more attracted to someone who is closer to being the right person. To make this self-correction in the kind of person we are attracted to or find interesting, we must clearly experience how far off the mark a shot was.

If we are way off the mark, then we know to compensate a lot. If we are closer to the mark, then we compensate much less. In a similar way, if someone is clearly far from our type, then we need to compensate a lot, but if he or she is close, then we should compensate only a little. Correctly assessing someone is important for fine-tuning our ability to be attracted to someone who is either right for us or at least closer to the target.

If you were blindfolded and every time you got closer to the target someone misdirected you, you would probably never hit the target. To self-correct after each shot, we need to get the correct feedback. With accurate information we can make the necessary adjustments in our next trajectory. Eventually we will just aim and hit the target.

GOOD ENDINGS MAKE GOOD BEGINNINGS

How we end a relationship and how we evaluate a date are essential to fine-tuning our ability to be attracted to the right person for us. The secret of making sure one relationship leads you to another one, closer to what you want, is to pay a lot of attention to how you end a relationship. How you end a relationship has an enormous impact on the quality of your next relationship. Good endings make good beginnings.

When you end a relationship feeling either resentful or guilty, it is much harder to move on to find a person who is right for you. Quite often, when a relationship ends, we may feel angry that our partner let us down or didn't fulfill our expectations. Women most commonly feel that they gave a lot to a relationship and they didn't get what they needed in return. As a result, they feel resentful. Men, on the other hand, tend to feel more guilt. They feel bad that the relationship didn't turn out well and guilty if their partner felt unfulfilled.

Although these dynamics—men feeling guilty and women feeling resentful—are common, it can also be the other way around. Generally the person who feels most rejected or abandoned feels resentful. The rejecter feels guilty. In either case, the result is the same. We end a relationship with a closed heart.

Without an open heart, it is much more difficult to find the right person. When our hearts are open, we are able to be attracted to and even fall in love with the right person, or at least make progress in finding someone closer to the right person. When our hearts are open, we can be assured that we are getting closer to our goal. When our hearts are closed, however, we tend to repeat the same experiences.

REPEATING PATTERNS

When we end a relationship with resentment or guilt, we are attracted to someone who will help us deal with unresolved feelings and issues. Everyone has the experience of making a mistake or doing something that he or she regrets. It is perfectly normal to think back and feel, "I wish I hadn't done that," or, "I wish I hadn't said that," or, "I wish I hadn't reacted that way," and then feel, "I wish I could go back and do it differently."

It is human nature to want to go back and fix things or change things that we regret. When we regret a relationship, our automatic tendency is to be attracted to another person we will regret meeting. We will repeat this pattern until we get it right. On the other hand, when we feel positive about a dating experience or an exclusive relationship that ended, we gain the ability to self-correct and move on. Instead of repeating the pattern the next time, we are attracted to someone closer to what we want.

STAYING TOGETHER TOO LONG

One of the reasons people end relationships with negative feelings is that they stay together too long. They do not recognize they are with the wrong person and move on. Instead, they try too hard to make a relationship work. They either try to change their partner or try to change themselves. In the process of trying to fit together, they make things worse. In trying to make a relationship that is close to the right one into the right one, they create frustration and disappointment. In the process of trying to make things better, they bring out the worst in their partner and themselves.

This explains why so often after breaking up, many couples find that they can be better friends. When they were together, they would fight because deep inside they were either trying to change their partner too much or changing themselves too much in order to make the relationship a marriage. After they gave up trying to make a relationship more than it was, they could relate in a much more friendly and loving manner.

When you try to fit a square peg into a round hole, it is just not going to fit no matter what you do. In the process of trying to make a fit when there isn't a real fit, unnecessary struggle and strife are created. At a certain point you need to recognize when a partner is not a fit and move on.

Bill and Susan dated for three years. After the first two

years, Bill was not sure he wanted to be with Susan and Susan tried to convince him that they could make it work. The longer they tried, the worse things became. Susan was always suspicious that Bill was interested in other women. Although he stayed faithful, she would ask him questions all the time about what he was doing, where he was going, and how he felt about her. Susan became closed and mistrusting, while Bill reacted by feeling trapped, irritable, and distant. Finally, after many bitter arguments about trivial things, they broke up, both feeling rejected and angry.

Instead of bringing out the best they had to offer, their relationship brought out their worst sides. They would argue and bicker all the time. Certainly they were also lacking good communication skills, but even that would not have saved their relationship. They were not right for each other, but didn't know how to end the relationship.

WHEN LOVE IS NOT ENOUGH

As Bill and Susan moved through the first three stages of dating, everything had been fine, but in the fourth stage it went downhill. As Bill got to know Susan, he began to think he was not right for her and she was not right for him. He loved her, but he didn't want to marry her.

This didn't make sense to him, and it definitely did not make sense to Susan. She would feel his hesitancy in continuing their relationship and confront him. She would say, "If you love me, then why don't you want to be with me? How can you just end this relationship? It's not fair. I thought you loved me. How can you love me and want to leave me? We have something special. You're just afraid of intimacy. You're not giving us a chance. . . ."

Bill's only answer was the same, "I love you, but I don't

feel you are the one for me." Susan could not hear this, and finally they had so many arguments that they broke up. They couldn't even decide where to go to eat without getting into an argument.

Neither Bill nor Susan knew that it was perfectly healthy to get to know a person, fall in love, and then discover that this person is not the right one. Instead of ending their relationship with love, they ended it because they had so many arguments that they just didn't like each other anymore. Without this important insight, many people end relationships by focusing on the negative instead of by focusing on the positive.

HOW DO YOU KNOW WHEN SOMEONE IS RIGHT?

Quite often single people ask, "How do you know if someone is right?" When you ask people who know they are with the right person, they will generally say something like, "Well, I don't exactly know what to tell you—you just know."

When soul mates fall in love there is simply a recognition. It is as clear and simple as recognizing that the sun is shining today, or the water I am drinking is cool and refreshing, or the rock I am holding is solid. When you are with the right person you just know. This knowing is not in any way dependent on a long list of reasons or qualifications. Soul love is unconditional. When the right person comes along you "just know," and you spend the rest of your life discovering why he or she is the right person.

While this answer is true, it is also very misleading. It could imply that if you don't "just know," you are with the wrong person. This is not necessarily true. The most accurate answer to this question is that you "just know" when you have created the right conditions to know, when your heart opens and you happen to be with the right person. If you open your heart and you happen to be with the wrong person, then you "just know" that you are with the wrong person.

This knowing who you want to spend your life with comes from opening your heart. Even if you are with the right person, you cannot "just know" if you do not first create the right conditions to open your heart to someone. Moving through the five stages of dating creates the right conditions for you to develop the ability to "just know" when the right person comes along. It also allows you to "just know" when you are with the wrong person. Once you are able to "just know," then the easy part is to find or be found by the right person. Each decision you make will lead you closer to hitting the target.

WHAT MANY SINGLE PEOPLE DON'T UNDERSTAND

Many single people don't understand this basic truth. They mistakenly believe that if you love someone, you should want to have a relationship with them. This is not right. The closer someone is to being the right person, the more you will be able to see him or her as worthy of your love, but still this might not be the right person for you. Just because you love someone doesn't mean he or she is the one for you.

Many people become confused when they fall in love. They think that if you love someone you should want to be together forever. If you break up, they mistakenly assume that you didn't *really* love them and as a result they feel betrayed. People do not realize that love is not enough. If they discover that their partner is not right, either they feel guilty ending the relationship or they unnecessarily focus on what does not work in the relationship in order to justify leaving.

Some people will automatically become more critical and

judgmental to justify ending a relationship. When couples don't know how to end a relationship with love, they bring out the worst in their partners and the worst in themselves. Not only is this unnecessary, but it makes it more difficult to find the right person next time.

WHAT IT TAKES

In most cases it takes both time and progression through the five stages before you can recognize your true life partner and soul mate. Certainly there are games and manipulations to make someone love you and want to marry you, but if a person is not right for you, then you will not necessarily live happily ever after. One of the reasons there is so much divorce today is that people do not move through the five stages. They rush through them or skip a few stages.

> There are games and manipulations to make someone love you and want to marry you, but this doesn't ensure that he or she will be right for you.

It was fine in previous generations to marry someone without first getting to know him or her, because the need for security was the basis of marriage. Our ancestors were primarily motivated to find a mate in order to secure their survival and the survival of children. In our parents' generation, they learned to be loving and grew to love each other. But this did not guarantee that romance would last.

For most couples in history, marriage meant the end of romance. Never in history has lasting romance been associated with marriage. If we are to find a partner with whom our love and passion can grow, he or she must be very special—someone picked out and recognized by our soul. It is a decision made in our hearts that sometimes feels as though it were made in heaven.

FINDING A SOUL MATE

A soul mate is someone who has the unique ability to bring out the best in us. Soul mates are not perfect, but perfect for us. While they can bring out the best in us, without good communication skills they can also bring out the worst in us, and vice versa. We are not just physically turned on to them; our soul gets turned on as well.

There are basically four kinds of chemistry between dating partners: physical, emotional, mental, and spiritual. Physical chemistry generates desire. Emotional chemistry generates affection. Mental chemistry creates interest. Spiritual chemistry creates love. A soul mate includes all four.

PHYSICAL ATTRACTION IS NOT ENOUGH

Physical chemistry alone is very short-lived. A man can easily be turned on by a seductive woman who promises sexual gratification without any strings. For many young men, just the opportunity for sex causes physical chemistry. After a few brief encounters of physical passion this chemistry will quickly dissipate.

I was amazed as a counselor to discover a striking pattern. Quite often women who were extremely attractive, who looked like models and movie stars, and in some cases were, would share the same complaint. Their husbands were not sexually attracted to them. I was dumbfounded. I couldn't imagine any available man not being attracted to these women. Yet it was true. I eventually realized why.

These women had been pursued by men who were primarily sexually attracted to them but didn't really get to know them. When a man feels sexual chemistry, quite often he *thinks* he knows a woman; he feels interested in her, he likes her, he even thinks he loves her. The real test is whether he still likes and loves her after he gets to know her. Although it may feel like love, it is not necessarily real or lasting. When a relationship passes the test of time, the love is real.

These men who stopped being attracted to their partners did not betray these women. Both partners were responsible. They put too much emphasis on the physical aspect of the relationship and didn't create the opportunity to know and love each other enough to discover if they were soul mates.

When physical chemistry is not backed up by chemistry in the mind, heart, and soul, then it cannot last or grow in time. Once the pleasures and passions of the body are experienced without corresponding passions of the mind, heart, and soul, the physical chemistry will dissipate. Physical attraction can be sustained for a lifetime only when it springs from chemistry of the mind, heart, and soul as well.

THE SOUL AND LASTING LOVE

The soul is that aspect of who we are that is most lasting. When the soul is attracted to someone and recognizes a mate, then with that person, because we experience a soul chemistry, the physical, emotional, and mental chemistry can also be sustained. Lasting physical attraction must find its source in our souls.

On the level of the soul, you are the same throughout your life. The person who was a little child is the same person you are now. You are you all of your life. The soul is that part of you that doesn't change. The way you physically look, the way you feel, and the way you think about things, however, do change.

The most change happens on the physical level. Everything on the physical plane is always changing. As we progress to the emotional plane, we change less. All adults can easily reflect back and still feel many of the feelings they had in childhood or young adulthood. On the mental plane, change is even less. We tend to be interested in the same sort of things our entire lives. Certainly there is some change, but definitely not as much as on the physical level. On the soul plane we are always the same.

The soul is who you are when you strip away the body, mind, and heart. Your soul has a potential that takes an entire lifetime to be fully realized. When a couple are soul mates, when their souls recognize and love each other and they are attracted to each other physically, emotionally, and mentally, then this love not only can last but can continue to grow and become richer as the years pass. This does not mean that everything will flow easily and effortlessly. It simply means you have the potential to be successful.

OPENING OUR HEARTS

In the early stages of dating, when our hearts are not fully open to each other, we depend on our feelings of attraction and interest to find the right person. Feelings of attraction and interest can only lead us into a relationship that meets our emotional needs. Once we begin to get our emotional needs met in a relationship, our hearts begin to open and we experience real love and intimacy. As we get to know our partner with love, it is still not certain that we will pick him or her as our soul mate.

We may feel a deep soul love, but still that person may not be the one. Finding a deep and lasting love does not mean that a person is the perfect person for you. When some people mistakenly assume that loving a person means marriage, they can never open up to feel the love in their hearts because they are not sure that they want to marry that person.

This catch-22 happens a lot to men. A man can sense that a woman wants to know if he loves her. He doesn't want to share those feelings because, if he does, she will expect him to marry her and be greatly hurt if he doesn't. In romantic movies, loving someone meant that you wanted to marry her. In real life, it is not always the case.

MARRIAGE IS A CHOICE

Marriage is a choice, but not like any other choice. You don't marry just any person you love. Instead, you first find love and then you are capable of making the right choice. As we have already explored, the experience of real love for a person doesn't necessarily mean he or she is the one for you. The experience of real love does connect us to our soul. With this connection, we are then able to know what our soul wants to do.

Choosing a soul mate is not a mental decision based on the pros and cons of a relationship. It is not an emotional decision based on comparing how a person makes you feel. It is not a physical decision based on how a person looks. It is much deeper. When our soul wants to marry our partner, it feels like a promise that we came into this world to keep.

It feels as if we are supposed to be together and share our lives.

When our soul wants to marry our partner, it feels like a promise that we came into this world to keep.

When our soul wants to get married, it feels as if we have no choice. We have to do it if we are to be true to ourselves. It is this kind of commitment that can sustain a lifetime of love. It empowers us to make the necessary sacrifices and overcome the inevitable challenges that come with marriage; it graces us with the experience of incomparable joy and fulfillment.

Many people mistakenly associate love with the right person for marriage because it is only when our hearts are open, and filled with love, that we can truly know someone and know the truth in our hearts. We can pick the right person only when our hearts are open, but it is also true that we can know for sure that a person is wrong only if our hearts are open as well.

With a clearer understanding of this, we are then free to end relationships without feeling guilty or resentful. Instead of feeling betrayed because someone loved us and rejected us, we can instead realize, "Yes, you loved me, but we were not right for each other. I was not the one for you. I feel disappointed and hurt, but I can forgive you and wish you well. Now I can move on to finding the right person for me." Let's look at an example.

When Bill Rejected Susan

When Bill rejected Susan, her attitude was, "We could have made this work if only you had made a commitment to me, if you had only gotten help. If you had cared more and tried harder, we could have made this work. If you had not given so much of your time to your work and been more supportive of me, then we could have gotten married and lived happily ever after. But no. You had to ruin everything and give up. My life is ruined by this. You were the person for me and now you have wasted three years of my life."

In personal counseling she would pine away, feeling, "How can someone you love so much not be the right one? Why does this relationship have to end?" When I assured her that she would find someone better, she just wouldn't believe it.

To some extent, almost anyone who has ever been rejected in a relationship that ended has felt some of Susan's feelings. Certainly, it is normal to have these kinds of feelings, but they must be released and replaced by positive feelings of love and forgiveness.

When Susan Got Involved Again

After about three months, Susan did get involved again. She fell deeply in love with Jack. Everything was moving along fine for about a year, but then Susan realized that Jack was wrong for her. She loved Jack, but as she got to know him better, she realized that he just wasn't the right person for her.

When she tried to end her relationship with Jack, he kept asking her to reconsider and try again. Susan felt guilty leaving Jack because he was feeling so hurt. They tried for a few more months, but eventually Susan saw that it was just going to get worse. She actually heard Jack say things about her that she had told Bill when he wanted to leave her.

It was then that Susan was open to knowing that you could love someone but not want to marry him. In personal counseling sessions, Susan was finally able to forgive Bill. She could now understand why he left. Before, she just didn't get it. With this new understanding, she was now able to think about Bill in a friendly way; she was able to release the resentment she felt in her heart.

She was also able to end the relationship with Jack without feeling guilty or bad. In her heart, she knew that Jack was not right for her and that if she was going to find the right person for her, then she would have to move on. In the past, she would have felt guilty and dragged out the relationship until things got really bad. This time she was able to move on, feeling compassion for Jack but not guilt. She was grateful for the time they had shared, but she was now ready to end the relationship.

Within three more months, Susan met Tom. They quickly moved through all five stages of dating. Within nine months, they were married. They are soul mates and have been living happily together for the last twelve years. They expect to share the rest of their lives together. Now Susan is very grateful that Bill was courageous enough to follow his heart and end the relationship. Bill also moved on eventually to find his soul mate.

Susan's story illustrates the importance of understanding that love is not enough and the importance of ending relationships in a positive manner. By eventually letting go of their resentments and feelings of guilt, Susan and Bill were able to find their soul mates.

PREPARING OURSELVES

The first challenge in the process of dating is to give up searching for your soul mate and instead focus on preparing yourself so that you can recognize your soul mate when he or she appears. Most people find or are found by their soul mates when they are not really looking. When you are ready your soul mate will appear.

> Most people find or are found by their soul mates when they are not really looking.

A big part of preparing ourselves is getting to know ourselves. As teenagers, we are still getting to know what it means to be masculine or feminine. Dating the opposite sex is exciting because we are getting to know not only the opposite sex but ourselves as well. When we are younger we date not to find a soul mate but to learn about ourselves and explore our feelings of attraction.

These feelings of attraction are generally crushes. We may think we love someone, but we are really infatuated. We are thrilled by the anticipation of being with someone, and then when we actually get to know the person we are not so excited. Certainly we are experiencing some genuine attraction, affection, and interest, but it has not yet ripened into real soul love. Going through this process is, however, an important part of preparing to find the right person.

Sometimes, after a relationship fails or if we feel rejected, even if we are much older, we will need to date for a while just to feel good about ourselves as a man or woman. Once we feel secure that we are attractive to the opposite sex, then we are ready to move beyond the first stage of dating and more seriously consider an exclusive relationship.

AUTONOMY IS THE BASIS FOR INTIMACY

In our twenties we are generally getting to know ourselves as autonomous beings separate from and not fully dependent on our parents. We need to experiment and explore who we are, what we like, what we don't like, what we can do, what we need, and what we don't need.

As we become more autonomous and
mature, we automatically begin looking
for more in our relationships.

Even at sixty-five, if we have just ended a long-term relationship or marriage, in many ways we are once again like a twenty-year-old. Our first test is to once again find a sense of autonomy. This sense of autonomy is the basis of intimacy. When we are on the rebound, instead of looking for someone to share with, we are like a hungry person looking for food. We are just looking for someone to feed us. To be ready for intimacy and thus able to recognize the right person, we must first be able to feed ourselves. Only then can we enjoy feeding and being fed by a partner.

Regardless of what age we are, as we begin to feel more independent and autonomous, we are not satisfied with dating just anyone attractive, nice, or interesting to us. We want something more than just a good time or fun together. We want a deeper and richer opportunity to know someone and to be known. Quite automatically we begin to feel the need to explore what a loving, exclusive relationship could offer.

SOUL MATES ARE NOT PERFECT

Another important insight about soul mates is that they are never perfect. They will not have everything on your list of ideal qualities. They come with baggage. They, like you, have good days and bad days. They may not look the way you thought they would look, they may have flaws that you don't like very much. They are not perfect, but when your heart is open and you know them, they are somehow perfect for you.

The love you spontaneously feel for a soul mate is the foundation for learning to share your life with someone who in many ways is very different from you. That love motivates you to cooperate, respect, appreciate, cherish, and admire that person. In this process, which is not always easy or comfortable, you become a better person. Your soul has a chance to grow.

When a caterpillar makes its transformation into a butterfly, it is not an easy process. The little butterfly struggles to break free of the cocoon. In that very process of struggling to get out, the butterfly exercises its wing muscles and builds up the necessary strength to fly. If you compassionately cut open the cocoon to make it easier for the butterfly, it will never gain the strength to fly. Instead it just dies.

If your life partner did not challenge you in some ways, the best would not be drawn from you. Soul mates are the perfect partners to bring out the best in us, and sometimes that is done by having to work through issues. In a marriage, you have to overcome all kinds of negative tendencies—being too judgmental, critical, selfish, compliant, demanding, needy, rigid, accommodating, righteous, doubtful, impatient, and so on. A soul mate gives you the opportunity to rise above these tendencies. When your dark side surfaces, you become stronger and more loving by exercising the love you feel deep in your heart to resolve an issue. In this process your soul, like the butterfly, has a chance to fly free.

WHEN YOU CAN'T MAKE UP YOUR MIND

If you are the type who expects perfection, you may never be satisfied with one person unless you are first able to open your heart. When we can't make up our minds about a person, the secret of success is to give the relationship a chance until you clearly "just know." Then if this is the right person, you get engaged. If not, you break up and don't look back for at least a year. Let's look at an example.

Richard is forty-seven years old. He has never been married, but has dated hundreds of women. He is attractive, charming, and successful, and he wants to get married. There have been some special ones, but he was never able to settle down. There was always something missing. This is how he describes these special women:

Sarah was wonderful; she was bubbly and energetic, everything that I am not. I like how I feel around her. We almost got married, but she didn't want to move and I didn't want to move.

Carol always loved me just the way I was. She loved being with me and we had a great time together. She was really so wonderful, I really couldn't ask for more, except that she wasn't bubbly and energetic like Sarah.

Mary was the most beautiful woman I have ever met. She was smart and successful, and I always felt proud when I was with her in public. I thought about marrying her, but she wasn't as accepting as Carol was. Carol liked everything about me. With Mary I felt I had to stay on my toes. I liked that feeling, but I don't think I could live my life like that.

Richard could go on for hours and hours comparing women. The bottom line was that he was expecting one woman to have it all. The more he experienced women, the more good qualities he wanted in his soul mate. Richard was always comparing because he was looking for perfection. He wanted all he could get.

THE IMPORTANCE OF EXCLUSIVITY

Besides not knowing that a soul mate is not perfect, the main reason Richard would get caught up in his head was that he was never just seeing one woman at a time. He was never in an exclusive relationship. He didn't give himself the chance to open his heart with just one woman. After being attracted to one woman, instead of staying with her during the uncertainty stage, he would feel uncertain and begin comparing and looking elsewhere. He always had a back door, someone he could be with if this one didn't work out.

Before he could open up to a woman and risk being rejected, he would have another one lined up. As a result, he never had the chance to be exclusive with one woman for more than six months. In all his special relationships, he would skip the exclusivity stage and move to stage four (intimacy) and then back to stage two (uncertainty).

While feeling uncertain he would then notice other women and pursue them. By moving back and forth between stages and between partners, he was never able to find the knowledge in his heart that a woman was either right or wrong for him.

Why Richard Couldn't Commit

Certainly there were childhood experiences in Richard's past that aggravated this tendency, but his inability to commit had roots in his failure to move through all of the first four stages. It had never been explained to him why it was so important to be exclusive as a preparation to recognizing the right person. He thought he should first recognize and be intimate with the right person and then be exclusive, rather than be exclusive (stage three) and then intimate (stage four).

Still, he looks back at many of the women he has loved and feels that four or five would have been perfect if only they were a little different. He still wonders, "Maybe she was the right one; maybe she was the best I could get."

Although Richard does not feel resentful or guilty, he does

feel incomplete. He isn't clear about whether any of these women was right or wrong. Unless he finally gives himself a chance to find out by being exclusive with just one, he will never find out.

Unless he learns that shooting in a certain direction is definitely wrong, he will never be able to self-correct and shoot in another direction to hit the target. In his mind, he is still thinking that four or five different directions might be the way to go. By ending relationships in an incomplete manner, he has unknowingly sabotaged his ability to find a soul mate. One of these women might already be his soul mate, and he doesn't even know it.

His only hope is to stop comparing and looking for perfection. He should find a woman to whom he is attracted, who clearly has some potential, and pursue her through the first four stages. Then he will finally gain the ability to "just know." Even if he "just knows" this one to be the wrong one, at least he knows. From there, he will find some completion to make sure his next relationship is closer to the mark.

WHEN A MAN CAN'T COMMIT

While Richard is incomplete about his past relationships, Jason, who is thirty-two years old, is seeing six women concurrently. He just can't make up his mind. He feels, "So many wonderful women, how can you decide?" It is hard for him to make a decision because he is stuck in stage two (uncertainty) and then jumps ahead to stage four (intimacy).

He will date a woman for a few weeks or months. As they really get to know each other and experience some real intimacy, his doubt comes up and he gets involved with one of his other girlfriends, since he has not yet committed himself to exclusivity. By going back and forth, he is not and will never be able to make up his mind and settle down.

Just as Jason is making a mistake to be seeing so many women, the women who date Jason are making a big mistake as well. They are willing to have sex with him and they are not in any way being assured by him that he is exclusive. These women make the common mistake of pursuing a man more than he is pursuing them.

Jason will talk to one partner about the problems in his life, which include his difficulties in his relationships with other women. This kind of intimate discussion is completely inappropriate and it ends up making the man more ambivalent. A woman should not behave with a man as if she is exclusive or intimate if he is still working through issues with other women. And she should not mistakenly believe that if she listens sympathetically to him, he will become convinced she is the one for him.

When a woman makes the mistake of dating a man and behaving as if she is in an exclusive, intimate relationship, when in truth the man is seeing other women, then it will be very difficult for the man to ever become clear and recognize her as his soul mate.

INCREASING DISCERNMENT

Each time we use dating as an opportunity to move through the different stages, our ability to discern and recognize the right person increases. Even the wrong person becomes the right person to help us self-correct and move on. Through making sure that you relate appropriately to the stage of the relationship you are in, your chances of eventually finding the right person for you go up dramatically.

This understanding of the five stages of dating will prepare you to recognize when true and lasting love is possible with a particular person and when it is not. The time you spend in any relationship is not a loss if you learn from it and complete it in a positive way. Each time you follow your heart and then plainly recognize that someone is not right for you, then you are definitely one step closer to finding the right person for you.

WHY COUPLES ARE WAITING TO GET MARRIED

Recent marriage statistics reveal that both men and women are waiting longer to get married. Some people worry that this is a problem, when really it is a sign of greater wisdom in young couples. They are waiting to get married. They are wanting to first get a sense of who they are, what they can do, what they want to do, and where they are going before deciding to make a marriage commitment. It is wise to first know yourself before trying to share yourself in a marriage.

> It is wise to first know yourself before trying to share yourself in a marriage.

When people get married before feeling autonomous, they run the risk of being too dependent on each other for love. They do not get the opportunity to experience sufficient independence to discover how they can be fulfilled without having a partner to depend on. Instead of taking a few more years to fully release their dependence on their parents and become dependent on themselves, they shift from their parents to a partner for love and support. By rushing into an intimate relationship, they can miss the opportunity to discover the inner confidence, self-assuredness, and autonomy necessary to make a marriage work.

Just as living separately from our parents is an important part of growing up, living separately from the opposite sex is equally important. Finding fulfillment through living alone or sharing a dwelling with friends of the same sex provides a strong foundation for eventually being able to share a life with someone of the opposite sex.

> **Just as living separately from our parents is an important part of growing up, living separately from the opposite sex is equally important.**

When we are not fulfilled through our work and friendships, then we are attracted to someone who can fill us up rather than someone we can share with. Instead of coming together to overflow, we come together primarily to fill up. With this understanding it becomes clear that being fulfilled as a single person is the basis of finding the right person and being successful in marriage.

THE WISDOM OF GOING SLOWLY

This does not mean that a couple cannot succeed if they get married early; it just means that there will be extra challenges. If a couple are in doubt, then—particularly if they are in their twenties—they should go slowly. The sad truth is that many married couples are soul mates but they do not know it. The process of dating and preparing to get married was in some way missed, and as a result they never really find their soul connection. This is not to say that once married they cannot find it, but it is much easier to find by thoroughly going through the five stages of dating.

Ultimately, taking the time to really get to know someone is the secret of success. The old saying, "To know him is to love him"—of her, of course—applies to a soul mate. Moving through the five stages ensures that you get an opportunity to fully know someone and experience the best of that person before getting married.

Certainly it is possible to be lucky and just get married right away to someone without going through all the stages, but for most people, to know they are with the right person and to ensure that after they get married the passion will be sustained, it is extremely useful to move through each of the five stages before getting married.

If you have perfected all the dating skills presented in this book, it does not mean that you can take *any* relationship through the five stages of dating and get married and live happily ever after. But by applying these insights you will gain the ability to recognize and find the right person for you and assist that person in recognizing you.

3

Stage One: Attraction

Although feelings of attraction are automatic, in
order to sustain attraction in a personal relationship we must
also be skillful in presenting ourselves in ways that are not
just appealing to the other sex but supportive as well. It is
not enough to say, "Here I am; take me as I am." The
alchemy of creating a loving relationship is a very delicate
balance of give-and-take. The blending together of male and
female must be done in gradual stages.

In stage one, quite often it is the anticipation that we can
get what we need or want from a relationship with a potential partner that tends to sustain attraction. Without a clear
message that we can get what we need, the attraction will
disappear. It can be so easy to misinterpret our date's
actions and reactions and be turned off simply because we
think and feel so differently. One of the biggest challenges
in the beginning of a relationship is to sustain the feeling of

attraction and give it a chance to grow as we get to know someone.

EXPRESSING YOUR MOST POSITIVE SELF

To sustain attraction in stage one, we must express our best and most positive self. Without an understanding of the customs and manners on Venus, a man can put his best foot forward and unknowingly turn a date off. Most men just don't understand the way women feel and what they are looking for. When a man is interested in a woman, quite automatically he treats her the way he would want to be treated. In many cases, that is not what a woman will appreciate. While trying to impress her he inadvertently turns her off. To various degrees, most men are simply clueless when it comes to understanding women.

> **Without an understanding of the customs and manners on Venus, a man can put his best foot forward and unknowingly turn a date off.**

For example, instead of taking the time to listen and get to know his date, a man talks about himself or his theories about life. He thinks this will impress her, and because she keeps asking questions, he thinks this is what she wants. When she does get a chance to talk, he mistakenly assumes she is asking for his advice and begins offering solutions to her problems or answers to her questions. Without even knowing why or how, he begins to turn her off.

Larry brought Phoebe to a restaurant for their first official date. I happened to be sitting next to them at another table. I observed that throughout the whole dinner Larry did all the talking. He spoke like a professor to his class. Phoebe always looked him the eyes, listened attentively, and with a little smile she nodded her head now and then. It was a sad sight.

When Phoebe would occasionally say something, instead of drawing her more into the conversation, Larry very quickly started expounding again. It was easy to tell that he really liked what he was saying, but it was also easy to see that Phoebe was being polite but felt bored and left out.

What could have been a delightful evening was a disappointment for both. They never connected because Larry did all the talking.

If Larry had understood Venusians, he would have asked Phoebe more questions to draw her out. If Phoebe had understood Martians, she would have just interrupted and talked more instead of continuing to politely listen and ask questions.

A man doesn't instinctively understand manners on Venus. In some ways he is like a bull in a china shop, oblivious of the effect he is having. He doesn't realize that a woman will feel most supported and impressed when he listens with interest rather than talking about himself or giving advice. This small insight can make a world of difference.

ASKING FOR HER NUMBER

What makes dating difficult is not understanding the opposite sex. A man wonders if he should ask a woman for her number or not. He wonders how to get it. He wonders if she is attracted to him.

He doesn't realize his power to win her over and become attractive to her. He doesn't realize how he starts becoming more attractive to her by:

- first initiating eye contact
- just noticing her

- politely and casually looking her over as she looks away
- being interested in getting to know her
- liking her
- being attracted to her
- taking the risk of introducing himself
- asking some friendly questions
- looking at her when she talks
- giving her his full attention
- complimenting her
- letting her know at the end of the conversation that he would like to call her (It can be so simple to say, "I'd like to give you a call.")

Whenever a man does something to make a woman feel special, in her eyes he becomes more attractive. Women have said in my seminars that even if they are not at first attracted to a man, his interest makes him more attractive. If he takes the risk of asking for her number or asking her out, she is inclined to say yes just because he took the risk. It makes her feel special and she feels flattered.

When a man can do all of the above without being dependent on getting anything else other than the pleasure of getting to know her, this makes him even more attractive. A woman can sense if a man's ability to feel good about himself is dependent on her responses to his advances. If she has to care too much about his needs, if she has to be overly sensitive not to hurt his feelings, then he becomes less attractive. When she is free not to worry about him, but simply enjoy the fact that he cares about her, then she becomes more attracted to him. Most men don't realize the incredible power they have to sweep a woman off her feet. The understanding of how we are different gives a man that power.

HOW WOMEN MISUNDERSTAND MEN

Women also misunderstand men. A woman often mistakenly assumes that if a man is the right man for her, he will know what she wants and will automatically consider her needs and do the things she does to show that he cares. When he doesn't fulfill this unrealistic expectation, then she becomes unnecessarily frustrated and discouraged.

For example, a woman will make the mistake of demonstrating her interest by asking a man a lot of questions. As he talks she continues to listen patiently. She assumes that if she listens with great interest, he will be more interested in her. This is true on Venus, but not true on Mars. The more a man talks, the more interested he becomes in what he is talking about. For a man to become more interested in a woman, she needs to do more of the talking and authentically share herself in a positive manner.

And how a woman talks can make a world of difference. On Venus, when two friends get together they enjoy the opportunity to share freely the mishaps, frustrations, disappointments, and complaints of the week. A woman's willingness to "share all" is actually a compliment to the other woman. It is a sign of trust, goodwill, and friendship.

> On Venus, friends enjoy the opportunity to share freely the mishaps, frustrations, disappointments, and complaints of the week.

While this gesture on Venus may be "putting your best foot forward," on Mars it is not. A man can easily get the wrong impression. When a woman dwells on negative feelings or problems in her life, instead of valuing her willingness to share openly, a man mistakenly assumes that she is difficult to please. Just as a woman is attracted to a man who shows interest in her, a man is attracted to a woman who clearly can be pleased. When she appears to be difficult to please, he may easily become turned off.

**A man is attracted to a woman
who clearly can be pleased.**

To create the ideal opportunity to experience the best a man has to offer and for a man to experience her best, a woman needs to be careful to share the positive side of her life and avoid dwelling on negative experiences. Conversation should be light, not heavy, focused on current events in the world and in their lives, but discussed in a positive manner.

This does not imply in any way that she should be fake. Authenticity is what makes anyone most attractive. Everyone has a positive and negative side, everyone has ups and downs, and everyone has a needy side and an autonomous side. Putting her best foot forward means sharing her most positive side, her up side, and her autonomous side. Later on she can share the other part. It is just a matter of timing.

To make the best impression and to get to know someone most effectively, it is important that we first get a chance to know the positive side. In the first three stages of dating—attraction, uncertainty, and exclusivity—it is best to focus on putting forth our best self. After getting to know our best sides, then in stage four, intimacy, we are ready to deal with the less positive sides of who we are.

**After getting to know our best sides,
we are ready to deal with the less
positive sides of who we are.**

Then, when we experience the challenges that come up in any relationship, we are much more capable of being accepting and understanding. Too much intimacy, too quickly, can cause women to become needy and men to pull away. Just as men have a tendency to rush into physical intimacy, women make the mistake of rushing into complete emotional intimacy.

WHEN A WOMAN GIVES ON A DATE

A woman commonly assumes that by giving a man the support she would want, he will become more interested in her. To put her best foot forward, a woman makes the mistake of treating a man the way she would want to be treated. She eagerly responds to his attentiveness by being overly interested in him. She responds to his consideration by being overly considerate of him; when he is of assistance to her she immediately wants to return the favor instead of just smiling and saying thank you.

A woman doesn't instinctively understand that after being receptive to a man's advances and appreciating his efforts, she doesn't owe him anything. She has already given him what he most wants. She has given him the opportunity to know her, please her, and connect with her. A woman needs to remember that she is the special one. It is the man's pleasure to have the opportunity to be with her. When she does not hold this attitude, it makes it difficult for a man's attraction to grow.

> After being receptive to a man's advances
> and appreciating his efforts, a woman
> doesn't owe a man anything.

When a man is attracted to a woman, he gets excited because he anticipates that he can make her happy and that in turn makes him feel really good; it brings the best of him out. The anticipation of more is very important to keep him interested. If he feels completely satisfied, then there is no distance for him to continue traveling to pursue her. Distance not only makes the heart grow fonder but gives a man the opportunity to pursue. Without movement and the opportunity for more, a man can easily lose the interest necessary to move through all five stages of dating.

> **Distance not only makes the heart grow fonder but gives a man the opportunity to pursue.**

When a woman feels attracted to a man, her feelings are very different. She gets excited because she anticipates that he could make her happy, and that in turn makes her feel really good. It brings the best out in her and makes her want to give to him.

A woman becomes excited because she anticipates receiving what she needs and then freely giving in return. A man becomes excited because he feels he can be successful in winning her over. When she is happy, he takes credit. Her fulfillment makes him most happy. His success in fulfilling her makes her most happy.

UNLOCKING THE CAR DOOR

When women do not understand men, they easily make the mistake of diffusing the attraction by continuing to give back, instead of increasing the attraction by continuing to receive. This tendency shows up most clearly when a man takes a woman on a special date. When he picks her up, she is beautifully dressed and looks great. He takes notice and tells her so. She is pleased. He walks her to the passenger side of the car, unlocks the door, and lets her in. After she is comfortably seated, he closes the door. She smiles and thanks him. Then he walks around to his side of the car to get in. What does she do? Does she reach across to unlock his door or let him unlock his door as well?

When a woman doesn't understand the dynamics of creating attraction and giving a man the distance he needs to pursue her, her tendency is to reach across the car, even if it is very uncomfortable to do, and open his door. Although this seems like the fair and loving thing to do, it is not. It is overgiving, it compromises her position, and it prevents the excitement of anticipation and romance from building in a man and in her as well.

> When a woman is too eager to please,
> a man doesn't experience the distance
> he needs to pursue her.

Some women argue that it would be selfish not to reach over to his side of the car and return the gesture. Quite often these are the single women in the audience and not the married ones. Now, certainly, if there is an unlock button on her side of the car, it could be okay to find it and push it, but to twist her body and reach way over, particularly when she is all dressed up, is neither graceful nor receptive. The whole point of the dating ritual is for the man to do little things to show his interest and caring and for the woman to receive him and take some time to discover how interested she is.

If she is going to reach over and unlock the door, then why would he have bothered to escort her to the car door in the first place? He is trying to be a gentleman and do something nice. She should let him be successful and gracefully receive and benefit from his gift.

When a woman reaches across to unlock a man's door it defeats the whole purpose of the date and confuses their roles. Instead, if she just happily waits, appreciating his attentiveness to her, there is a greater opportunity for the attraction to grow.

When a woman reaches across to unlock a
man's door, it defeats the whole purpose of
the date and confuses their roles.

A man is often so used to women reaching across and making things comfortable and easy for him that when a woman doesn't reach over, he may be a little surprised and grumble inside. He may think, Humph, I unlocked her door. Why didn't she unlock mine? He may even be momentarily distant and aloof. Then he will realize, Oh, she didn't reach across because it is awkward and uncomfortable. Even more important, when he looks over and sees that she is gracious, happy, and fulfilled, he takes credit. Now he starts to feel a little proud: Yes, I opened the car door, I am taking her on a date, and she is pleased. As his positive feelings come up, the grumbles go away and his attraction and respect for her go up.

WHY WOMEN GIVE TOO MUCH

A woman will tend to give too much in the beginning of a relationship when she doesn't understand how men think and feel. A man hungers for the opportunity to make a woman happy. It fulfills him to make her happy. Her happiness is his happiness. This, however, is not the way women are. A woman is not primarily fulfilled by making a man happy. A woman needs to feel she is getting what she needs in a relationship. Then she can freely and happily give her love. When she is getting her needs met, then and only then is his happiness hers.

When men feel good about themselves, they are most motivated to please a woman. The more a man's life is in order, the more he hungers for a woman to share it with. Although he may feel very autonomous and independent, he begins to feel empty. He is missing something. That something is satisfied through fulfilling a woman or making her happy. A woman need never feel obligated to please a man. By giving him the opportunity to please her more, she allows a man to be most fulfilled.

> **A woman need never feel obligated to please a man.**

This concept is hard for women to understand, because when a woman feels autonomous and independent, instead of feeling a need to care for someone, she feels the need for someone to care for her. When she feels empty and hungers for a relationship, she has already spent most of herself giving to others. Romance for her is the opportunity to relax and let someone else take charge of her needs.

When she feels empty, she feels a need to receive. If she was feeling empty and continued to give, then it would make her very unhappy if she didn't get something in return. A simple smile and a thank you from the man she was giving to would not be enough. When a man feels empty, and can succeed in fulfilling a woman's needs, a simple smile and a thank you from her are plenty for him.

FALLING IN LOVE RIGHT AWAY

Besides not understanding men, there is another reason women tend to give too much. Sometimes a woman will see something or even imagine something about a man that triggers a surge of confidence in her. She feels, This is the man of my dreams; he is the one for me; he is perfect for me. It is as though she falls under a spell. In this state she responds to him as if she were already getting everything she could ever want. She is lovingly responsive and receptive to whatever he does. The excitement certainly brings out the best in her and makes her very attractive, but it can also prevent him from continuing to feel a strong attraction for her.

> **When a woman falls in love,
> she may feel as if she is already getting
> everything she could ever want.**

She feels so satisfied by his presence that she begins to think, He is so wonderful. What can I do to be worthy of him? How can I earn this love? What should I do for him? How can I make sure he likes me? How can I be most attractive to him? These kinds of thoughts then lead to action. As she proceeds to pursue him, he becomes less interested in her.

A wise woman approaches the situation differently. Even if she does fall in love, she is careful to remember that even though it feels as if she were in an exclusive relationship with her ideal partner, she is not. Even if he has the potential to be the man of her dreams, he is not yet. She needs to remember that they are in stage one. He is not even exclusive with her (stage three), nor does she really know him (stage four), and they definitely are not engaged to be married (stage five). It is vitally important for a woman to remember what stage their relationship is in and respond appropriately to that stage. Having a clear awareness of the stages of dating helps us to keep this balanced perspective.

4

Stage Two: Uncertainty

When someone is more special to us than others, we automatically move into stage two, uncertainty. When we begin to feel that we would really like to get to know someone and have an exclusive relationship, it is quite natural suddenly to shift and not feel so sure. For some that shift is like an earthquake and for others it is a mild tremor. Sometimes the size of the shift or the suddenness with which it occurs is a signal that this person has good potential.

We could actually be dating our soul mate, but in stage two of dating we may not know it. Whether the person is wrong or right, in stage two the experience is uncertainty. Unfortunately, many singles do not recognize this as a necessary stage and *mistakenly* assume that if they are not certain, this must not be the right person for them. They think that if they have found the right person, the gates of heaven should open and bells should ring.

> You could actually be dating your soul mate,
> but in stage two of dating you may not know it.

When a man moves into stage two, he can easily make the mistake of thinking, If I am not sure, then I should keep looking around and testing. He doesn't realize how this tendency can prevent him from ever finding the confidence that he is with the right person.

Looking around and dating many women may be fine for stage one, but in stage two this tendency is counterproductive. This is the time for a man to temporarily stop dating others and to start focusing his attention on his special partner. Stage one is a time to meet and get to know a variety of people; stage two is the time to focus on one. This is the time to make a decision to give the relationship a chance.

WHEN THE GRASS LOOKS GREENER ON THE OTHER SIDE OF THE FENCE

During this stage of uncertainty, the grass temporarily looks greener on the other side of the fence. For a man, other women may begin to seem more appealing. Men tend to have a visual picture of their perfect mate, but very rarely is that picture ever correct. It is a fantasy picture of a man's ideal partner. Not until he begins to experience real bonding with a woman in a way that makes him feel successful will the power of that picture weaken and be replaced by a real person.

As long as a man has not experienced the reality of making a woman happy, he will compare her with a fantasy picture. He may begin to question his feelings: "I like her, but she is not my picture." As a man continues to know a real woman and feel a real bond of desire, affection, and interest, then his need for his partner to look like his fantasy picture subsides. The spell is broken when his heart opens and he feels a special connection with his partner. This process takes time, even if he is with the right person.

> **As long as a man has not experienced the reality of making a woman happy, he will hold a fantasy picture.**

In stage two, even if the grass on the other side of the fence begins to look greener, the man's new objective is to look and dig a little deeper on his side of the fence, to stop looking at the grass and dig for the gold. He may or may not find it, but he will *never* find it if he doesn't start digging.

To dig deeper he needs to ask himself these questions:

- Could I possibly be the right man for her?
- Could I possibly have what it takes to make her happy?
- Do I care for her?
- Do I want to make her happy?
- Does her happiness make me happy?
- Do I miss her when I am away from her?

When, over time, a man discovers an affirmative answer to each of these questions, then he is ready to move on to an exclusive relationship.

WHY MEN BEGIN TO DOUBT

When a man does not understand Venusians, he can make the mistake of thinking he can't make a woman happy. In reality he may have the ability, but because he misinterprets the way she thinks and feels he reaches a faulty conclusion.

For example, on a date while driving through an expensive neighborhood, a woman might say, "Oh, look at that beautiful house; I'll bet they have a swimming pool. Oh, I love swimming pools."

She is simply sharing herself, but his reaction may be something like, Wow, this woman has expensive tastes; I don't know if I could keep her happy. He mistakenly assumes that because the thought of a mansion and a swimming pool makes her happy, he will have to provide it all for her to be happy. At this point, he starts to think that she may be the wrong person for him to pursue.

In stage two, it is very important for the man to do little things for the woman so he can repeatedly test and experience the idea that he has the power to make her happy. A man bonds with a woman through being successful in providing for her happiness, comfort, and fulfillment. His doubts are dispelled not primarily by what she does for him, but by how she responds to what he does for her.

> A man's doubts are dispelled not primarily by what a woman does for him, but by how she responds to what he does for her.

Traditionally, this is why men have been the ones who provide on a date. The man gets the woman's number, the man calls her up, the man asks her out, the man comes up with a plan, the man picks her up, the man opens and shuts the car door, the man drives and navigates, the man buys the tickets, the man escorts the woman to her seat, the man takes responsibility for her comfort and happiness, the man pays the check. The man gives and the woman graciously receives.

These little things that a man provides on a date give him a chance to test the waters and to see how much he likes making this woman happy. She also gets to taste how it feels to receive his support. In this way, he bonds with her and she bonds with him. In the next stage, exclusivity, after they have bonded, she can begin sharing the expenses and doing little things for him as well, but on a romantic date he should be the main provider.

Without an understanding of these stages, a man sometimes gets stuck in uncertainty. Instead of testing to see if he can make a woman happy and win her over, he begins to question whether she can give him what he wants. When a man focuses on what he wants, he is sure to miss the perfect woman for him. When he focuses on the question, "Am I the right man for her?" then he will find clarity to either move on to exclusivity or end the relationship and start again with someone else.

> When a man focuses on what he wants, he is sure to miss the perfect woman for him.

WHEN WOMEN ARE UNCERTAIN

When a woman moves into stage two and feels uncertain, she reacts differently from a man. While a man tends to question whether he wants to pursue a relationship, a woman tends to question where the relationship is going. Quite often, she senses the man pulling away. To find reassurance, she makes one of two common mistakes. Either she starts asking questions about the relationship, or she may try to win him over. Both of these approaches can push him away or prevent him from feeling confident that he is the right guy for her.

> **While a man tends to question whether he
> wants to pursue a relationship, a woman tends
> to question where the relationship is going.**

In the uncertainty stage, when a woman doesn't understand a man, she may easily begin to panic. During the attraction stage he was coming on so strong, and now he is not. If she doesn't understand the stage of uncertainty, a host of feelings may arise. These are some common reactions.

WHAT A WOMAN ASKS

- Did I do something wrong?
- Is there someone else?
- Does he still care?
- Will he call?
- Am I doing the right things?
- Am I doing enough?
- What can I do to regain his attention, interest, affection, and desire?

Unfortunately, all of these questions lure her in the wrong direction; she begins to pursue him. When a man stops pursuing, a woman's task is to resist the enormous urge to find out what has happened or to do something about it.

For a woman, the stage of uncertainty should be a time to reflect on what she is getting from the man, not on what she could get. This is a time for the woman to stay open to his future advances, but more important, it is a time to fill up her life with the support of friends. This is a time to test whether he is really the right person for an exclusive relationship.

**When a man stops pursuing, a woman's task is
to resist the enormous urge to find out what has
happened or to do something about it.**

It is in this stage that the old saying "Absence makes the
heart grow fonder" applies. If he pulls away, she should
gracefully allow him take his distance. A woman needs to
remember that men are like rubber bands. They pull away. If
you don't run after them, they will spring back. After he
springs back a few times, he will have the certainty that she
is the one with whom he would like to pursue a steady or
exclusive relationship.

By giving the man the space to pull away and then once
again become more interested, a woman also gets to know if
this man is the one with whom she would like to have an
exclusive relationship. If she can fill up her life with the support of friends and family and she still misses him, it is a
good sign.

HOW TO AVOID PURSUING TOO MUCH

In the uncertainty stage, both men and women must be careful not to react to their partner's uncertainty by pursuing too
much. A man who doesn't take this time to pull back can
smother a woman by his insistent pursuit of her with
promises of love. When a woman says no to his advances, he
must be careful to pursue gently and respectfully. Persistence
is good, but it must be done in a nondemanding manner.
Trying to make her feel guilty for not spending more time
with him can be a real turnoff. As a result, she can build a
wall of resistance that prevents her from discovering that she
may want to have an exclusive, steady relationship with him.

If a woman's reaction to uncertainty is to pursue a man, it can actually prevent him from moving through his uncertainty to discover whether he wants to invest in a relationship or not. This is why, traditionally, women don't call men. The wise woman waits for him to pursue her. Yet there is a time for a woman to call. It is foolish to wait passively. A wise woman can create the opportunity for a man to pursue her.

WHAT TO DO WHEN HE DOESN'T CALL

If, in the uncertainty stage, a man does not call for a while, it is a good idea for the woman to give him a call but not to pursue him or tell him how she feels about being ignored. Instead she can casually let him know that all is well. She can call just to say hi, to thank him for something, or to ask a question that he has some expertise about. It is just a short, friendly sounding call, so he clearly gets the message that she is not harboring any resentment because he didn't call. The worst thing she can do is to call him and interrogate him about his feelings about her and the relationship.

> The worst thing a woman can do is to call a
> man and interrogate him about his feelings
> about her and the relationship.

Sometimes when a man is in stage two he temporarily forgets about a woman. Two days, two weeks, or even two months can pass by in a flash, and then suddenly he remembers how much he likes a woman. He thinks about calling but anticipates that he will be scolded or rejected for taking so long to call. So he decides to not call and moves on. If he has received a friendly call, then he gets the clear message that he is not in trouble. This then frees him to consider pursuing her again.

Just as time slows down for women in uncertainty, time can speed up for a man.

When a woman does not understand men, it is easy to conclude that a man is a real jerk if he doesn't call her. This is not really the case at all. There are many reasons a man doesn't call. With a more complete understanding of the way men think and feel, a woman can assess a man's instinctive behavior and not take it so personally. In Chapters 15 and 16 we will explore in much greater detail why men don't call and how a woman can call a man without turning him off.

THE PRESSURE TO GIVE BACK

When a man comes on strong in stage one and then pulls back in stage two, a woman sometimes feels pressure to give back sexually. She has received so much that she feels obligated to return the favor. She hopes that by responding in a sexual manner and fulfilling his desires, she will regain his interest. By giving more of herself than she is ready to give, however, she can actually sabotage a relationship. More is not always better.

A woman can best move through the stage of uncertainty if she can enjoy a man's advances without feeling obligated. If she has not been used to feeling pursued and romanced, then she may feel even more obligated. When people are starving and they don't have any money to buy food, then quite naturally they might feel, "I will give you anything for this food." Likewise, when a woman feels loved and adored, she might feel, "I will give anything for this to continue." This attitude is unhealthy.

A woman needs to understand that by receiving and responding in a warm and friendly way to a man's romantic gestures she is already giving back to him. This basic understanding is crucial, and women today are missing it. Quite often a woman feels that she is not giving enough in return, and then she feels obligated to give more.

When she senses that the man wants more, instead of just being flattered by his desires, she sabotages the dating ritual by feeling the pressure of obligation and giving in to being more physically intimate than is appropriate to their relationship. Instead of letting him continue to please her, she shifts to trying to please him. Inevitably her position is compromised and he loses interest.

How Sharon Felt Obligated

Sharon described it this way: "At first Kevin was so wonderful. He listened to everything I said. He was such a gentleman. I loved everything he said. He was interesting and funny. We had such a good time. Then, after an evening of passion, everything stopped."

Sharon felt embarrassed. She thought they were soul mates destined to get married, but Kevin was just in stage one, attraction. He was still dating other women as well. Sharon said, "It hurts so much, I'd rather not try again. I don't need a man that much."

After learning about men, however, Sharon realized how she had misinterpreted the signals. His intense attentiveness had meant to her that he must have been her soul mate. The truth is that they had only known each other for a few days. Although she thought they were going to be exclusive, they hadn't even gone through the uncertainty stage.

After taking a Mars/Venus workshop, Sharon confided that she felt really stupid. She said, "Sure he said he loved me. But there's nothing wrong with that. He just didn't love me enough to stay. The real reason I feel hurt is that we had sex and then he rejected me. If we hadn't gone all the way sexually and we had just kissed and touched, than his rejection would not hurt so much. If we had just dated for a few weeks and then he didn't want to pursue a relationship it would have been fine."

At a certain point, Kevin was being so wonderful that Sharon started feeling obligated to give him everything he wanted. After all, he was giving her what she wanted; it seemed only fair for her to return the favor. But was he really giving her everything she wanted? Sharon wanted to get married. Was he giving her that?

She said, "I want to get married. When a man gives me all of what I want then I will give him all of what he wants. Until my wedding night, I am remembering that I am not yet married."

Sharon realized that she didn't have to give up dating men because it hurt too much. She could just be more discerning in how far to go sexually. Sharon learned that physical intimacy doesn't have to be all or nothing. It can slowly increase over time.

Physical intimacy doesn't have to be all or nothing.

By reaching this conclusion, Sharon was able to complete her relationship with Kevin. She didn't feel like a victim but instead was grateful for the insight. She now clearly saw how she had set herself up to feel hurt. She forgave Kevin and wished him well. This lifted her spirits and she went back to dating with a new approach.

She felt her need for a man but didn't feel any hurry to pursue a more intimate relationship. Instead of giving up dating men, she gave up feeling obligated. She had a good time flirting a lot and dating until the right guy came along. When they became exclusive, she practiced having sex without going all the way. Eventually they got married, but this time she waited until she was ready to be fully physically intimate.

NEED AND OBLIGATION

Sharon's story illustrates a very important point. Quite often a woman denies her feelings of need for a man because she doesn't want to feel obligated. But by clearly realizing that she is under no obligation, she can begin to freely flirt with men and enjoy receiving what men can offer. She can feel her needs without feeling obligated. The more receptive and responsive she becomes, the more attractive she will be to the kind of man who will want to marry her.

> By clearly realizing that she is under no
> obligation, a woman can begin to freely flirt with
> men and enjoy receiving what men can offer.

When a woman has a tendency to feel obligated in response to a man's advances, it prevents her from being receptive. Younger women, particularly, feel a pressure not to let a man pay on a date so that they don't feel obligated to have sex. This is the woman's way of saying that he should not get his hopes up.

She senses his desires and wants him not to get the wrong idea. The problem with this approach is that he will get the idea that she is not receptive at all and lose interest. By denying the part of her that needs a man's affections, she will decrease her own ability to feel attractive and attracted.

Just because a woman enjoys a man's gifts does not in any way obligate her to give more than a smile or a thank you. Women commonly confuse a man's hope that he will "get lucky" with the expectation that she should be physically intimate with him.

> Just because a woman enjoys a man's gifts
> does not in any way obligate her to give more
> than a smile or a thank you.

Most men do not *expect* a woman to be physically intimate; they just *hope* to get lucky. They don't think, Well, I paid for dinner, so she should have sex with me. Still, sometimes a woman will refuse to let a man pay for dinner because she doesn't want him to get the wrong idea. This is insulting not only to him but to herself as well. If she feels that a man is trying to buy her sexual favors, then why go out with him at all?

THE DESIRE FOR INTIMACY IS INNOCENT

It is innocent for a man to want to be intimate physically and it is just as innocent for a woman to feel swept off her feet by a man's strong interest and passion. While most men only hope to get lucky, there are some who expect it. They have had sex with women who are just looking for a good time, and so they expect this from all women.

They expect it because they see it on TV, in the movies, and in magazines, and they assume that all women are just as fast as men. Without an understanding of what it takes to make a relationship work, it appears that fast sex is a heavenly antidote for a frustrated love life. Nothing could be further from the truth.

By clearly understanding the wisdom of going slowly and moving through the five stages of dating, both men and woman will enjoy the dating process more and eventually find true love. When a man is used to fast women and then he meets a woman who wants to go slowly, it is normal for him to grumble a bit. If, however, there is more than just physical chemistry between them, he will respect her wishes and go slowly.

Instead of refusing to be receptive to all his advances, a woman should just politely and firmly say no to the sexual part if she is not yet ready. If he can respect her, then he is worthy of her. If he cannot and stays annoyed, then he is just not ready to be in a serious relationship and she does herself and him a favor by rejecting him.

> If a woman is not ready she can still be polite
> and firmly say no to a man's sexual advances.

When a man wants to be more physically intimate and a woman doesn't know how to say no because she doesn't want to hurt his feelings, she needs to remember that she is not obligated in any way. All he really needs is to feel successful in fulfilling her and to hope that one day it might happen. She can simply say, "I like this, but I am not ready for more. This is as far as I go for now."

Saying no to sex doesn't mean that a couple should have no sexual intimacy. Men need physical intimacy in order to open up and feel their love and desire, and to feel committed. Just as women are stimulated by a man's romantic interest and good conversation, men are stimulated by a woman's sexual responsiveness. To be stimulated, however, they don't have to go all the way.

FOUR DEGREES OF PHYSICAL INTIMACY

A woman can say yes to different degrees of sex without having to go all the way. This is a very important insight, because to avoid intercourse, many woman will not be physically affectionate or sexual at all. For a woman to feel comfortable being physically intimate, she needs to share a clear picture of how far she wants to go, and she must get a clear message from the man that he will respect what she wants.

It can be very uncomfortable or difficult for a woman to say no to a man when she is in the heat of arousal. When she is kissing him and he wants to go further, she doesn't always want to be saying no. To facilitate clear conversation with a man about sex, baseball can provide some helpful examples.

Getting on First Base

There are basically four degrees of sexual or physical intimacy. As in the game of baseball, each degree can be likened to getting onto another base. Getting on first base has to do with kissing and affection. At first, people casually or unintentionally touch. They may spend many minutes gazing into each other's eyes while sharing a meal together. Then he holds her hand, puts his arm around her, or gives her a kiss. Gradually their kissing becomes more lengthy and passionate.

As they get to know each other, he feels very comfortable putting his arm around her and holding hands in private and in public. In private they may spend hours cuddled up together or passionately kissing and pressing their bodies together. Although there is a lot of passion, they purposefully restrict the stimulation to lots of kissing, cuddling, embracing, and rolling around and alternately lying on each other.

Getting on Second Base

Second base is heavy petting. In this stage they begin to stimulate their more erogenous zones. There are basically three zones of exploration. The first zone is from the neck and shoulders up, plus arms, hands, and feet. The second is from the waist up and the third is from the waist down. Second base includes exploration in zones one and two. Slowly they will begin to explore and touch each other. At first this exploration is done with clothes on, then with less clothing on, and then with nothing on.

Getting on Third Base

Third base is the full stimulation of the genitals without intercourse. It includes touching, caressing, and stimulating each other in all three zones. Although the man does not penetrate the woman through intercourse, they give each other pleasure through mutual stimulation. They both eventually enjoy the orgasmic bliss of two souls uniting in love.

The woman commonly makes the mistake of rushing to third base to satisfy the man because she can feel his longing and desire. This is a mistake. Ideally, before she gives him an orgasm, she needs to first be open and receptive to having her own orgasm. When she also feels her longing to have an orgasm and she experiences one, then by giving him an orgasm she is not giving too much or going too far. In this sense, by listening to her own body she can know how far to go.

Sliding into Home Base

The fourth base or home base is intercourse.

*   *   *

With a clear understanding of the four bases, a woman can definitely and accurately communicate to a man how far she is willing to go. This clarity allows her to move from feeling uncertain to getting more involved with a man.

How far the woman goes should always be her choice. To make this choice she needs to be sure that her willingness is not coming from a place of obligation or sympathy for the man's need, or from a rebelliousness to authority. She needs to listen within herself to determine when she is ready. A clearer understanding of the five stages of dating will help both her and him to understand why waiting is so important.

HOW TO SAY NO

Rachel had no problem saying no. She chose to stay a virgin until her wedding night, when she was twenty-eight years old. At a certain point while dating, as she started to feel the pressures building to be more physically intimate, she would simply say, "Look, I just want you to know I am a virgin and I plan to stay that way till I get married. I like kissing and touching, but that is all." By establishing her limits she then felt free to open up and be more physically intimate as she and the man she was dating also became more emotionally and mentally intimate.

Andrea had a different approach. After a kiss became very steamy, she would say clearly, "I don't want to go any further. I am not ready. I need more time." As time passed, she would let a man know when she was ready to go a little further.

Cathy would just say very quickly, in a friendly tone, "No, I don't want to do that. I am not ready. I just want to kiss."

The best approach is always to be clear and definite. Being vague doesn't work. Many men hear a clear invitation to keep advancing when a woman says, "I don't know. Maybe we should wait." He will continue until he gets a clear no. Just as a man needs to be respectful of a woman's boundaries, a woman also needs to consider the messages she is giving.

When a man is touching a woman, moving his hand away to say no is generally misinterpreted as "Not yet; I am not ready." If she means "Don't do that again tonight," then she needs to say that with words. If he doesn't respect that first no, then she needs to immediately get up and leave. She can be polite and also be clear about setting that boundary. She could just get up and say, "I really like you, but I am not ready for this." Then she should go home, or at least to another room.

WHEN WAITING TO GET INVOLVED IS A MISTAKE

Without a clear understanding of how to say no and set limits on how much sexual intimacy she is ready to share, a woman may not bother dating until she meets a man that she doesn't have to say no to. She waits to meet Mr. Perfect. She decides to refuse dates and not flirt until she feels right away that a man is right for her.

Mary shared these feelings: "For me the most difficult part of breaking up is knowing that I will have to once again undress in front of another man."

Although she was just being funny, she had given up. Mary didn't feel comfortable saying no or yes to a man's advances, so she decided that she was going to wait to get involved. She said, "I just can't keep getting involved with the wrong men. From now on I am not going to date a man unless I know he is right for me."

This expectation is totally unrealistic. With this attitude,

Mary could wait her whole life and stay single. Knowing that a partner is right happens only in stage four, the intimacy stage; it is totally unrealistic to make that a prerequisite. In stage two, it is perfectly normal to question whether a partner is right for you.

At a certain point in the uncertainty stage, if you have been careful not to pursue other relationships, both the man and woman will be ready to move on to having an exclusive relationship. Either you become more interested in getting to know each other or you don't. Even though you may not be sure, if a part of you wants to pursue the relationship and if you want to prepare yourself to know for sure, then it is time to move on to stage three and have an exclusive relationship.

5
Stage Three: Exclusivity

When we are able to feel that our dating partner has the potential to be a mate, or if we just feel that we want to get to know the person better and give the relationship a chance, we are ready to move into stage three, exclusivity. In this stage, we make a commitment to focus on having a primary romantic relationship and avoid nurturing any romantic relationships on the side.

In stage three, we build a foundation that allows us to open our hearts and truly love someone. Before this stage, we are just reacting to the anticipation of getting what we need and testing to see if we want to get involved. Now we actually have a chance to give freely and fully and experience getting what we need in return.

> Having a primary romantic relationship and
> avoiding any romantic relationships on the side
> will build the foundation for truly loving someone.

Most dating couples in this stage unknowingly sabotage this opportunity to experience the best of their partners and themselves. As soon as they become exclusive, they relax and no longer put their best foot forward. This is a big mistake. In this stage, we must make a deliberate effort to keep doing the little romantic things that allowed us to move successfully through the first and second stages.

After a couple become exclusive, they often become too comfortable and begin to take each other for granted. The man stops pursuing the woman because he feels he has won her over, and the woman tends to expect more, since they are now exclusive. This creates predictable problems that can all be avoided.

WHEN THE PURSUIT IS OVER

A man may do everything to win a woman over, but once he has passed the finish line, he turns off his engine, parks his car, and celebrates. In stage three, exclusivity, he mistakenly assumes the pursuit is over. Somebody needs to tell him that the race is not over. He has only just shifted into third gear. He still hasn't reached his top speed. He still has fourth and fifth gears. To move beyond third gear, he needs to focus on being the best partner he can be and continue to lead the relationship.

Most men think that you do the little romantic things only until a woman accepts you and then you can relax. A man does not instinctively realize that it is his romantic attention that fuels a woman's attraction for him. If a man relaxes too much, a woman will not get the fuel she needs to continue responding to him the way she did.

A man needs to remember that even though they are exclusive, the pursuit is not over. Without an understanding of the stages ahead, he also begins to run out of fuel. By clearly keeping his goal in mind, he will find the energy and intention necessary to do his best.

This effort is similar to his lifting weights or going the extra mile to make a project at work successful. By putting forth the effort, he will bring out the best in a woman. Her warm and friendly responses will give him the fuel to keep going.

MARTIAN EFFICIENCY

On Mars, they instinctively try to be efficient. Their motto is, Never do anything you don't have to do. If someone else will do it, then relax. Save your energy for the emergency. Put off what doesn't have to be done so that you can do what has to be done. Get from point A to point B as quickly as possible. Do less and accomplish more. Invest your resources so that you will not have to work later. These are all Martian tendencies.

Why is it that men tend to wait till the last minute to do just about anything? It is because they feel that if they wait long enough, quite often either the problem goes away or someone else solves it for them. If that doesn't occur, then the problem becomes necessary to solve, and so the man dedicates the time and energy to do it.

To make sure they don't waste energy, men automatically prioritize. Unless something gets to the top of the list, it just doesn't get done. They wait to dedicate their energy to something until they clearly know that it is necessary. Men do what they believe is required of them. The problem is that they don't necessarily know what is required, particularly when it comes to romantic relationships.

This is why it is crucial for a man to understand women. Otherwise he just doesn't know what is required to make a relationship work. When he assumes he is doing enough and the woman is not happy, he quickly gives up and loses his attraction because he thinks either that something is wrong with her or that she is the wrong partner for him. It may just be that he has the wrong approach.

KEEPING THE EDGE

Without an understanding of the basic strategy of stage three, a man will mistakenly assume that he has done all that is required of him to win his partner over. Now he thinks he can relax and live off the interest from his original investment. By relaxing in this manner, he loses his momentum and the relationship ceases to bring out the best in him and his partner. He becomes increasingly passive in the relationship and loses his edge.

This can happen in any area of a man's life. It clearly happens all the time in the world of work. After becoming successful, big companies lose their competitive edge. They become too comfortable and stop researching innovative ways to stay ahead of the competition. They become too soft and complacent. They lose the power and good fortune that come from hard work, effort, sacrifice, planning, researching, and taking reasonable risks. To keep the edge, to maintain their sharpness of focus, they need to sustain those behaviors that made them number one.

By putting forth his best effort, a man eventually experiences his edge. He reaches the limit of his potential. The result of reaching to express all that he can be is greater creativity. The automatic consequence of pushing to his limit is more power. He gains the power and creativity to do more, be more, and achieve more.

By fully expressing his potential, he allows that potential to expand and increase. Now to reach his new limits he must do more. If he does not utilize this opportunity to develop and express increased power and creativity, he loses the edge. Only by continuing to express his potential as it grows can a man keep his edge.

This same dynamic is particularly true in stage three of dating. By continuing to take the time to research what a woman might like and put forth the effort to plan and deliver a romantic date, a man ensures the growth of affection and interest in his relationship.

He discovers how much more a relationship has to offer. He finds a confident, purposeful, and responsible part of himself he did not know. He experiences a self-assured, receptive, and responsive part of his partner he could not have known. By sustaining his edge in his relationship, he creates the opportunity for real love to spring forth.

A RELATIONSHIP IS LIKE AN INVESTMENT

A man automatically looks at a relationship like an investment. He puts his energy in and hopes to get something out of it. This is why he takes time to pick the right person for himself. It would be foolish to invest everything in the wrong investment. Once a man picks a partner with whom to be exclusive, he mistakenly assumes that he now has made the investment.

A man needs to have a more realistic perspective. In stage three, he is still just earning the capital to invest. In stage four, he picks the investment, and in stage five he invests it. When he makes it through all five stages, then he has invested successfully in his relationship. He can live out the rest of his life benefiting from his deliberate efforts and the hard work often required to move through the five stages.

In stage three, a man needs to realize that much more will be required of him, but not more than he can do. His best is good enough. As he gradually grows and can give more, his partner can put forth more of herself in a healthy manner. As they gradually prepare themselves in this way to experience the growth of true intimacy in the next stage, a man's orientation toward the relationship has a chance to change.

HOW A MAN'S EXPERIENCE CHANGES

By continuing to put his best foot forward, a man experiences that he has the power to bring out the best of his partner. He also likes doing it. Although it requires effort and attention, he is strengthened by it. When a man feels confident and purposeful, he enjoys exerting himself.

Just as working out and exercising his muscles will make him stronger and will eventually feel good, a man finds that he has a tremendous power to provide in stage three. The relationship muscles he builds in stage three give him the strength to move through stages four and five.

By deliberately putting forth his energy and attention to fulfill a woman's romantic needs long after a woman has accepted him, a man trains himself to experience that the little romantic gestures of dating are not just to win a woman over but are actually required and necessary to sustain her responsiveness.

Instead of planning a date because he knows she will be impressed, he plans a date because it nurtures the woman he cares for and that makes him feel good. As he experiences repeated success in stage three, giving in romantic ways becomes automatic for him.

Giving still requires effort and risk, but the reward makes it all worthwhile. His reward is the pleasure and pride he feels when he succeeds in making his partner happy.

HOW MEN CHANGE

Without an understanding of the importance of continuing to make romantic gestures, a man will unknowingly stop doing the very things that made him so attractive in the beginning. Let's look at a few examples of how men change.

Johnny and His Plans

In the beginning of their relationship, Johnny used to plan dates in advance. He would research what was happening, get ideas, and suggest his plans to his girlfriend, Vanessa. She was generally very pleased by his ideas and they had many wonderful dates.

After they became exclusive, everything quickly changed. Johnny stopped planning dates in advance. He waited till Friday and would then ask Vanessa what she wanted to do. Since they had less time to plan, they started doing more casual things, like renting a video and making popcorn. There was nothing wrong with this. After all, not every date has to be special. Variety is good. For a while, Vanessa and Johnny had a good time not going out.

But as this continued, they gradually started to lose interest in each other. After taking a Mars/Venus dating workshop, Johnny realized what had happened. He realized that he had stopped planning dates. In the workshop, he learned that women love it when men plan dates. Women love a man with a plan, and Johnny had stopped planning. He didn't even notice the change. He stopped making plans because his initial reason and motivation for planning were gone.

In the beginning of the relationship, he would plan in advance to make sure he would get a date. He didn't want Vanessa to book up her weekend, so he would plan things with her way in advance. When it was clear that they would be exclusive, she naturally left her weekends open to be with him. He then had no reason to plan and make dates in advance.

Johnny learned a new reason to plan in advance. When he planned in advance, not only did Vanessa feel more provided for and special, but she also had a week to think about the date and look forward to it. Most men don't realize how important that is to a woman. She loves to look ahead, to prepare, to get ready, and to talk about it with her friends. By learning about women, Johnny was once again motivated to plan in advance. He said this one change put the juice back into his relationship.

Why Bob Stopped Talking

For several dates, Bob was very talkative with Sarah. He talked about his job, his goals, his values, his parents, his brothers and sisters, his past, his spiritual beliefs, his interest in sports, his daily experiences, and his reactions to the news, and he talked about his past as it related to different experiences that he was having. He was a dream partner. Women love men to share the way they think and feel about things. They had many wonderful conversations.

When they moved into stage three, Sarah was expecting things to stay the same and even get better, but the opposite happened. Bob stopped talking as much. At first, she thought he was probably distracted by some problem at work, but eventually she concluded that he was just losing interest in her.

Sarah suggested that for fun they take a Mars/Venus workshop. She thought that if they took a class together on communication, she would understand what to do. After the workshop, everything changed. She heard that statistically men talk more on the third date than any other date in their whole relationship. She was relieved to recognize that Bob's lack of interest in talking to her was not about her or their relationship at all, but was quite ordinary.

Men may talk a lot in the beginning of the relationship because, in a sense, they are on a job interview. They are giving their date a verbal résumé of who they are by sharing what they think, feel, and value. Once a man gets the job and he is exclusive, a shift takes place because there is no longer any reason to keep talking.

Talking has served its purpose. Now that they know each other, they can get on to being and doing things together. Men talk most on the third date because it is after their third date that they decide to be exclusive. As in baseball, it is generally three strikes and a man either gets on base or is out.

On Mars, talking is not an end in itself. Men generally don't call each other up and say, "Let's go to lunch and just talk." If they do, it is because they have something in particular that's pressing to talk about. When invited to lunch to talk, a man will ask, "What's up?" or "What is it that you want to talk about?"

Women, on the other hand, *will* call each other up and say, "Let's have lunch." They don't have to have a specific reason to talk. There are not specific topics to discuss or pressing problems to solve. They don't even bother asking. They know lunch means talking about whatever.

Bob, like many men, had stopped talking because he had no reason to talk. He had fully introduced himself and he had gotten the job. After taking the seminar, he realized that in stage three he needed to keep doing the things he did to win her over. One of the most important things was to keep talking as he had talked on the first few dates.

Why Jerry Stopped Listening

Quite often in the third stage, some men make the mistake of not listening to or looking at their date as much. Stephanie complained, "Once we started going steady, Jerry stopped listening. I could be talking and he would just look away. I couldn't believe it." Stephanie assumed that he was another jerk who came on strong and then became passively interested.

Jerry, like many men, made the mistake of relaxing too much in stage three. He had no idea that he was turning Stephanie off. As a result, she felt offended and ended their relationship. It was important for Stephanie to understand why this happened or her opinion of men would stay jaded. In a Mars/Venus workshop she learned how she had misinterpreted Jerry's feelings.

While doing business, a man will always focus directly on the person talking to him, but in a relaxed social setting this tendency changes. When two best friends have lunch together, they are not in any way offended if one looks away.

Particularly in a relaxed social setting, a man feels most comfortable looking around while a person is talking. This is why bars always have a TV going. Men don't feel offended at all when the person to whom they are talking is watching and listening to a game at the same time.

After Stephanie learned more about Martian customs, her feelings about men began to soften. She learned that Jerry had stopped doing a lot of the things he used to do because he *was* convinced that he wanted to pursue a relationship with her.

In the beginning, he looked directly at her because he was still doing business. He listened intently to get to know her because he was gathering information to make the decision. He focused on her to figure out if he wanted to be with her. Once he made the decision that she was the one, the problem had been solved; he could now relax and look away while she talked. By not understanding what women enjoy most in a man, Jerry had sabotaged his relationship.

Why Ross Stopped Giving Compliments

Naomi complained, "After four or five dates, Ross stopped giving me compliments. After he let me know that he wanted to see only me, his affection just turned off. I thought we were really getting close. I couldn't understand why, if he liked me so much, he would stop complimenting me. After a while I was so annoyed that I refused to date him anymore. He became so stingy with his affection."

Many men in stage three will automatically stop complimenting their partner. A man mistakenly assumes that because he is being exclusive, she doesn't need to hear his compliments anymore. He thinks the fact that he wants to be only with her is already making a statement that she is more special than other women.

From a man's point of view, giving compliments is a way to communicate the message that he is attracted to a woman, that he finds her attractive. Once he clearly believes that she understands this message, then he may no longer feel the need to give more compliments. From his perspective, there is no point to it. He thinks, "Well, we are going steady; she should know that I think she is pretty." Because Ross made this simple mistake over and over again, his relationships never progressed beyond the third stage of dating.

Tom and His Comfort Zone

Louise questioned, "Why is it that we keep doing the same things? In the beginning our dates were fun and interesting, but now Tom just wants to do the same things over and over."

Louise didn't realize that Martians are creatures of habit in many ways. When they find a formula that works, they just keep doing it over and over. Their thinking is, Why risk failure by changing things when you have a surefire formula for success?

Quite often, as soon as a man reaches stage three, he finds his comfort zone. He will tend to repeat the things he has done to get there, and not try new things. If he has taken her to a particular restaurant and she liked it, then he will continue to go back. He does not realize that one of the main reasons she liked it was that it was new and different. Women like variety. They like to try new things and have new experiences. By continuing to take risks and try new things, a man is assured of successfully moving through stage three.

Jose Stopped Offering to Help

Maria complained, "As soon as we started being exclusive, Jose stopped offering to help me do things. He would come over to my apartment and watch TV while I was making dinner. In the beginning, he would always offer to help. Then, I couldn't believe it: He started treating me like a servant. He expected me to do everything for him."

Before they were exclusive, Jose wanted to let Maria know that he was happy to help her with anything. To make sure she knew his intentions, he offered to help with washing the car, carrying bags, moving boxes, driving her places, making dinner, and fixing things around the house. Then he stopped.

Maria mistakenly assumed that he now expected her to

return the favors he had given her, to help him. She was fine with this for a while. Women are always happy to give back what they feel they have received. But after a while she became very resentful. She was doing things for him and he was doing nothing for her. He had stopped offering to help.

Maria didn't understand the real reason Jose stopped offering his help. He assumed that by now she would know that he was happy to help. Now that they were closer, he mistakenly thought that if she wanted his help she would ask for it. When she didn't ask, he just assumed that he was giving enough and she didn't want any more.

In stage three, a man should remember that a woman feels most loved and supported when he offers to be of assistance. It is most romantic for a woman when a man anticipates her needs and offers to help. Even if she doesn't need his help at the time, she will feel supported just because he offered.

> It is most romantic for a woman when a man
> anticipates her needs and offers to help.

While the wise man continues to offer his support, a wise woman practices asking for support. No matter how perfect a man is, he is still from Mars. Even if he is deeply in love with a woman, he will still not instinctively know what a woman really needs or when he should offer to help. He could be completely willing but just not know what he should be offering or when he should be offering it.

A WOMAN'S GREATEST CHALLENGE

In stage three, a woman's greatest challenge is to practice the art of asking for support. Women are taught to be desirable, but not to desire. It is hard for them to ask for more. The biggest mistake a woman makes in stage three is to assume that now a man will do things without her having to ask.

Women are taught to be desirable but not to desire.

In this stage, a woman must break through this limiting conditioning to discover that she is actually more desirable when she expresses her desires. A woman becomes more attractive when a man clearly knows what she wants. He can then feel confident that he can fulfill her. If she just waits for him to know the right things, she may be waiting her whole life.

WHEN TO ASK FOR SUPPORT

The best time to ask for support is when a man stops offering it. This simple truth can be very confusing to women. When a man stops offering his support, a woman mistakenly assumes that this is the worst time to ask. Like Maria, a woman doesn't realize that a man may be very willing to help but is waiting to be asked. Instead of asking for support, she quietly does something herself or postpones her needs. Although making sacrifices is a part of a relationship, women tend to make too many.

When men don't do the right things, it is because they don't know what to do or they don't realize how important a certain thing is on Venus. It has little to do with how much or how little they care. Stage three is the perfect time for a woman to become more direct and begin asking for support. At this time it is also the best kind of support she can give a man. Just as a man's little romantic efforts reassure a woman that she is special, a woman's little requests encourage him to continue giving her what she needs.

WHEN WOMEN MAKE SACRIFICES

For a while, a woman is even happy to make sacrifices and give more in a relationship. On Venus, this is a sign of love and also one of the ways to ask for support. When a woman gives more, it is clearly also a sign that she is not getting her due share. Another woman will immediately notice and insist on helping. To her, it is obvious that when a woman is struggling to carry a box, she is asking for help.

For a man it is not always so clear. In stages one and two, he will offer his help to assure her that he is willing to help, but in stage three he assumes that if she wants help she will ask.

When a woman gives more instead of directly asking, it gives a man the wrong message. He is led to believe that either she doesn't need his help or he is already giving enough.

> A man automatically assumes that
> when a woman is not asking for help,
> she must be getting enough.

Without this understanding of how men think differently, a woman keeps giving to a man until she feels resentment inside. As her resentment builds, she feels increasingly entitled to ask for more. Eventually she does ask for more, but because she is feeling so resentful, she asks in a demanding tone or complains before making her request.

WHY MEN RESIST A WOMAN'S REQUESTS

At this point, a man will resist her request. His resistance is also misunderstood. It is not that he is resisting giving the help; he is resisting her resentful attitude. He is resisting the negative picture her complaints are painting of him. Although she thinks she is just sharing her feelings, he interprets her behavior as unfair blaming and manipulation.

From his perspective, he feels criticized for not giving enough and unjustly judged as unsupportive. He rejects her feelings because he has been happy to help. He clearly got the message that he was doing plenty, and now she turns on him by not appreciating what he brings to the relationship.

All of this predictable turmoil and conflict can be avoided when a woman recognizes that stage three is the optimal time to ask for support. This is when she has the most negotiating power. In stage three, a man is actually most receptive to her requests.

> **In stage three, a woman actually
> has the most negotiating power.**

If a woman waits too long to ask, then when she finally does, in a later stage, the man may get the feeling that she is asking for more because he has not been doing enough. This is not a pleasant experience for a man. He likes to feel that he is a great guy in a woman's eyes, and very happy to go the extra mile for her. A man is actually much more motivated to say yes to a woman's requests when she asks him for support with an attitude that is free of strings, expectations, and obligations.

When a man cares about a woman, even if he doesn't want to do something, he is happy to do that very thing if he gets a clear message that it will make her happy. If he gets a complaining or resentful message that he *should* do it, he is resistant and may refuse to do more until he is first fairly acknowledged and appreciated for what he has already provided.

DISCOVERING HER POWER

Long before a woman gets to stage four (intimacy), when it is appropriate to share negative feelings, she must first discover her power to ask for what she wants and get it without needing to complain. A woman needs repeatedly to experience that a man is already willing to be of assistance. With this awareness, as she opens up more in stage four, she will not feel the need to use her negative feelings as a way to motivate a man to fulfill her requests. Instead she will open up as a way to experience greater intimacy and to find relief.

Many women turn men off by making the mistake of focusing on their negative feelings before making a request. On Venus they commonly talk and share their feelings about a problem before asking for a solution. While this approach may work with girlfriends, it does not work with men. These are a few examples:

Don't Say	Do Say
"We never go out."	"Would you take me out to a concert next weekend?"
"We never do anything fun anymore."	"Let's do something fun this weekend. Let's have a picnic on the mountain."
"I'm tired of hanging around town all the time."	"Maybe we could go to the beach this weekend. What do you think?"

By learning to ask for what she wants in a positive way, a woman will eventually develop one of the most important skills she needs for having a successful relationship with a man.

WOMEN CHANGE TOO

Women are very aware of and verbal about the way men change in a relationship, but they are not as aware of the way they change. Women change, too. They think that now that they are in an exclusive relationship, a man will automatically do even more. The woman's expectations increase. In anticipation, she feels inclined to do more for him. While this may seem like a good idea, it is not.

As she feels she is giving more, she is no longer as excited and appreciative of the little things he does. Instead of growing in appreciation, she begins to take her partner for granted. Instead of delighting in how supported she feels, she begins to feel obligated to even the score.

Since he has been doing things for her, she feels she should do things for him. She eagerly begins doing little things for him, she becomes more accommodating, she opens her schedule for him, she makes plans for him, she makes reservations for him, she worries for him, she waits for him, she tries to please him, etc. By beginning to do more, although he may like it, she unknowingly takes the wind out of his sails.

THE SECRET OF SUCCESS

It is fine to give to a man, but what is great is to receive. The secret to success for a woman in the third stage is to continue receiving. This is the time for her to focus not on doing things for her partner but on receiving. By being receptive and responsive to what a man offers, she is actually giving the relationship the best chance to grow.

As long as she doesn't give more than she feels he is giving, then she will not begin expecting more in return. To be most receptive and open to him, she needs to focus on trusting him and not giving him any advice, accepting him just as he is, not trying to change him in any way, and appreciating what he offers regardless of how much better she might like something else.

Her role is to give him the opportunity to keep succeeding; his role is to keep succeeding. In stage three, learning to create a receptive attitude can be as challenging for a woman as it is for a man to continue giving when his automatic tendency is to relax. Just as a man tends to take for granted that a woman is getting what she needs because he is being exclusive, women take for granted that men should be more giving and supportive.

DON'T TAKE YOUR DATE FOR GRANTED

It is easy on a first date to be responsive. After a woman has been dating a man for a while, when he still makes some of the same mistakes, then she can easily make the mistake of being too critical. Rather than focus on what she can do for a man, she needs to focus on creating a receptive attitude. Without making a conscious decision to put her best foot forward, she can easily begin to expect his support in a way that takes him for granted.

She can easily forget to be responsive. Being responsive is at first automatic, but then a woman must consciously make a choice to focus on and express her positive responses. After expressing her positive responses becomes an automatic habit, a woman is ready to move into the intimacy stage of a relationship. Here are some examples from dating couples who came for counseling or participated in Mars/Venus workshops.

When Tom Was Late

In the beginning, when Earl was late, Dawn would think, Well, he is just getting used to where I live. A few months later, when Earl did it again, she got more upset with him. Instead of focusing on the fact that he got there and being happy to see him, she became upset. Earl felt Dawn was too demanding.

Once Dawn discovered her mistake, she didn't give him a disapproving look or complain the next time he was late. That evening they had a great date. After he kissed her good night, he apologized and thanked her for not minding that he was late.

Dawn learned the importance of being responsive to a man's efforts and saved her relationship. It is these little misunderstandings that can prevent a couple from moving through the five stages of dating.

When Joel Emptied the Trash

In the beginning, Joel used to empty Veronica's trash, and she was happy and responsive. Later she started occasionally doing his laundry, and she felt the least he could do was to keep emptying her trash. When he emptied the trash for her and she had no positive response, he immediately noticed. When he asked if she noticed that he had emptied her trash, she just argued. She said, "I don't expect you to be excited when I do your laundry, so why do I have to make a big deal out of it when you empty my trash?"

Veronica won the argument, but Joel stopped emptying the trash. She just didn't understand that men are different and they lose their feelings of attraction for a woman when she is not responsive. Eventually, she learned that when she was responsive to Joel and appreciated his efforts with positive responses, not only was he happier, but he became more interested in doing things for her. This kind of support made her even happier and more responsive.

When Michael Didn't Call

In the beginning, Michael didn't call Terressa on a regular basis. She was understanding because they were not yet exclusive and Michael had a very demanding work schedule. After about ten dates, she began to feel he should be calling her more. When he did call, though, she was not that excited, and when he didn't call enough she would even get upset with him. After a while, Michael said, he didn't think much about calling her and then the thought of her expecting him to call turned him off.

After a while he said, "Look, if you want to talk to me then you call me." For a while, Terressa called him, but she was disappointed that he was distant and distracted, and didn't seem interested. After taking the Mars/Venus workshop, Michael realized that by calling or even surprising her with a little card, he could let Terressa know she was important to him and that he was thinking of her. Even if he didn't have much time or much to say, he could call and say hi and ask about her day.

Terressa learned to be appreciative that he was thinking of her and to be responsive to his call. She learned to appreciate the ways he was showing his caring and he started calling her more, not because he had to but because he wanted to.

When Darrel Opened the Car Door

In the beginning, when Darrel took Linda on a date, she smiled and was really delighted when he opened the car door for her. After about six dates, she began to expect it and stopped smiling. She responded as if it was his job. He was the man and he should just do it. After a while, he would sometimes forget to open the door for her.

Although it is important for a man to show his affection

for a woman by doing little things like opening the car door, it is just as important for a woman to pay attention to the little things he does and respond in a way that reveals her good feelings for him.

After the workshop, they both changed their attitudes. Linda said, "I could never understand why he would want me to acknowledge the little things he did. I didn't understand, so I thought he was just being too demanding. Now that I understand my appreciating the things he does is the best way I can show him my affection, then I am happy to do it. It has made our relationship so much more fun and light."

When Gary Took Lisa Out for Dinner

In the beginning, Gary brought Lisa to a nice restaurant and she was particularly appreciative. She was happy to be there and enjoyed the food a lot. Gary was particularly impressed by how responsive she was. After several dates, she was not so appreciative. The thrill of going to restaurants was over. She stopped being responsive and instead started being rather negative. Instead of looking at what was good she responded to what was missing.

After a while Gary wasn't inclined to pick restaurants anymore. Instead of suggesting where to go, he just asked her where she would like to go. He felt, If she's going to be so picky, then I'll just let her pick the restaurant. After a while, they lost their feelings of attraction. At the seminar, they became inspired again to express their affection for each other.

When he would suggest a restaurant, Lisa was very careful to share in a responsive manner her most positive feelings. It was not that she was faking it. She had always had the capacity to bring up her positive feelings, but once Gary became more familiar, she was just relaxing and letting herself vent the frustrations of the day through focusing on the negative.

Certainly, sharing the frustrations of the day is an important part of a relationship, but it should not be attempted until stage four of a relationship. In stage three, both partners develop the habit of expressing their most positive side. Once that becomes automatic, then they are ready to balance the scales by sharing their negative feelings as well. Then she will have the sensitivity to make sure he feels acknowledged for providing such a nice dinner and he will have the understanding that she is not being critical of him.

When Ed Paid for the Tickets

In the beginning, Ed paid for the theater tickets and Elaine seemed impressed and appreciative. After they had dated for a few months, she got used to his paying for dates and began to respond as if he was supposed to do it. Even though up to stage four the man *is* supposed to, it should never be taken for granted, even if the woman is also doing things for him.

After Elaine realized that she was taking Ed for granted, she was immediately able to respond differently. Not only did she start smiling and thanking him, but she was careful to be responsive whenever he did something for her. When he planned a date, she was careful to say she was glad that he had taken the time to plan it.

Sometimes even if she thought it wasn't such a great idea, she appreciated his effort and went along, only to be surprised that she had a really good time. She began really to appreciate not having to think and plan all the time. That in itself was more important than planning the perfect date. Ed loved it and was always thinking of things they could do together, since she was so positive in her response. Instead of getting a list of things that could be wrong or go wrong, he got her support. This brought the fun back into their dating.

When Rick Complimented Colleen

In the beginning, Rick used to compliment Colleen. She used to smile and let it in. As they continued to date, when he complimented her, she stopped responding. She would sometimes say things like "Oh, I really don't like my hair this way," or "I can't believe that; this dress is really on the way out," or "I really didn't have time to get ready," or "Oh, you're just saying that; I must look awful." After a while, Rick just stopped complimenting her. He didn't even know that the change had occurred.

In the workshop he learned the importance of compliments and so he started giving them again. He asked Colleen just to let them in and say thanks. Colleen was open to learning about their differences and was willing to practice responding in a positive way to his compliments. After a few months, she said not only that she liked them more, but that she had started to believe them.

REALIZING THE PURPOSE OF STAGE THREE

Without understanding the purpose of the third stage, a couple can easily miss creating the experiences that will determine the outcome of their relationship. Each partner must experience the best the other has to offer. Both need to experience that they have the power to give of themselves and be successful.

In stage three, they need to create a history of dates where he has succeeded and she feels supported. In the future, when a partner is not so giving or receptive, they can easily trust that it is just a temporary setback and that they have the power to create a positive experience again.

This is not a time to evaluate your partner at all. Instead, it is a time to evaluate how you are doing and what you can do to be your best self and bring out your partner's best. To this end, men make romantic gestures and women focus on being receptive and responsive. If the outcome is that they are inspired to be their best, then they are ready to experience the real and lasting love that can grow only in the fourth stage, intimacy.

THE WISDOM OF WAITING

The wisdom of waiting to be intimate is that a man's desire has a chance to grow into the higher levels of expression. When a man takes time to move through the first three stages of dating, his physical desire expands into the emotional desire to please the woman. His desire to please her in turn develops into a genuine interest in who she is. This interest in who she is then has a chance to turn into love. When his physical desire is also the expression of his love for a woman, then this is the best time to experience increasing degrees of intimacy.

Having an exclusive relationship provides the foundation for lasting intimacy. A woman creates intimacy by honestly sharing more of who she is, and a man experiences increased intimacy by successfully supporting and nurturing more of who she is. As she discloses herself more, he can gradually get to know her. If he continues to be supportive as he gets to know her better, then the love he feels in his heart has a chance to grow.

6

Stage Four: Intimacy

When we are able to feel and experience the best in ourselves and in our partners, we are then ready to experience all of them and allow them to experience all of us. When we feel a chemistry with a partner on all four levels—physical, emotional, mental, and spiritual—then we are ready for intimacy.

These different levels of chemistry can be easily explained.

- Physical chemistry creates desire and arousal.
- Emotional chemistry creates affection, caring, and trust.
- Mental chemistry creates interest and receptivity.
- Spiritual chemistry opens our hearts, creating love, appreciation, and respect.

When we are turned on to a partner on all four levels, we are ready to move on to stage four.

By getting your needs met in the earlier stages, you are able to discover how much spiritual chemistry or love you feel for someone. Using the right dating skills cannot make you love someone more or make him or her love you more, but dating skills *can* assist you in discovering how much love you have for a person.

CHEMISTRY IS NOT CREATED

Chemistry on any level cannot be created. You cannot make someone physically attracted to you. All you can do is create the right conditions for that person to discover what chemistry is possible. You cannot just drill a well anywhere and find water.

When a woman in a restaurant gets up and walks to the rest room, a man gets to see her. Either he feels the chemistry or he doesn't. The same woman viewed by different men will evoke different degrees of attraction and interest.

In a similar manner, we cannot create emotional, mental, or spiritual chemistry. It just is. What we can do is create the right conditions for people to discover how much they love us or how much they find us truly interesting or how much they want to make us happy. All we can do is make sure we have the opportunity to feel chemistry to the degree it exists.

By setting up the right conditions in the earlier stages, we give whatever chemistry is potentially there a chance to be felt. When you have seen the best of a person over time, then your heart has a chance to open. With enough love in your heart, you are then prepared to experience the worst of that person and still come back to a loving connection. You are able to hold him or her in your heart even though you may be frustrated or disappointed.

THE POWER OF LOVE

When our hearts are open and we love, respect, and appreciate our partners, we are capable of supporting them even when they are not as perfect as we might have thought in earlier stages. Spiritual chemistry gives us the power to overcome the judgments, doubts, demands, and criticism we may sometimes experience. Even if our hearts temporarily close down, we can more easily find our way back to that love with the solid foundation of many loving and positive experiences.

Through repeatedly coming back to love, you will eventually gain the confidence and self-assurance necessary to pick your special partner for life in stage four. After getting married, you will be prepared when the big challenges of a relationship arise. Instead of going through the power struggles many couples experience, you will be able to draw on that spiritual chemistry to find the right compromise, to apologize when necessary, and to forgive your partner for not being perfect.

THE STRATEGY OF STAGE FOUR

In this fourth stage the strategy is slowly to become more intimate, revealing more and more of who you are. This is the time to relax more and just get to know each other. It is not necessary to keep up your guard and be as positive as in other stages.

A woman can open up more and communicate how she feels even when she is not in a good mood. It is fine for her to talk about the things that she doesn't like in her life and in the relationship. It is sometimes even better for her to interact with her partner when she is not in a good mood. She does not always have to be so positive when they are together.

This is a great relief for a woman. Now she can turn to her partner and share her vulnerable side; she can relax and be the rest of who she is. As she is able to share more of herself, how she thinks and feels, and a man continues to feel love, interest, caring, and desire for her, then she is ready to experience increasing physical intimacy as well. As a woman slowly opens up to experiencing more intimacy, she has a chance to rise up in waves of increasing fulfillment and pleasure.

Likewise, in this stage the man feels a relief as well. He has been looking forward to more physical intimacy. As the woman experiences the ability to open up and share all of herself mentally and emotionally, then they both rejoice in the opportunity to experience that love physically as well. A man's heart has a chance to open fully as he experiences increasing physical intimacy.

WOMEN ARE LIKE WAVES

One of the challenges of this stage is for men to understand that when a woman rises up she also comes crashing down. Women are like waves, as I explain in Chapter 7 of *Men Are from Mars, Women Are from Venus*. As a woman becomes more vulnerable in the relationship, then quite naturally her feelings tend to rise and fall. For many weeks she may feel very loving and happy, but then suddenly, after the wave reaches its peak, the wave crashes and she hits bottom.

> Increased intimacy makes a woman feel more
> vulnerable, and as a result her feelings will tend
> to rise and fall like waves.

When a woman's wave crashes, she has very little to give, temporarily. This is when a man is required to draw from his skills of stage three and continue giving his best without expecting an immediate return. He has to remember he has the power to provide for her happiness. When a man mistakenly assumes that he can't make a woman happy, he becomes very discouraged.

The many positive experiences of stage three prepare a man for this time when he doesn't seem to be as successful. A man can minimize his discouragement and frustration when the woman's wave inevitably crashes by understanding that women are like waves and by having many positive memories of times when he has been successful. Then, instead of feeling he can't do anything, he knows exactly what to do and has realistic expectations about the outcome.

> **When a woman's wave crashes, a man may mistakenly conclude that he can't do anything to make her happy.**

As the wave rises, a woman is able to give and express more and more love. When it crashes, regardless of how wonderful her partner is, she will temporarily lose (to different degrees) her ability to be as loving. She is suddenly not as self-assured, receptive, and responsive.

At those times, the man makes the mistake of trying to fix her. He tries to talk her out of feeling the way she does instead of taking the time to be more considerate and supportive in a way that works on Venus. Rather than giving solutions, a man can be most successful if he provides increased understanding and empathy. When her wave is crashing, what a woman needs to feel most is that she is not being judged or rejected for not being as loving.

> **When the wave crashes, a woman needs a man's love the most.**

When a woman feels supported, she doesn't necessarily feel better right away. It takes time. If she is on her way down, then a man's support will just make it easier for her to hit bottom. Once she hits bottom, if she feels his support, her wave will rise up again.

WHEN THE WAVE CRASHES

These are some common examples of how a woman feels when her wave crashes.

1. She Feels Overwhelmed

She may suddenly begin to complain about her life. Instead of feeling rejected, a man needs to listen and be understanding. After she has talked about all that she has to do, a man must resist giving a solution and give her a compliment.

If she says, "I have no time to go out. There is so much to do. I just can't do it all:" . . .

DON'T SAY	DO SAY
"Just don't do so much. You should relax and take it easy."	"You give so much of yourself for so many people. Let me give you a hug."
"Forget it and come out with me. We can have a good time instead of being miserable."	"There *is* so much to do." Then listen with empathy as she lists everything.
"You worry too much. It will all work out. Let's just go out and have a good time."	After listening for a while to everything that needs to be done, either offer to help or ask, "Is there anything I can do?"

Once she feels heard, a man offers his help. He must be careful not to expect his support to take away her discouraged feelings. She is not going to say, "Oh, thank you so much for offering to help; now I feel so much better." She can say that only when her wave is on the way up.

When the wave crashes, a man has to know that a woman's ability to appreciate him is at an all-time low. When the wave comes back up, she will then feel a lot of appreciation. Anyone can be loving when a person is in a good mood. The real test of love is to be there for her when she hits bottom. When a woman is down and a man is there for her then he is always remembered and appreciated. These are the times when a woman actually grows in her ability to trust her partner's love and support.

2. She Feels Insecure

She may suddenly begin to ask a lot of questions about the relationship or about how he feels. She may ask questions about how much he loves her or how he feels about her body. These questions are not to be taken literally. Don't try to solve her problem through reason. She is just looking for reassurances.

If she says, "Do you think I look fat?" . . .

DON'T SAY	DO SAY
"Well, you certainly don't have the body of model, but those women starve themselves."	"I think you are beautiful and I love you just the way you are." And then give her a hug.

DON'T SAY	DO SAY
"You shouldn't be so hard on yourself. I'm not."	"You look great just the way you are. I adore you." And then give her a hug.
"If you really want to lose weight then you should get help."	"You sure turn me on. I think you are a knockout." And then give her a hug and a kiss.
"If you would come with me to work out then you would feel better about your body."	"You look wonderful to me. I love your body." And then give her a hug and kiss.

If she says, "Do you think we are right for each other? Do you still love me?" . . .

DON'T SAY	DO SAY
"Well, I think we still have several things to work out."	"Yes. I am madly in love with you. You are the most special woman in my life."
"Well, time will tell. That's why we're dating."	"Yes. You are the most fantastic woman I have ever met."
"Why else would I be dating you for a year?"	"Yes. I love you more each day."
"How many times do we have to go through this? I think we have already had this conversation."	"Yes. My love for you grows each day I know you better."

*If she says, "How can you love me? My life is so
disorganized. I am falling apart." ...*

DON'T SAY	DO SAY
"Well, sometimes it is hard. I really wish you would not make such a big deal out of things."	"Well, I love you and I am here to hold you together. You do so much. Let me give you a hug. I sure love you."
"Your life is not falling apart. You just need to be less emotional."	"Well, you can fall right here in my arms anytime. I love you. You can call on me whenever you need me."
"You take on too much. If you would relax more, then things would not be so bleak."	"I love you because you are so giving. You give so much of yourself. What can I do to help?"
"If you wouldn't get so upset about things, it would be a lot easier to love you."	"I love you because you are special to me. I don't care if you're falling apart. I'm here for you."
"If you would prioritize your time better, then your life would not be falling apart. If you . . ."	"I love that you need me. I love being here for you. I have some time, let me do this for you . . ."

3. She Feels Resentful

Quite often, as her wave rises, a woman will happily give
of herself without realizing that she is also expecting more in

return. On her way up, she is not expecting more, but if she has given more than she feels she has gotten, she will feel resentful when the wave crashes. She may be resentful toward practically anything: her partner, her life, her job, his job, the weather, the waiter in the restaurant, her parents, the traffic, and so on. A man must be careful not to judge her or condemn her for being too negative or unreasonable, and he should not try to talk her out of her feelings.

If she says, "I hate my boss. I can't
believe how much he expects me to do.
He left me a memo saying . . ."

DON'T SAY	DO SAY
"I don't think your boss means to wear you out. He likes you."	"I think it's really unfair. How can he say that?"
"He probably doesn't know how much you're already doing. He just expects you to do your best."	"He doesn't recognize how much you do. You do so much. What does he want?" Then listen and let her talk more.
"You should tell him you just can't do more. Just say no."	"It's awful—doesn't he see how much you're doing?" Then listen and let her talk more.
"You should tell him how busy you are. Then he wouldn't give you so much more to do."	"Hummph, he expects too much. You deserve some time off. When do you rest?" Then listen and let her talk more.

If she says, "This waiter is really a jerk. We have
been waiting for our check for fifteen minutes." . . .

DON'T SAY	DO SAY
"Well, they're busy today. I am sure he's doing his best."	"I can't believe it. Those people at that table over there got their check and now they're leaving. I'll go find him."
"It's not his fault; they're short of staff."	"Yeah, he's ignoring us. I can't believe they have so few waiters."
"Don't worry, we're not in a hurry. We can still make the movie."	"If he doesn't come soon we could be late to the movie. I'll try to get his attention."

When a woman is feeling resentful, the last thing she
wants is for a man to minimize the problem about which she
is upset. She primarily needs to talk it out, vent her frustrations, and feel that someone is on her side. This is what intimacy is all about. She needs to feel that he is her ally.

To feel most loved, a woman needs to open up, share all of
herself, and experience that she is still loved. Learning to cope
with a woman's tendency to move up and down like a wave is
one of the most difficult challenges of dating for a man.

A WOMAN'S GREATEST CHALLENGE

Women also have a challenge with their male partners. Just
as women move up and down as a result of intimacy, men
move back and forth. When a man experiences increasing

intimacy, he begins to switch back and forth between wanting to get closer and wanting to pull away.

To move into a woman's life without losing his sense of self and sense of autonomy, a man moves back and forth between feeling a strong desire to get close and a desire to get away and be on his own. The more intimate a man becomes with a woman, the more he will sometimes feel a need to pull away.

As long as he hasn't yet become intimate, as in stage three, a man continues to feel a desire to be close, he plans to make her happy, and he is interested in getting to know her and express his love for her. He doesn't feel this need to pull away nearly as much.

Once he moves into stage four and experiences increasing intimacy, he will feel the need to pull away as well. To whatever extent he has given up parts of himself to move closer, he will feel a need to be autonomous. No matter how wonderful a woman is, as they get closer, a man will periodically pull away before he can get closer.

When a man experiences increasing intimacy, periodically he needs to pull away before he can get closer.

The more intimate a man feels with a woman, the more he will eventually feel a need to pull away. He can then return to her with even more love. Each time, after he pulls away, his love has a chance to grow when he returns.

THE IN-AND-OUT URGE

This basic in-and-out urge is in all men. It is associated with a man's high levels of testosterone, which all men have and women don't. Since this isn't a woman's basic experience, it is difficult for a woman to instinctively support a man in this process. As a result, she can unknowingly sabotage the growth of a man's love and attraction for her.

When a man pulls away, it is very important that she not pursue him or try to get him back. She must be careful not to be rejecting when he returns. A man needs to feel that she freely accepts his tendency to pull away.

Women mistakenly assume that more intimacy is better. When a man pulls away, a woman thinks something is wrong and wants to experience more intimacy. The wise woman learns to give a man his space and trust that he will once again find his hunger to be with her on his own. She understands that "absence makes the heart grow fonder." She even encourages him to spend time with his friends away from her. By giving him distance, she lets him feel his desire to pursue her and win her over and over again.

MEN ARE LIKE RUBBER BANDS

When a woman accepts a man's need to pull away, she sets the right conditions for him to find within himself his desire to be close to her. As I explained when discussing stage two, men are like rubber bands. When they pull away they can only stretch so far before they come springing back. By supporting a man's tendency to pull away, a woman ensures that he can find the love in his heart to come back.

Each time he comes back to her, he will love her more. His need to pull away will diminish slowly over time. It will always be there to some degree, but it becomes less extreme. A man's tendency to pull away is most extreme when he experiences intimacy before he is ready. If a man gets close to a woman before he has experienced chemistry on all four levels—physical, emotional, mental, and spiritual—he may not come back when he pulls away. If he has not experienced enough love, then the rubber band breaks. Let's explore an example.

Love at First Sight

When Derrick, thirty-two years old, first met Rochelle, who was thirty years old, he fell in love. It was love at first sight. Within a few dates they were already feeling and acting like soul mates. Derrick would call several times every day. They spent weekends together sharing everything. Derrick had never felt so passionate. Rochelle had been swept off her feet. Their relationship was romantic; they just couldn't get enough of each other.

Then after three weeks, Derrick stopped calling. Rochelle couldn't understand why. She worried that something had happened to him. She called him at work, but nothing was wrong. He was friendly, though definitely different. He didn't even plan a date with her. Rochelle was offended. She couldn't believe he could change so quickly from hot to cold. She acted nice but was devastated inside. She felt hurt that he talked to her as if she were just a friend.

She waited for two days and he still didn't call her. She couldn't believe it. She never wanted to see him again. She then proceeded to call and let him know how she felt. After a very uncomfortable call, they ended their relationship. She felt hurt and resentful, while he felt bad for hurting her.

He hadn't meant to lead her on. He had thought she was the one. All he knew was that one morning he woke up next to her and all he could feel is that she wasn't the one. He felt an almost uncontrollable urge to get away. As they had breakfast together, he began comparing her with the ideal woman in his mind. She just didn't measure up to what he wanted. As suddenly as he had fallen in love with her, he was now no longer in love with her.

He didn't know what to do, so he didn't do anything. When she called again and he heard how much he hurt her, he agreed to end the relationship. He felt sorry, but that was all he could do. He couldn't change his feelings and he definitely didn't want to keep hurting her.

Getting Hot and Then Cold

Six months later, after taking a Mars/Venus workshop, Derrick learned that men were like rubber bands. It suddenly made complete sense to him why he had been so hot and cold with Rochelle. He had gotten really close and experienced being intimate with her. Then while he was pulling away, she called him. He couldn't reassure her of his feelings for her because he was not feeling them. He assumed that she was just the wrong person for him. He wondered what would have happened if they had taken more time to get to know each other instead of rushing into stage four of the relationship. Although he wasn't feeling a deep hunger to be with her, as before, he did miss her. He decided to call her and explain what he thought had happened. They went to dinner to discuss the insights he had gained in the workshop.

One thing led to another and they continued to date each other. This time, although it was hard to refrain from having sex, they went more slowly. They decided to experiment to give their relationship a chance and took the time necessary to move through the different stages of dating.

When they finally reached the fourth stage, Derrick started feeling his need to pull away again. Like a stretched rubber band, he would spring back. This time, his need to pull away was not as intense because he had taken enough time to develop their relationship. When he pulled away it was only a few days before he started to miss her a lot. Derrick and Rochelle had developed enough of a relationship so that when he pulled away the rubber band didn't break. After about a year, they got married, and to this day they are very happy together.

THE FOUR DOORWAYS TO INTIMACY

There are four doorways to connecting and experiencing true intimacy. As discussed earlier, they are physical, emotional, mental and spiritual. Until we have prepared each of these different aspects of who we are, we are not ready to become deeply intimate in a relationship. If we rush into being too intimate before we are ready, the results will be counterproductive.

The first three stages of dating prepare us to experience intimacy. As we take the time to experience and develop physical, emotional, mental, and spiritual chemistry, we become capable of getting closer. If we become physically or emotionally connected before we feel mentally or spiritually connected, then we may feel incomplete.

We wake up the next day wondering who that person was with whom we just connected. Instead of wanting to get closer, we will want to get away. Or it may go the opposite way. We might feel, That felt good but something was missing; I need more.

When couples connect too soon, the man generally ends up pulling away, while the woman feels more needy. Some neediness and some pulling away are fine, but when we are not prepared on all levels, these two reactions are even stronger.

A man may pull away so intensely that he doesn't come back to the relationship. A woman will feel so needy that she will begin to pursue the man as he pulls away and turn him off. By first opening all four doorways, a man and woman become ready to experience true intimacy.

When couples rush into intimacy, the tendency for a man to

be like a rubber band and a woman to be like a wave is intensified. If they take time, her waves will not be so extreme and his rubber band will not be so long. They will have their ups and downs, but they will be more manageable.

WHY WAITING IS SO IMPORTANT

Through fully experiencing stage three, men and women are able to move through all the four doors to intimacy. For many men, it comes as a surprise when they experience that mental and emotional intimacy can be as fulfilling as physical intimacy. When a man eventually tastes the fulfillment of experiencing complete physical intimacy with someone with whom he also shares emotional, mental, and spiritual intimacy, he cannot go back.

Just to have sex when he could make love is like eating junk food when he could have a Thanksgiving feast. Why settle for less? It may take more time and energy, but it is real and lasting. By taking the time to move through all the five stages, a man ensures that when he does give all of himself it will yield the greatest return.

SWITCHING ROLES

As a man succeeds in being there for a woman, she will feel it's safe to become more vulnerable. This very process of a man's being there for a woman not only helps the woman but also helps a man open up to his feelings. By learning to respect and understand her feelings, he becomes more in touch with his own. Naturally, he will want to share more with her. Once she has gotten what she needs to open up and share herself, it is fine for a man to switch roles temporarily and allow a woman to be there for him.

In stage four, it is fine to switch roles occasionally. If the man has always planned the dates, she can do it now and then. If he has always been a good listener, now she just listens. If he has always initiated romance, now she initiates it sometimes. This switching of roles is an important step, but it must be done with caution. It is too easy for a man to sit back and receive and for a woman to give too much. When roles are switched, it should be done consciously, with an awareness that it is just occasional.

WHEN MEN FEEL AND TALK A LOT

Some men are already in touch with their feelings. They are very open and ready to talk. These men can unknowingly sabotage a relationship. A woman needs to feel first that a man is there for her; then she can be there for him without losing herself. When a man needs a woman more than she needs him, it can be a real turnoff. By making sure that he never talks more than the woman, a man creates the right balance in the relationship.

> **The man should be careful never to talk more than the woman.**

When a woman senses a man's need for support, it can actually prevent her from feeling her own needs. This is a big difference between men and women. When a man is there for a woman, he gets more in touch with his own feelings and needs. When a woman is there for a man, it may cause her to lose touch with her feelings and needs.

FINDING BALANCE

When a couple switches roles too much, a man may become like a wave and a woman may become like a rubber band. The problem with this is that when a woman is like a rubber band she may not spring back automatically like a man. When a man is like a crashing wave, it makes a woman feel overly protective of his needs and she tends to forget her own. He also runs the risk of becoming too soft and sensitive. To avoid this, couples need to find the right balance for them. Too much switching of roles can kill romance. In the right measure it is wonderful.

A man can go to his partner to share his intimate and private thoughts, feelings, needs, wishes, and wants, but he must be careful to do this only when she has gotten her needs satisfied first. He must also be careful not to be overly sensitive. If he tends to get more upset about things than she does, it can prevent her from getting in touch with her true sensitive feelings. This then can prevent them from experiencing the deep intimacy that can be felt only when the woman opens up and the man enters in to support her.

A man needs to be careful not to be too needy of a woman's time, energy, and nurturing support. It is way too easy for her to be accommodating and then, later on, resent the fact that she feels she is not getting the support she deserves. She may feel the need to pull away, but she doesn't happily spring back. Instead she feels pulled back by obligation. This can prevent a couple from moving on to the fifth stage of dating: engagement.

MOVING ON TO THE FIFTH STAGE OF DATING

By getting to know each other more intimately, when the time is right, we can easily recognize whether our partner is to be our soul mate. So many times people ask, "How do you know?" The answer is: Move through the first four stages and you will know. At a certain point, you will know whether this person is for you. At this point, you are ready to move on to the fifth stage of dating.

7

Stage Five: Engagement

Having prepared ourselves in the earlier stages of dating, we gain the ability to know if we want to marry our dating partner. We recognize our partner to be our soul mate. Not only are we in love; we love this person so much that we want to spend the rest of our life with him or her.

This recognition is only a glimpse. Although we are certain that our partner is right for us, this knowledge can later be doubted or forgotten. To make sure it is lasting, we must acknowledge and commit ourselves to it. It is important to strike while the iron is hot; otherwise, when it cools down, we may miss the opportunity.

> When we are finally able to
> recognize our soul mate,
> in the beginning it is only a glimpse.

By making the commitment to get married, we automatically strengthen and support this recognition. By acting on this feeling and becoming engaged, we make this delicate realization becomes more solid, real, and grounded. It must be carefully nurtured and protected, like a little sprout shooting forth in spring. With the appropriate care our love has a chance to grow stronger.

THE IMPORTANCE OF THE PROPOSAL

Most men don't realize how important the proposal is to a woman. On Venus, second to a wedding ceremony, the proposal is the most cherished memory of a lifetime. Some men rebel against this idea because they don't realize how important it really is. Besides being one of the most important gifts a man can ever give, a proposal paves the way for a great marriage.

> On Venus, second to a wedding ceremony,
> the proposal is the most cherished memory
> of a lifetime.

At difficult times in the future, it will be so helpful for the couple to look back to that very special moment and remember how they felt when their hearts were innocent, without any baggage, and they sincerely pledged their love to each other.

It is a wonderful gift for a man to create a memorable occasion. It will happen only once, so it's a good idea to put some extra thought into it. For the rest of her life, a woman will tell the story of how her partner proposed. A man should privately ask his married friends for some good ideas.

THE CHALLENGE OF STAGE FIVE

The greatest challenge in stage five is not to rush into taking on the responsibilities of marriage. Many marriages fail not because couples picked the wrong partner but because they did not prepare adequately. When the inevitable stresses and problems of moving in and sharing a home and life together arise, they begin to doubt that they are with the right person. They lose touch with the very special feelings of love and commitment they felt in stage five.

The engagement stage is an opportunity for the couple to create lasting memories of their special love for each other. It is a time to practice the most basic skills of loving before putting them to the test of marriage. Being engaged is like a warm-up period before more rigorous exercise. It is a time to stretch your relationship muscles so that when you put them to the test and exercise them, they will be ready. An engagement prepares you to succeed in marriage.

> **Being engaged is like a warm-up period before more rigorous exercise.**

When couples take at least five to eight months to bask in the certainty of their love, then they are ready when the big tests come later. As the stress of marriage increases, we are able to once again find that love in our heart because we have had many pure and untainted experiences of love for our partner and his or her love for us. Being engaged provides a strong and necessary foundation for taking on the challenges of moving in and sharing the complexities of life with a partner.

> Being engaged provides a strong and
> necessary foundation for taking on the
> challenges of moving in and sharing the
> complexities of life with a partner.

THE GIFTS OF ENGAGEMENT

The gifts of engagement are equally important but different
for men and women. A woman will be more successful in
marriage by remembering the clear and loving feelings she
experienced while being engaged. For the rest of her life, she
will be able to reach back and reconnect with the part of her
that trusts, accepts, and appreciates her partner.

The special commitment her partner makes to her helps
her to find the part of her that is self-assured, receptive, and
responsive. Later on, when life becomes mundane and routine, she will be able to reach back and find the part of her
that can create romance and is inspired by giving and receiving love.

During the engagement, a man also collects a series of
experiences and memories that will affect him for the rest of
his life. When he experiences his partner without the stresses
of marriage, but with the clear recognition that he wants to
share his life with her, he is able to feel his most confident,
purposeful, and responsible self.

Without the pressures of marriage, a man has many
opportunities to experience his power to provide. This confidence gives him the power and commitment to solve the
problems and resolve the conflicts that will arise in the
future.

> **Without the pressures of marriage,
> a man has many opportunities to successfully
> experience his power to provide.**

Being engaged gives a man the future ability to connect with the most noble part of who he is. At times of stress, he is able to reach back and remember the promises he made when his heart was open. He is able to reconnect with that part of him that deeply cares, respects, and cherishes his partner.

THE TWO MOST IMPORTANT SKILLS

Being engaged is a stage for couples to celebrate their love in preparation for getting married. During this window of time, we have the greatest ability to learn and practice the two most important skills of staying married: the ability to apologize and the ability to forgive. By practicing these two skills before the more difficult challenges arise, couples are then ready to get married. These two skills are like the two wings of a bird. Without both wings the bird of love and peace cannot fly.

Apologies and forgiveness are interdependent. When one partner apologizes, that makes it easier for the other to find forgiveness. When one partner is very forgiving, that makes it easy for the other to be more responsible and apologize. It is difficult for a man to apologize for his mistakes when he does not sense he will be forgiven. It is equally difficult for a woman to forgive a man's mistakes when he does not apologize. One cannot exist for long without the other.

When Men Apologize

To develop these skills most effectively, a man should first focus on being responsible for apologizing for his mistakes and a woman should first focus on being responsible for forgiving the man for his mistakes. Although both men and women must be able to apologize and forgive, by maintaining this particular approach, they will be most successful.

When a man can apologize for a mistake and be forgiven, then he automatically becomes forgiving of his partner. As he anticipates her love and acceptance, he can more easily acknowledge and learn from his mistakes. When he does not have to consider whether he will be loved, then he is free to consider what happened and how he could do it differently in the future.

A man's ability to self-correct in consideration of others is directly linked to how accepted he feels. When a man feels punished by his partner, it is difficult for him to become more considerate and sensitive to her needs. When men can apologize, not only are women happier, but the man also gets what he needs most—her trust, acceptance, and appreciation.

When Women Forgive

When a woman can forgive in response to a man's apology, she gains the ability to be more accepting and trusting. Without his apologies, she cannot easily grow in her ability to trust and accept a man the way he is. If he is unwilling to consider his mistakes, a woman will dwell on his mistakes until he does. She takes on the responsibility of improving him instead of staying focused on herself and improving her attitude.

> **When a man is unwilling to consider
> his mistakes, a woman will dwell on
> his mistakes until he does.**

A relationship thrives when a man focuses on correcting his behavior to be more considerate and the woman focuses on correcting her attitude toward his behaviors. By practicing forgiveness, a woman discovers her power to bring out the best in a man and herself. By finding the forgiving part of herself, a woman will connect with her most loving self.

THE PERFECT TIME TO PRACTICE

Engagement is the perfect time to practice giving apologies and finding forgiveness. Certainly it would be easier for the woman to do all the accommodating and apologizing and the man to be easygoing and forgiving, but they would not be prepared for marriage. Too often married women complain that their husbands never apologize, while married men complain that their wives are unforgiving and punishing and never forget anything they do wrong.

To correct this tendency we need to nip it in the bud. A man in stage five does not mind making apologies. This is primarily because he hasn't experienced years of being blamed and rejected for his mistakes. In stage five, he still anticipates being forgiven. That is why this is the best time for him to practice.

> **When a man focuses on his mistakes
> and not hers, he discovers a tremendous
> power to make her happy.**

A woman in stage five doesn't mind practicing being forgiving. After all, unlike her married counterpart, she hasn't experienced her partner's repeating certain mistakes for years. In stage five, she anticipates that he will continue to be considerate of her needs. As a result, she is most open to practicing forgiveness.

When a woman deliberately chooses to focus on creating a positive and receptive attitude by forgiving, she then discovers how much a man really wants to please her and support her. She begins to trust that he really is doing his best and that he can provide more and more of what she wants. She experiences and learns that her love, not her punishments, brings out the best in him.

MARRIAGE IS A MAGNIFYING GLASS

Engagement is the best time to practice because we are not yet married. It is still practice. It is still warming up to the real thing. Marriage is like a magnifying glass. Everything becomes bigger. Our love grows, but our problems and pressures become bigger as well. By practicing before marriage on issues that come up, both partners become more receptive.

In this stage, the man feels completely accepted after the woman has just agreed to marry him. It is at this time that he is most confident and responsible and therefore more willing to make apologies for his mistakes. The more he apologizes and gets forgiven, the more he will feel free to acknowledge his mistakes and correct certain behaviors in the future.

The more a man apologizes and is forgiven, the more considerate he becomes.

A woman is also more receptive to a man's mistakes. By clearly expressing her forgiveness when a man asks for it, a woman gives him the messages he needs to be the best he can be. The ability to forgive is the most important skill for a woman to have. With this power, she can keep letting go of little resentments that eventually build up and prevent her from being loving and responsive. In a similar way, the ability to apologize is the most important power a man can utilize.

WHY MEN DON'T APOLOGIZE

One of the reasons men don't apologize more in relationships with women is that apologies to women don't work—or at least men don't think they work. On Mars, when a man says he is sorry, he is saying he made a mistake. The other man happily accepts his apology. He feels, Okay, now that you admit you are wrong and I am right, we can be friends again. If there is a problem on Mars, it is usually the end of the discussion when one person finally apologizes.

On Venus it is the opposite. When you say you are sorry, the discussion begins. When a man says he is sorry to a woman, she will proceed to tell him in great detail why he should be feeling sorry.

> To find forgiveness, a woman needs to
> talk about her feelings until she feels that
> a man understands why she is upset.

He becomes very frustrated with this response because he expects his apology to be the end of the discussion. When she starts talking, he feels that his apology did no good. When his apology doesn't work, he does the next best thing he knows. He tries to make her feel better by explaining why she doesn't need to be upset. On his planet, if you have a good explanation, then the other person feels better right away.

If I am late for a meeting on Mars, I explain that there was an accident on the bridge and I was stopped for forty-five minutes. The other Martians feel better immediately. If I said I was stopped for two hours in gridlock, they would feel even better. If I said, "My daughter accidentally cut herself and I had to rush her to the hospital," they would not be upset with me at all. On Mars, the better the explanation, the better the person listening feels and the more forgiving he becomes.

EXPLANATIONS DON'T WORK ON VENUS

On Venus it is different. Explanations can make things worse. When a man gives a good explanation, he assumes that it should make a woman feel better right away. It has the opposite effect. She hears that he thinks she doesn't have the right to be upset. On Venus, before a woman feels better, she first needs to feel that the man understands that she has a valid right to be upset.

She cannot simply accept his explanation as a means of making her feel better; she needs first to talk about how it made her feel. She wants to be understood; then she is ready to do the forgiving. She doesn't even need a good explanation. She just needs to feel that he truly understands why she is upset.

These are some examples of Martian explanations and how Venusians may react:

HE SAYS	SHE HEARS
"I'm sorry that I was late. There was a huge accident on the bridge. The traffic was terrible. It was so hot and it took so long, I was stuck behind this huge truck . . ."	"I have a good reason for being late, so you shouldn't be so upset about this. You should be happy that I made it here at all."
"I'm sorry I got mad at you, but you were so critical of me. You said . . ."	"You were being so critical of me; You made the mistake, so you should be apologizing to me."
"I'm sorry I didn't call you back. I'm under a lot of pressure at work. You wouldn't believe the deadline I have to finish this project. I just don't know what to do . . ."	"You shouldn't be upset with me; instead you should feel sorry for me. I'm under so much pressure at work."
"I'm sorry that I forgot to get the tickets for the symphony. The weather was just so good I thought we could go sailing instead. This is the best time of the year to go sailing . . ."	"You shouldn't be upset with me; my idea of going sailing is a better idea. You should be happy with this plan."

HE SAYS	SHE HEARS
"I'm sorry that I left you for a while at the party. I didn't think you would feel left out. I was just talking with some old friends. I certainly didn't mean to hurt you. I thought . . ."	"You shouldn't be so sensitive. If you were normal you would not have felt so hurt. I didn't do anything wrong. I was just talking with some old friends."
"I'm really sorry about the things I said. I was just really offended by the way you spoke to me. When you said . . ."	"There was no good reason for the way you spoke to me. I said some mean things, but not any worse than you. You were the one who started it . . ."

To become more adept in the art of apology, a man needs to remember that with women explanations don't work. There is another approach that works like a magic charm.

THE ART OF APOLOGIZING TO A WOMAN

The art of apologizing to a woman has three steps.

1. Say You Are Sorry

When a woman is upset she first wants to hear that you are sorry. When you say you are sorry it signals to her that you are open to hearing her feelings. Briefly say you are sorry without giving any explanation. The least number of words creates the best effect.

2. Listen to Her Response

When you say you are sorry, then she feels you care enough to give her the opportunity to talk about her feelings.

Once she has talked about her feelings, you must be careful once again not to give any explanations or argue with her in any way.

If she then wants to talk further, you should just listen to her response. If she doesn't say anything, then you can move to step three.

Listening to a woman when she is upset is not supposed to feel good. If it doesn't feel very good to listen, that is okay. It is to be expected. Either you can choose to feel bad for a few minutes or she will make you feel bad for weeks anyway. When a woman feels upset, she needs to experience in some measure that you feel the discomfort she is feeling.

3. Respond with a "Nadjective"

When you make a mistake, use a negative adjective—a "nadjective"—to describe yourself or what you did. While listening to a woman talk in steps one and two, reflect on sincerely coming up with the appropriate nadjective to describe yourself at the time you made the mistake, instead of planning an explanation. These are a few examples of different nadjectives and how they may make a woman feel.

YOU SAY	SHE FEELS
"I'm sorry that I was late. . . . I was really *inconsiderate.*"	You're right. You were inconsiderate. Okay, you know how I feel. That feels better to me. I can deal with your being late sometimes. You don't have to be perfect. I just need you to think of me as well. I can forgive you. It wasn't such a big deal.

YOU SAY	SHE FEELS
"I'm sorry about the things I said yesterday . . . I thought about it and realized that I was really *overreactive* . . ."	That's right, he did overreact. Wow, he is being so responsible. I am really impressed. We probably both overreacted, but he admitted it. That is really good. He really did go away and think about our conversation. He knows how I must feel. . . . Well, he wasn't so awful. I can forgive him.
"I'm sorry I didn't call you back sooner. You're right; I was really *insensitive*."	Hmm, he really gets it. I guess he really isn't as insensitive as I thought. Maybe he does care about me. I can forgive him for that. I don't need him to call me all the time.
"I'm sorry that I forgot to get the tickets. It was really *selfish* of me."	It sure was. He didn't even think of me, he just thought about himself. . . . Hmm, maybe he isn't as self-absorbed as I thought. He doesn't have to do everything I want. A relationship is give-and-take. I can forgive him.
"I'm sorry you felt excluded at the party. . . . I was *inconsiderate*, it was really *mean*."	That's right, it was inconsiderate and it was mean. . . . In a way, he's really very considerate to realize that. I can forgive him. I'm sure he didn't mean to leave me alone.

You Say	She Feels
"I am really sorry about the things I said. I was really being *defensive*."	He *was* being defensive. I thought he didn't hear a word I said. I guess I was wrong. He is trying to hear what I am saying. I can forgive him. At least he cares enough to try to understand me.

In these six examples, the man apologized using one or more of these six nadjectives: *inconsiderate, insensitive, self-ish, mean, defensive,* and *overreactive.* These are the six most important. Certainly a man can come up with others, but these will do.

A woman never gets tired of hearing these nadjectives after a sincerely felt apology. It is like saying "Thank you," "Good idea," "That makes sense," or "Thank you for your patience" to a man. He never gets tired of hearing these phrases.

HOW TO FORGIVE A MAN

Just as it is important for a man to find the right words to apologize on Venus, it is equally important for a woman to express her forgiveness in a manner that works best on Mars. Just to say "I forgive you" can be taken by some men to be a put-down. If you express a receptive attitude that accepts a man even though clearly he made a mistake, he then feels most forgiven. These are some examples of phrases that can send a man to Martian heaven:

He Says	You Say
"I'm sorry that I was late. . . . I was really *inconsiderate*."	"It's okay. Give me a call next time, all right?"
"I'm sorry about the things I said yesterday. . . . I thought about it and realized that I was really *overreactive* . . ."	"Apology accepted. . . . It wasn't so bad. We were both upset. I appreciate that you thought about it."
"I'm sorry I didn't call you back sooner. . . . You are right; I was really *insensitive*."	"It's fine; I just didn't know what had happened." At this point she *is* receptive to his explanation.
"I'm sorry that I forgot to get the tickets. . . . It was really *selfish* of me."	"It's all right. You owe me one. Next time let's go to the symphony."
"I'm sorry you felt excluded at the party. . . . I was *inconsiderate*, it was really *mean*."	"It's no big deal, but it does feel good to know that you didn't mean to do it. I'm sure you'll make it up to me" (said with a smile).
"I am really sorry about the things I said. I was really being *defensive*."	"Thanks, you really didn't have to say that. I appreciate that you were trying to understand."

When a woman expresses her forgiveness with any of the above phrases, it frees a man from becoming defensive and allows him to be more responsible and considerate of her needs. These are some examples of how a man responds to a woman's forgiveness:

SHE SAYS	HE THINKS
"It's okay. Give me a call next time, all right?"	Wow, she is so accepting. Well, next time I need to remember to call. That's a reasonable request.
"Apology accepted. . . . It wasn't so bad. We were both upset. I appreciate that you thought about it."	Wow, she is being so loving. I shouldn't get so defensive with her. Next time I will try to hear her point of view better.
"It's fine; I just didn't know what had happened."	She is being so nice. I really appreciate that in her. I should call her more often.
"It's all right. You owe me one. Next time let's go to the symphony."	Umm. I really was selfish. Next time I am going to do something really nice for her.
"It's no big deal, but it does feel good to know that you didn't mean to do it. I'm sure you'll make it up to me" (said with a smile).	Well, it is a bigger deal than I thought. Next time I will be more considerate.
"Thanks, you really didn't have to say that. I appreciate that you were trying to understand."	She is so wonderful. Where did she come from? I love Venus.

In each of these examples a woman's forgiveness and acceptance motivate a man to continue trying to do his best in their relationship. By minimizing his mistakes, she makes him take her feelings and sensitivities more seriously. It takes a while for a man to understand how a woman may react differently to situations.

MAKING UP SO YOU DON'T BREAK UP

These techniques of apology and forgiveness can be used at any time throughout the five stages, but definitely they should be practiced as a prerequisite for marriage. As the potential problems and conflicts increase, it is vitally important to know how to find resolution and compromise. Without the practiced ability to make up, you may eventually break up. If you get into the habit of apologizing for the little things, then when the more difficult situations arise it will be much easier.

SINGLE AGAIN

Some people who are single again may not feel the need to get married. They are divorced and their children have grown up. To them there is no apparent reason to get married. In past generations, marriage was just to raise children. They believe they can have a deep and meaningful relationship without a lifetime commitment.

Likewise there are couples who do not plan to have a family. They also do not necessarily recognize the importance of getting married. In the past people got married primarily to ensure the survival and security of the family. If they are not planning a family, then why get married?

As we have already explored, times have changed. Today we get married to find more than survival and security. We get married to find personal fulfillment. Certainly a couple can share a deep and meaningful relationship, but unless they eventually move to stage five, their love will not continue to grow. Romantic love requires a soul commitment to thrive.

WHY MARRIAGE?

Marriage is the acknowledgment that our partner is special to us on all levels and that we are committed to the growth of love in the relationship. Marriage is a promise that we will hold our partner as more special than anyone else for our lifetime.

Without this commitment, something very important will be missing. For a woman to give a man the kind of special love, appreciation, acceptance, and trust that he wants, she must feel confident that her needs will also be met. She needs to feel that he adores, cares for, understands, and respects her so much that he will always be there for her. By settling for anything less, they will have less. The love they feel in their hearts will not have a chance to develop fully and be expressed.

REAL AND LASTING LOVE

The love we feel when we are engaged is not only real and lasting but also infused with hope. It is like a seed that contains the vision of possibilities for our future. It is the foundation on which we will build our lives. To nurture that seed and give it a chance to grow, we must take the time in stage five to celebrate our love.

Moving through the five stages of dating could be compared to baking a cake. Mixing all the ingredients together happens during the first four stages; then, stage five is the equivalent to putting it all into the oven. For the cake to rise there needs to be enough baking time. Taking several months in stage five gives us a chance not only to feel the warmth of our love but to make it solid.

Finding true and lasting love doesn't mean we will be able

to feel it all the time. Everything in the world moves in cycles. Night follows day, the tide moves out and then in, what goes up eventually comes down. Likewise, when the heart opens it also closes. The commitment of marriage helps us each time to open our hearts once again.

Each time we act and react in a manner that will keep this commitment of the soul, we once again open our hearts and align ourselves with our highest purpose.

HOW WE EXPRESS OUR SOUL

The desire to share our lives with someone is the expression of our soul. In practical terms, it is our soul remembering its highest purpose. By making a commitment to fulfill that purpose, we align ourselves with the power within us to be successful not only in our marriage but in our lives as well.

> **When we can make decisions from an open heart, then we are able to create a better life.**

In spiritual terms, the desire to be married is our soul remembering the sacred promise we are here to keep. It is God's will within us being felt. When we fully commit ourselves to keeping that promise we align ourselves with God's will.

All of the pieces in our lives begin to fit together when our hearts are open. By keeping our promise to love and cherish our partner above all else, we are able to open our hearts again and again. By making sure we keep our soul's promise, we are able to bring the spiritual into the material world. When we live in love, we bring the kingdom of heaven on earth.

THE SEED OF GREATNESS

The seed of greatness is our ability to know, speak, and keep our word or our truth. One power is physically to keep our word by doing what we say we will do. Another power is emotionally to support the people we care about most. Another power is to uphold and live in accordance with what we believe to be right and just. The highest power is to act, feel, and think from an open heart. When our hearts are open, we are able to act in accordance with our highest purpose, which is to love.

When we can do what we say we are going to do, we gradually find the power to manifest our dreams. When we can express the best of who we are, we gradually create the good fortune to attract in our lives all the opportunities we need. When we can act, feel, and think in accordance with what our soul wants to do, we can manifest greatness in our everyday lives.

By keeping our soul's promise, we infuse our lives with meaning, grace, and purpose. Marriage is the acknowledgment of that promise, and making sure a marriage works is the fulfillment of one of our soul's highest purposes. By making this commitment, we harness our inner power to make love last in our lives.

8
Making It Through the Five Stages

When either partner skips the earlier stages of dating, this can make it more difficult to get married. To get through the five stages of dating, it is important to respect the whole process. Each stage creates certain opportunities and challenges. The positive experience of each stage provides the basis for successfully meeting the challenges of the next stage. In school, it would have been very frustrating to take advanced algebra courses without first learning the multiplication tables. In a similar way, there is great wisdom in fully preparing yourself in each stage before moving on.

Without a clear understanding of the five stages, it is tempting to skip a stage, particularly when the challenges of that stage begin to show up. Instead of facing the challenges of stage one, a person might skip ahead to experience the benefits and promises of the next stage. The problem is that when the challenges of the next stage surface, a person is unprepared and tends either to lose interest or to go backward.

For example, in stage one, because we don't want to experience the possibility of rejection or failure, we may move too quickly into stage two, uncertainty. As a result, in the initial period of dating, we become overly picky before pursuing or flirting with a potential partner. Instead of being open to what a person can offer, we begin to test a person too soon. We are looking for certainty that this is the right person with whom to be exclusive instead of just having a good time dating.

Quite commonly, people skip stage two. Instead of risking the loss of a partner because they are not sure, they just move right into the higher stages. Instead of taking some time to test the relationship before getting more intimately involved, they panic and give in to the pressure of not knowing and behave as if they know for sure.

Instead of feeling secure that a man is the right man for her, a woman skips ahead by trying to prove to him that she is right for him. When the man feels uncertain, he may feel the pressure to show how committed he is as a way to impress her when in truth he is not ready. As they get more involved, they will both have a tendency to go back to uncertainty. He may tend to become indifferent and distant, while her tendency will be to become more needy and hungry for reassurance.

When a woman reacts to a man in stage one (attraction) as if she were in stage five (engagement), it is as inappropriate as it would be to ask a man on the first date how many people he wants to invite to the wedding, or how many children he wants to have. In most cases, when a woman reacts as if she were in a higher stage, that will make it more difficult for a man to progress though the stages.

The appropriate response when one falls in love in stage one is to stay in stage one and restrain yourself from reacting and responding to your partner in a manner that would be automatic in stage five. Then, after a few more dates, move into stage two (uncertainty) and try to maintain a sense of uncertainty. Even if her heart is jumping for joy or he wants to fly to Vegas to get married, they should proceed slowly, with caution, and let the relationship pass the test of time.

> **If you are quick to fall in love,**
> **be careful to proceed slowly and let the**
> **relationship pass the test of time.**

A woman needs to remember that she is the jewel and a man provides the right setting for her to shine. Instead of focusing on pleasing him because he makes her so happy, she needs to let him continue to please her with his actions. Instead of stopping her life for him, she needs to let him demonstrate his interest by making adjustments in his schedule for her.

> **A woman is the jewel and a man provides**
> **the right setting for her to shine.**

When a woman allows a man to make little sacrifices for her, he begins to feel that she is more special. She does not have to do anything to earn his interest. He is already interested. The more he gives and she graciously receives, the more interested he becomes. Without this insight, a woman can unknowingly prevent a man from wanting more of her by giving too much in reaction, being too eager to please, too enthusiastic, too accommodating, and too available. When a man feels he is winning a woman, she becomes increasingly attractive. He is able to find the necessary motivation to move on to the next stage.

WHEN A WOMAN MOVES FASTER

When a woman falls in love and behaves as if she is completely won over, as she would be in stage five of a relationship, a man will tend to stay in whatever stage he is in. There is no motivation to move ahead. When a woman moves faster through the stages, a man will tend to put on the brakes.

On Mars there is a very strong belief and instinctive tendency not to deviate from a formula that works. If throwing the ball a certain way wins the prize, then why risk changing? "Don't fix it if it isn't broken" is a fundamental Martian strategy. Women do not realize this difference, because on Venus it is just the opposite. If something works well, then they think, Let's see how we can make it better. When a relationship is giving a woman everything she wants, she is motivated to make it even better, but a man thinks, Okay, I can relax; I must be doing enough.

> On Mars there is a very strong belief
> and instinctive tendency not to deviate
> from a formula that works.

When a women reacts to a man as if she is in stage five and he is not, he will not be as motivated to move on to the next stage. He will tend to relax and stay put in whatever stage he is in. This is true whenever a woman reacts strongly in a stage beyond the stage he is in. Let's explore a few of the possible examples.

IF HE IS IN STAGE FOUR (INTIMACY) and she reacts as if she is in stage five (engagement), then he might feel, Why should we do anything to upset the applecart? Everything is fine. Let's not change anything. In this case, her being in a higher stage may prevent him from feeling the depth of longing, deep in his soul, necessary for him to decide that he wants to share his whole life with her. As a result, he may never feel a need to propose and become engaged.

IF HE IS IN STAGE THREE (EXCLUSIVITY) and she reacts to him as if she is in stage four (intimacy) or stage five (engagement), then his reaction might be, This relationship will be just fine for a while. Although he remains exclusively committed, he is not wanting more. His tendency will be to coast and take her for granted. He will have a greater tendency to give up doing all the little romantic things he did in the earlier stages. This passivity will cause him to keep noticing other women and eventually prevent her from feeling her love for him. When her bubble bursts, they will tend to go their separate ways.

IF HE IS IN STAGE TWO (UNCERTAINTY) and she reacts to him as if she is in stage three, four, or five, then his reaction might be, I sure don't want to disappoint her or hurt her; I'd better not call. I don't want to lead her on. Or he might think, She expects a lot. I don't think I'm ready for that. Although it is perfectly normal for a man in stage two to doubt a woman, if she is reacting from a higher stage, his desire to become exclusive will be influenced by the imminent possibility of hurting her if he were to end the relationship or of disappointing her if he did move on to the next stage.

The sad truth here is that the more he likes her, the more he will avoid getting involved because he might eventually hurt her. Yet if her reaction to him is also uncertainty, he does not have to worry about eventually hurting her if he were eventually to become exclusive and then break up. This freedom assists him in finding the confidence necessary to explore a relationship in the next stage, exclusivity.

> **The sad truth is that the more a man likes a woman, the more he will avoid getting involved because he might eventually hurt her.**

Let's look at a more extreme example. If a woman is desperately in love with a man or hopelessly dependent on him, the man is obviously going to think something like this: She seems so sure that I am the one for her. Well, I don't know. If I get involved more, I could be leading her on by feeding her hopes. She would really be devastated. I like her too much to do that to her. I don't think this is the right relationship for me. I'm not ready for this.

On the other hand, if a woman seems open at first to a man's advances and then later seems a little unsure about moving on to stage three, she becomes more attractive to him. If he is the one convincing her, he will not have to feel so bad if the relationship doesn't turn out well.

> **When he doesn't have to worry about how difficult it will be to get out of a relationship, a man is much more inclined to get involved.**

When a woman seems unsure and the man feels he is convincing her, then he can relax, knowing that if things don't work out and he stops convincing her, she will not want him. This actually frees him to make the commitment. A woman would not think this, because if she feels she has to persuade a man to love her, then when she wants to relax and be taken care of, he may not find that he loves her. This is just another reason why throughout the five stages men are to pursue and women are to create the opportunity to be pursued.

IF HE IS IN STAGE ONE (ATTRACTION) and she reacts as if she is in stage two (uncertainty), it can have the effect of making her seem too difficult. He may think, How can she reject me when she doesn't even know me? She must not be the right kind of woman for me, or, She is too critical or judgmental for me.

If she reacts as if she is in stage three (exclusivity), she may easily compromise her value to him. Imagine that you went house shopping and found a house you liked and the seller said, "You like it? It's yours. You pay me whatever you like." The chances of getting a respectable offer are very low. This situation is similar to the old joke by Groucho Marx, "I wouldn't want to belong to any club that would accept me as a member." However you look at it, when a woman sells herself cheap, she comes out looking easy.

If a woman reacts as if she is in stage four or five, it can cause a man to get really close and then back off. The promise of intimacy makes a woman very attractive, but the experience of too much intimacy can easily cause a man to lose interest. Even the best dessert can make you sick if you eat too much. A woman's challenge is to reveal herself in stages, not all at once.

WHEN A MAN MOVES FASTER

If a man behaves as if he is completely won over, it can be easier for the couple to move through the five stages, but still he runs the risk of turning her off. Quite often a man will be so persistent that he will smother a woman in promises. Although he is tempting and she feels flattered, she tends to mistrust him. She cannot be assured that he loves her because she knows he doesn't really know her. She knows he hasn't seen her on a bad hair day.

A woman needs to trust that she can get what she needs in a relationship. She is not easily impressed by a man's strong feelings. On Venus they tend instinctively to know that feelings are always changing. She needs assurance that his feelings will not change as they really get to know each other. Taking the time to react and behave appropriately for each stage of the relationship will ensure that a man can nurture in a woman the trust she needs to feel before moving to the next stage. Let's explore a few examples.

IF SHE IS IN STAGE FOUR (INTIMACY) and he behaves as if he is in stage five (engagement), then she might become turned off and think, He is acting as if we were married and I haven't even agreed. I don't feel that he will be supportive of my needs if I marry him. He doesn't even consider my feelings. In this case, his acting as if they are engaged can turn her off and prevent her feeling that she can fully surrender herself to this relationship. Before a woman responds with a yes to his proposal, she needs to feel that her feelings will be respected.

IF SHE IS IN STAGE THREE (EXCLUSIVITY) and he behaves as if they are in stage four (intimacy) or stage five (engagement), then her reaction may be, He wants too much from me; I'm not ready to share this much. I'm starting to feel obligated to do more. I don't know if I can give him everything he wants. I'm still just getting to know him. I'm not ready. Although a woman greatly appreciates a man's attention and his desire to be with her, when he comes on too strong she may become like a Martian and want her space.

When a man's advances consistently make a woman feel she is not ready, her tendency to move on is restricted. As a woman begins to experience that she can and will get the support she needs, then she will become ready to move on to the next stage.

IF SHE IS IN STAGE TWO (UNCERTAINTY) and he behaves as if he is in stage three, four, or five, then her reaction might be, How can he want me so much? He doesn't even know me. When he really gets to know me he will leave me. I don't want to be hurt. I don't want to get my hopes up. He thinks I am so perfect and I'm not. I can't trust his instincts. Although it is perfectly normal to doubt a man, when he comes on too strong, it can prevent a woman from trusting him enough to move on to an exclusive relationship.

Once again, the sad truth is that the more he likes her the more she will pull away and mistrust him simply because he doesn't realize the importance of respecting each of the stages. When a woman senses that a man is making sure he is the right person for her, then that attitude helps her find the assurance she needs in order to move on to an exclusive relationship.

Quite often men complain to me that women are not attracted to nice guys but that they get involved with guys who don't even seem to care. First of all, it is a myth that women don't get involved with nice guys. How many women whisper to a friend before they walk down the aisle, "I am so excited. . . . He's such a jerk"?

It is a myth that women don't get involved with nice guys.

One of the reasons men think women don't like nice guys is that when women reject men they almost always say, "You're nice, but I would just like to be friends." It is easy to conclude that women reject nice guys.

Every time a nice guy is rejected, he then mistakenly assumes it is because he was nice. This experience is compounded by the recurring situation of a woman complaining about a past relationship. If she is complaining, then she tends to focus on what a jerk the guy was. So once again a nice guy can't figure women out and wonders why she got so involved with a jerk. The answer to this question is that when she first met him she thought he was nice.

Women like nice guys, but they are turned off when a man seems too nice. When a woman is in stage one or two and a man behaves as if he is in stage three, four, or five, then she can easily lose interest. She feels he wants too much, he expects too much, and he gives too much, so she feels obligated to give back more than she is ready to. If he is too nice, then she is afraid of getting involved and hurting him. If he is really nice, she may also feel afraid that when he finds out that she is not always as nice as he, he will abandon her.

When women seem to be attracted to men who "don't really care," it is because these men are clearly in stage one or two, which is the appropriate stage to begin a relationship. When a man pursues a woman but is not yet sure about exclusivity and beyond, it can make him very attractive.

He is attractive to her because for a woman to open up and get to know a man she must also feel it is safe to back out and be unsure. When a man comes on really strong, it can make a woman feel she doesn't have the right to feel uncertain. As a result, she never gets the chance to find the assurance from within herself that she is ready to move into an exclusive relationship.

WHEN A WOMAN IS IN STAGE ONE (ATTRACTION) and a man behaves as if he is uncertain, then she may feel, He must not care that much. Even though I am attracted to him, I'm tired of giving out my card; I want a man to pursue me. Other times she may feel, Maybe he's just really shy; I'll flirt with him, and if he still doesn't ask for my number I'll give him my card. In either case, his being uncertain will prevent her from feeling more receptive to him. In some cases it may prompt her to pursue him, and then inevitably the attraction will dissipate.

When she is in stage one and he behaves as if he is in stage three, four, or five, once again it is very hard for her to trust him. She senses that he needs so much from her that she is turned off. Or she may sense that he wants her so much that if she were to say no he would be hurt. She then feels protective of him, similar to how a woman feels protective of a child, and the attraction is automatically lessened. This is when she wants to be just friends.

In all of these examples, a couple's ability to move through the five stages is restricted when one partner is too eager. It can also be that both partners are too eager and they skip stages together. This does not necessarily mean that they will not make it through all the stages, but it does mean that they will not gain the insights and ability necessary to build a strong foundation for the relationship to grow. They may even get married, but because they were not prepared, the inevitable problems and challenges that arise will be more difficult to deal with.

In general, men tend to become passive when women give more to the relationship, while women tend to be mistrustful and close up when a man gives too much. Neither men nor women should withhold their affections and responsiveness to each other, as long as they are appropriate to the stage of dating.

Since everything these days is so fast, we tend to move too fast in dating. We must be careful not to give much more than our partner is giving. For all the reasons listed above, it becomes clear why so many people today have such a hard time getting together.

LIVING IN THE PROMISE

Quite commonly, a woman makes the mistake of anticipating what a man will give her if she is loving to him. In a sense, she lives in the promise of getting his love, and so she becomes more loving. If someone you trusted told you that you had just won a million dollars, you would probably become really excited. You would feel like a millionaire. After calling to make sure the check was on the way, you would probably go out and begin spending some of your money. You would begin acting like a millionaire. If you discovered later that it was just a hoax and you were not a millionaire, not only would you be disappointed, but you would also be in debt.

When a woman lives in the promise of a man's love, because she believes that she will get what she needs, she is happy to give in advance. The more she gives in advance, the happier she becomes because she assumes she will get it all in return. When she gives in advance and not in response to what he has given, then it has the effect of making him less interested.

It is a mistake to believe that if she turns him on, fulfills his every need, and happily accommodates his wishes, he will do the same for her. Some women are taught that for a woman to get a man to love her, she should be pleased by everything he does, wait on him hand and foot, and laugh at all his jokes. Although this might work if he did this for her, when a woman gives in this way, she unknowingly lessens the attraction.

Men can also live in the promise. A man can fall in love with a woman and feel that he is the right man for her, that he holds the key to her ultimate happiness. Because he anticipates making her so happy, he behaves as if she is perfect. He behaves as if he is certain that he can make her happy. As we have discussed, when a man's behavior is too strong and he promises too much too quickly, it can backfire and cause a woman to close up.

By taking the time to move together through the five stages of dating, both men and women can minimize the illusions of living in the promise. By overcoming the challenges of each of the stages, we can learn the necessary lessons of love.

9
When the Clock Keeps Ticking and He's Not Wearing a Watch

Quite often a woman will feel the pressure to get married when her partner is happy to stay in stage four. She may hear the clock ticking because she wants to get married and have children and her childbearing years are running out, or she may just feel that something is missing in their relationship if they don't get married.

As we have already discussed, many men don't realize the importance of going all the way emotionally by getting married; if they are going all the way physically, they are satisfied. After all, he thinks he is getting everything he wants, so why should he risk moving on to the next stage? He doesn't know that by making a lifelong commitment to her not only would he get more on an emotional level, but she would get what she needed as well.

Marriage is to women what sex is to men. If a woman told a man she only wanted to go to second base with him, he would instinctively feel something was missing. He would want to go all the way sexually. Similarly, a woman wants to go all the way emotionally and get married. It is a common tragedy—a woman wants to get married and a man doesn't want to make that step.

> **Marriage is to women what sex is to men.**

When a woman is ready for stage five and a man stays in stage four, at a certain point the woman will make the mistake of either passively accepting his wants by denying her need to get married, or demanding that he marry her. Neither approach tends to work, as men don't respond well to ultimatums. Besides, what woman feels thrilled when her partner gives in to her pressure and agrees to marry her? A marriage proposal, just like a woman's acceptance of the proposal, should be a free and joyful expression of our heart's desire, not an obligation.

> **Men don't respond well to ultimatums;
> a marriage proposal should be the free and
> joyful expression of our heart's desire.**

Fortunately, there is another alternative to giving an ultimatum or denying one's need: a woman can move back a stage. Instead of being in stage five and demanding that her partner move on with her, she can move back to stage four—intimacy—and share how she feels in a nondemanding way without blaming him. Men respond much better when they are seen not as the problem but as the solution.

> **Men respond much better when they are seen
> not as the problem but as the solution.**

Margarette was thirty-four and had been dating Stephen for three years. She realized, however, that she had been responding to Stephen as if they were happily married although he had not even proposed. With an understanding of how she had contributed to the problem, she was able to share with him her feelings in a nonblaming manner.

She shared her feelings with Stephen:

> Recently I have had a lot of uncomfortable feelings. I realized that I am starting to doubt whether we will ever get married. I hope that someday I will get married, but I am starting to feel as if that may never happen. In my heart I feel that you are the one for me, but now I am starting to doubt that. I do not want to pressure you into doing anything that you don't want to do; I just need you to know why sometimes I am feeling distant. One part of me loves you very much and another part of me is not sure that I want to continue our relationship.

After a few conversations like this, Stephen surprised Margarette with a marriage proposal on a romantic occasion. If Margarette had given him an ultimatum or threatened to leave him, he might never have proposed. By releasing her demands and clearly communicating her feelings, Margarette created the opportunity for Stephen to solve the problem.

WHAT TO DO WHEN YOU HAVE MOVED TOO FAST

If you have moved too quickly through the stages, the solution is generally to move back to the appropriate stage. This is easier said than done. Exercise caution; an ounce of prevention is worth a pound of cure. When you have moved ahead too fast and you decide to move back, your partner may feel that you are taking something away. This can in itself create new problems.

When a man has been very attentive to a woman and he pulls back to stage one or two, it can hurt her a lot. Likewise, when a woman has been physically intimate with a man and she pulls back, he can easily feel that he is being unfairly punished. In both cases, a mutual understanding of the wisdom of the stages can make this necessary transition easier. It is best, however, to think ahead and not move too quickly in the first place.

A clear awareness of each of the stages assists us in making the decision to move back and express ourselves in an appropriate stage. Also, when our partner has advanced too far we have the language and understanding to ask him or her to slow down. It is quite common in matters of love to be so enthusiastic that we make mistakes. Wise people forgive themselves or their partners for these mistakes and try again.

HOW TO AVOID DIVORCE

Although most single couples are unaware of this formula, it is applied all the time to save marriages. When a married couple plan to get a divorce they are generally advised to separate for several months before doing so. In some states it is even a law that before a couple can get a divorce they must first separate for six months. Quite often during that time they reconsider and decide not to get a divorce.

Separation is just moving back to an earlier stage. A separated couple may go back to stage one and date others as if they were not married at all. Sometimes after dating others for several months they decide to get back together. By moving back to an earlier stage of dating they get something they were missing and are now able to make their marriage work.

When married couples separate, they are moving back to an earlier stage of dating.

At other times couples agree to live separately but not to date others. This is like going back to stage two, uncertainty. They live on their own without looking for others to date and consider if they want to get back together. They occasionally go out and explore how it feels to be together without being so dependent on each other. Eventually they may decide to move on to the next stage and get back together, or they may split up.

Other couples may decide to separate and date each other again as if they are in stage three or stage four. When this is the case it is particularly difficult for a woman to connect with her loving and romantic feelings if she doesn't have the opportunity to experience greater emotional intimacy. Similarly, a man needs to experience intimacy on the physical level of the relationship in order to experience his loving and romantic feelings.

To ignite romantic feelings a woman needs emotional intimacy while a man needs physical intimacy.

Certainly a woman should open up sexually only to the degree to which she is comfortable. However, accommodating a man's needs to is very helpful in making sure that he has a chance to open his heart again. A man should not expect a woman to be as responsive as she once was, and should be grateful that she is willing to accommodate his needs.

Meanwhile, he must make some sacrifices to accommodate her need to experience emotional intimacy. She will need to talk about the problems she has experienced throughout their marriage. While this may be difficult for him, he should give her the opportunity to share her feelings, and he should listen nondefensively. She should not expect him to be thrilled by this requirement, but should be grateful that he is willing to do his best to accommodate her needs.

Quite often going to a marriage counselor can make this process much easier. The more she can talk freely, the more she will be able to feel her love again. By making a deliberate effort to accommodate each other's needs at this difficult time they can reignite the love and passion they used to feel.

However, going backward is always more difficult than going forward. If couples initially take the time to move through the stages, they can create a solid foundation so their house will not get cracks. By devoting time to overcoming the challenges of each of the five stages they can avoid having to face divorce.

WHEN TO KEEP MOVING BACK

When a woman wants to get married and her partner is resistant—and moving back to stage four doesn't work—she should move back to stage three; if that doesn't work, she should move back to stage two or even one. By moving back gradually she and her partner can experience the earlier stages of the growth of love.

In this way a man can gain the strength and clarity to either end the relationship in a positive manner or make a marriage proposal. It will also give the woman the strength and clarity to either end the relationship if he doesn't propose or respond with a big yes if he does.

In order to move back to stage three, a woman would have to let her partner know that she didn't feel the relationship was going where she was going. She would need to let him know that she loved him but that she did not want to be as open and vulnerable to him. She would see him less and just focus on how she could respond to what he gave her in the most loving way she could.

WHEN SHE REJECTS HIS PROPOSAL

If, however, she moves back to stage three and he does eventually realize that he wants to marry her, she may suddenly feel resentful that he took so long to propose and then reject him. Although she moved back to stage three so that he might propose, when he does she suddenly has a change of heart. She feels either angry with him or uncertain. Instead of being receptive to his proposal, she rejects him.

While on Mars this doesn't make sense, on Venus it does. Sometimes a woman is so concerned about getting a man's love that she doesn't realize how hurt she feels to be rejected. She automatically suppresses her hurt and resentment. When he finally does give her the love she wants, she is suddenly faced with a surge of resentment and hurt or just feels a temporary numbness.

These feelings must be handled very delicately. With this new insight into the five stages, she can see beyond her immediate reactions and realize that it is her hurt talking and not her heart. If she doesn't say yes to his proposal, she should as least ask him to propose again in a month. By taking some time to explore her feelings she can release her temporary feelings of hurt and resentment and find the deeper soul love in her heart.

....

**With this new insight a woman can see beyond
her immediate reactions and realize that it is her
hurt talking and not her heart.**

....

When Raj first met Tina, he fell in love with her. He knew
that she was his soul mate. They were very passionate and
within a few weeks were in stage four. He had never felt so
deeply in love. But it was too much too fast, and Raj found
himself pulling back. He was feeling uncertain and started to
have doubts. Tina, who had been swept off her feet by his
love, was now feeling deeply hurt. She called Raj, but he
didn't return her calls.

Months later, Raj realized that he had made a mistake. He
wanted Tina back and tried calling her, but now she wouldn't
return his calls. Each time he called she would listen to his
messages and feel her hurt. Fortunately, during counseling
Tina was able to learn that she felt that hurt because she still
loved him. She had resisted getting involved again because she
didn't trust his love. She felt, "How could he really love me if
he could pull away so easily? He was so cold and indifferent
to me."

By understanding the five stages, Tina was able to understand
how she had also contributed to the problem. She learned that
by going more slowly this time she could trust his love. She
learned that Raj had pulled back because he had gotten close
too quickly, not because he didn't love her. Raj and Tina were
lucky to get back together. Without this understanding, many
men and women bounce back and forth and miss each other.

MOVING BACK TO STAGE TWO: UNCERTAINTY

When a woman moves back to stage three and her partner
does not propose, after a few months she will generally begin

to doubt that he is the right one for her. This is the time to move back to stage two, uncertainty.

To make this shift she might share her feelings like this: "I am sorry that I don't love you the way I did. I know I love you, but because you don't want to get married, I am closing down. I don't trust that you are the one for me. I need to pull back into myself to decide what to do. I am not ready to date others. I would still like to date you if you call, but I need more time on my own. I am just not sure." By making this transition and taking this time to be in stage two, she will benefit in two ways.

The First Benefit of Uncertainty

The first benefit is that it connects her to the truth that he may not be the right person for her. This awareness can give her the clarity, strength, and courage to break off from him in a positive manner. Instead of feeling cheated she will eventually feel grateful that she didn't marry the wrong person.

There is no better way to complete a relationship than with positive feelings of gratitude. If she does not feel grateful for his inability to commit, then she has not yet accepted that he is not the one for her. She is still blaming him. As we have already discussed, this negative attitude may prevent her from moving on to find the right person for her.

By giving herself the permission to feel uncertain and doubt him, she will eventually understand why he is also uncertain about getting married. This understanding will allow her to forgive him. From this place of forgiveness she is much more discerning in knowing who is right for her.

The Second Benefit of Uncertainty

The second benefit of moving back to stage two is that a woman gives her partner the space he needs to determine if he is the right person for her. By creating more distance between them, she gives him a chance to experience how much he loves her. Quite often a man feels how much he loves a woman when he is directly faced with the possibility of losing her.

> **Quite often a man feels his love when he is directly faced with the possibility of losing a woman.**

When she takes on the position of being uncertain, it frees him to find the certainty in him. Quite often a woman can unknowingly prevent a man from feeling his desire to be with her because she desires him too much. By being too interested, she can actually take away his desire and make him less interested.

As she takes the time to feel uncertain, he will suddenly become more definite about the relationship. Either he will realize that she is the one for him or he will realize that she is not and break off the relationship. In either case the result is greater clarity for both of them.

WHY A MAN'S FEELINGS CHANGE

Often, a man will realize how important a woman is to him after she rejects him. This is not necessarily because he has a neurotic need to feel in control or because he has low self-esteem and seeks the love of a woman who doesn't love him; it is simply because he needs distance to feel his longing and desire. When a woman gets too close to a man, he doesn't have the opportunity to feel his desire.

When couples move too quickly to experience intimacy, a man doesn't experience again and again how much he wants to be with a woman. In some cases he will realize how special she is to him only when she backs off and stops pursuing him. Quite often a man will pull back and then—once the woman has let go—he springs back with greater desire and love.

> A man will pull back, and once the
> woman has let go he springs back
> with greater desire and love.

This reaction is very confusing to a woman. When he comes back, she feels it is too late. She is unable to bend back to him because it is hard to believe that his sudden rush of love is real. She feels hurt and is afraid of getting hurt again; she thinks that if she goes back he will just lose his newfound interest. Without understanding how she contributed to the problem, she cannot trust that his love will be lasting.

Understanding of the five stages gives her the insight necessary to overcome her fear of intimacy and open her heart to trust his love. Once she clearly understands how she contributed to the problem, she can make sure it doesn't happen again.

Instead of feeling like a victim at the whim of her partner's changing feelings, she feels assured that she has the power to get what she needs. She can trust her partner's love when she feels the power to create the right conditions for their love to grow.

> Instead of feeling like a victim at the
> whim of her partner's changing feelings,
> a woman can feel self-assured.

With this deeper understanding, a woman does not have to reject a man to create the distance for him to fall in love with her. If they have moved ahead too quickly, she can recognize her mistake and begin moving back through the stages. By slowly moving backward she can create the required distance without having to break up or threaten to break up. While this is not the ideal procedure, it is better than having to break up again and again until she learns to allow love to grow more slowly.

Perhaps the man wants get married and the woman is not ready. As we have already discussed, he should just move back to stage four and share his feelings in an intimate but nondemanding manner. If this doesn't work, he should slowly move back through the stages, being careful not to hurt his partner's feelings. Remember that this is a very delicate situation and should be handled with great sensitivity and consideration. Whether he is moving back or she is, reading *Mars and Venus on a Date* together or getting the assistance of a relationship counselor can make this process much easier.

10
Men Are Like Blowtorches, Women Are Like Ovens

When Martians and Venusians get together without understanding that they come from different planets, it is quite easy for a woman to misinterpret a man's interest and experience repeated frustration and disappointment. Often a man will suddenly become physically attracted to a woman and then just as quickly lose interest. He is like a blowtorch that can heat up really fast and then turn off in an instant. This Martian tendency is easily misinterpreted because women are not like blowtorches. Women are like ovens. They slowly heat up and slowly cool off.

A man's physical attraction heats up right away, while a woman takes more time.

A woman assumes that if a man is physically attracted to her, he is also interested in pursuing a relationship with her.

She confuses his attention, interest, and attraction with affection or love. When this "love" is not lasting and he quickly loses interest, a woman can easily feel disappointed and unnecessarily begin to mistrust men. Unless she learns how men and women think and feel differently, she may become closed to men and thus limit her chances of finding the right man for her. Without this crucial understanding, dating for many women is a very dissatisfying and discouraging experience.

> **Women commonly confuse a man's interest as the intention to pursue a relationship.**

Certainly when a man is attentive to a woman, he could also be interested in having a relationship with her, but quite often he is not that discerning. To a certain extent, when he is enamored of a woman, he just likes what he sees and he wants to touch. Then he behaves in ways that most women mistakenly assume to be clear signs and signals that he is interested in having a relationship.

A MAN'S PASSIONS

Without even considering what kind of person a woman is, a man can feel a strong, passionate desire to be with her. Then, once he gets to know her, he may find that he doesn't even like her, nor is he interested in getting to know her better. Yet when he sees her he feels a strong physical chemistry and will do almost anything for the opportunity to be with her, impress her, and make her happy. As he gets to know her, his interest and affection may quickly dissipate.

This is commonly known as the morning-after syndrome. One day she is beautiful and radiant in every way; the next day, after a closer look, her toes are too big. Once he gets to know her, his passion dissipates, he finds something wrong with her or realizes that she is not the one for him, and he moves on. He has no idea that she thinks they are about to get married. Anyone on his planet would know that he was just physically attracted, but someone from Venus could easily misunderstand his intentions and think he was promising much more.

A WOMAN'S PASSIONS

A man's strong physical passion, interest, and attention are easily misunderstood because women come to relationships the other way around. Women are first attracted to some aspect of who a man is and not just his body. A woman first feels interested in getting to know a man, then she feels affection, and then she feels strong physical attraction and desire. The more a woman feels mentally and emotionally attracted to a man, the more physical chemistry she will begin to feel. Since this is her experience, she mistakenly assumes that when a man is physically attracted to her, he must be mentally and emotionally attracted as well.

It is hard for a woman to understand how men could be so different, but they are. On Mars, they are first attracted by the physical. The more physically attractive a woman is to a man, the less he needs to think or discern. He automatically behaves as if she is the most special woman in the world, and she believes it. He is just being in the moment and feeling his attraction. What she doesn't know is that the next day he could be with someone who turns him on and feel the exact same feelings of attraction. Without this understanding of our differences, women assume that men are either deceptive or just superficial.

WHY VERY ATTRACTIVE WOMEN ARE VERY ANNOYED

The more physically attractive a woman is, the more annoyed she may become with men. Men who have no deep interest in her are constantly pursuing her. Although a woman may feel flattered by a man's attentions, after a series of disappointments, it can become a source of resentment as well. These are some common frustrations of women who became sexually intimate too quickly:

Jill complained, "I can't believe the men I meet. At first they are so charming and interested and then they just turn off and you never hear from them again."

Jane said, "I can't trust men. They are so selfish. They pretend to be very interested and then when they get what they want they are gone."

Karen shared, "I don't even like to date anymore. When a man is so giving, I feel obligated to give him what he wants, and then I get nothing. I would rather get nothing and be alone than give myself and then get nothing."

Carolyn questioned herself: "I don't know what I do, but as soon as a man gets to know me, he doesn't like me. I don't think any man could love me."

Nancy wondered, "Why is it that the men I meet are all jerks? At first they stick to you like glue and then the next morning you feel that they want to get away from you. I called one guy the next morning and he asked why I had called! I can't even imagine saying that to someone."

Yvette asked, "Why do I attract men who only want one thing? They are always so nice in the beginning, and then after having it their way, they don't even call."

These women have a right to be upset. They innocently responded to a man's advances and then felt disappointed or betrayed. They felt in some ways tricked by his sudden shift in interest. What these women don't realize is how they are also a part of the problem. In each example, the women misinterpreted a man's behavior and mistakenly assumed they were further along the five stages of dating.

To correct this problem, a woman needs to understand what makes her special to a man. Then she can proceed correctly in each of the stages of dating. Without correctly interpreting the signals, she will mistakenly conclude that she is in stage four when from his side he is still in stage one.

WHAT MAKES A WOMAN SPECIAL

There is something special about every woman, but what makes a woman more special to a particular man is the special chemistry he feels for her. This chemistry cannot be created. It either exists or doesn't exist. An apple seed is an apple seed. It can't become anything other than an apple tree. The only thing we can do is make sure we recognize its needs and give it a chance to grow. Too much water can rot the roots, while not enough will starve it. How we approach a relationship can either prevent or support the growth of attraction.

> We cannot create chemistry, but we can
> either prevent or support its growth.

A woman first feels that she is special to a man when he feels physically attracted to her. A woman must remember that she is not that special, because there are a lot of women to whom a man can feel physically attracted. It is a good beginning, but it doesn't necessarily mean anything more. To him, in that moment, she may be the ultimate woman of his dreams. In this case, he may believe and behave as though he were in love with who she is, but only time will tell, by giving him an opportunity to get to know her.

A woman becomes more special to a man when he finds that not only is he physically attracted to her, but he also likes her. There are many women to whom he can be physically attracted, but only a smaller group with whom he can also be friends. A woman becomes even more special to him when he also finds that he is mentally attracted to who she is as a person. There are only a few women for whom he can feel all three levels of chemistry.

She becomes still more special when he is able to see her as an imperfect person but also lovable. Even at difficult times in their relationship, when he is not getting what he needs from her, he is able to still see the good in her and feel his love for her. This kind of unconditional love makes her very special. Then, within this very small and special group, his soul picks one to share his life. It is then that a woman is most special to a man.

WHAT MAKES A MAN SPECIAL

A man becomes more special to a woman in a reverse manner. She is first mentally attracted to him. She looks at some aspect of who he is and what he is doing with his life and feels some chemistry. This is the largest group of men from which she picks. Then she finds that some men are more special. She begins to feel emotional chemistry; she begins to feel affection for a man and like him as a friend as well.

While there may be many men with whom she feels mental chemistry, there are fewer men who cause her to feel emotional chemistry. At this point, she may discover that she also feels a physical attraction. It might happen slowly or it might happen very suddenly. Quite often, it happens when he gives her a kiss. That one little gesture of affection can suddenly make it clear to her that he is more special. When a shy man postpones the kiss, it may actually postpone or even prevent a woman from feeling her physical chemistry for him.

> **Sometimes it is a man's kiss that triggers in a woman her feelings of physical attraction.**

Many of the traditional dating rituals between men and women are really just opportunities for a woman to assess her feelings for a man. When a man does little things for a woman, like open the door, compliment her, ask her out, plan a date, or even give her a good-night kiss, it allows her gradually to experience different levels of chemistry.

WHEN WOMEN ARE ATTRACTED TO THE WRONG MEN

Sometimes a woman meets a man and suddenly feels all four levels of chemistry. She particularly feels an immediate physical passion for him. This is a clear sign that this woman is attracted to her fantasy of the man and not the man himself. When this is the case, a woman needs to learn to be more discerning. If she feels strong physical attraction, she should not immediately assume that the man is right for her. Although there is a chance he could be right for her because she is turned on immediately, it is a clear sign that she does not yet know him. She is attracted to the illusion of who she thinks he is.

If a woman has a history of being turned on to the wrong guys, then when she enters a room with thirty men and one man turns her on like a blowtorch, she should run the other way. If she does choose to engage in a relationship with him, she should be very careful to get to know him before she becomes intimate.

....

**If a woman enters a room with thirty men
and one man turns her on like a blowtorch,
she should run the other way.**

....

This phenomenon helps explain why therapists commonly hear this comment from single women: "Whenever I'm passionately turned on to a man right away, he turns out to be the wrong one. Why do I keep picking the wrong kind of men?"

These women would do well to experiment with having a relationship with a man who doesn't turn them on right away to see if in time the passion grows. Katherine, a forty-six-year-old single businesswoman, was amazed to hear this. All her life, she had rejected men who didn't turn her on right away. Many men had approached her, but if she didn't feel something physical right away, she wasn't interested. This understanding helped her realize why she had not found her soul mate.

WHEN A WOMAN OPENS HER HEART

After a woman begins to feel all three levels of chemistry—mental, emotional, and then physical—her heart begins to open to a man. Now she can truly experience how much love she has for this man. As they move through the fourth stage of dating and intimacy and she continues to feel an unconditional love for him, then he becomes even more special. All four levels of chemistry grow together until her heart fully opens and she can realize that he is the one for her.

A man should not be discouraged if a woman is not immediately interested in a physical way. A man needs to remember that a woman is like an oven that slowly warms up. If she just wants to be friends at first, it doesn't mean that he does not stand a chance. Quite often women who have found their soul mates say that at first they were just friends and that the romance came later. Their husbands point out that the potential for physical attraction, from their side, was almost always there.

MEN FEEL PHYSICAL ATTRACTION FIRST

When a man meets his soul mate, there is almost always a spark of physical attraction to start with. When it is not there, it could simply be that he doesn't understand the importance of having standards. He simply follows his attractions and doesn't learn to become more discerning about whom he picks. A man temporarily loses his ability to feel physical attraction for a woman who could possibly be his soul mate when he consciously chooses to pursue other women whom he clearly knows are not his type.

The more a man pursues women he could not love, the less he is able to feel physically attracted to a woman that he could love. By learning from his experience to distinguish between the women to whom he is attracted, a man gets closer to finding the right person for him.

> **The more a man pursues women that he could not love, the less he is able to feel physically attracted to a woman whom he could love.**

The more discerning we become about whom we are willing to share a relationship with, the closer we get to finding our soul mate. Although a few people hit the target in a few tries, most of us go through the normal process of trial and error. Through repeated self-correction, we eventually meet the right person. This process of increasing discernment develops in predictable stages. By understanding the four levels of discernment, you can sense how close you are to finding a soul mate. Let's explore these levels in greater detail, first for men and then for women.

LEVEL ONE FOR MEN: PHYSICAL ATTRACTION

At the first level, it is quite normal and natural for a man to be physically attracted to many women. He is particularly attracted to the way a woman physically looks: her walk, her body, her hair, her smile, her eyes, her height, her legs, her rear, her breasts, and the overall shape of her body. Men tend to like one or two particular features. For example, one man may particularly be attracted to legs while another insists on blond hair.

This physical attraction is the first and lowest level of discernment for men. Generally a young man starts out on this level. Even a more mature man may regress to this level when he is on the rebound from a relationship. A hungry man is not picky about what food he eats.

Since this physical attraction is mindless, a man's low level of discernment is enormously influenced by what he sees on TV and in movies and magazines. We are bombarded with images of a particular type of woman who always appears sexually receptive, responsive, and self-assured. We are hypnotized to want one type. This attraction has nothing to do with whether a woman is his soul mate. A young and undiscerning man can even feel physical chemistry by looking at a naked store mannequin.

Basically one female body type is heavily marketed to be the most attractive to men. As a result, a man associates a certain body type with sexual receptiveness and is automatically attracted to that type. Women also tend to consider that body type to be the most beautiful and worthy of love because it is that body type that gets a man's attention, which they mistakenly assume is his affection.

As a man matures and moves through the first three stages of dating, he automatically becomes more discerning and discovers that he is also attracted to women who don't look like the seductive women on TV and in the movies and magazines. When a man finds his soul mate, she is rarely the type he was most attracted to at the more undiscerning level.

While physical attraction is the foundation for a man's discernment to build on, it is still mindless. A woman needs to remember that even if he does not know anything about her except how she looks, he will suddenly start to feel physically attracted. His attraction has nothing to do with who this women is, nor does it reflect a willingness or desire to know her or have a relationship with her. He only wants to see more, touch more, and feel more.

LEVEL TWO FOR MEN: EMOTIONAL ATTRACTION

After some dating experiences with some of these women the man is attracted to, he starts to find that he likes some better than others. This is an important step. Just as he is able to feel a physical attraction, now he will begin to feel an emotional attraction as well. When he experiences a woman, he will not just feel physical attraction but will also sense how much he likes her.

At level one, physical attraction, he may *think* he likes her because he likes how she makes him feel, but at level two, emotional attraction, he can know if he really likes *her* and not just how she makes him feel. When a man feels emotional chemistry, he feels friendly and affectionate toward a woman not just because he feels physically attracted; he wants to be close because he likes her as well.

Emotional chemistry has a lot to do with a person's personality. Personality is how you relate to the world and others. Quite often, opposite personalities are attracted to each other. Some men like a woman with a bubbly or perky personality, while others like a more stable or relaxed personality. The possibilities are really endless. We can be attracted to someone like ourselves, but generally we are most attracted to people who are *not* like ourselves.

For example, a very stable personality with somewhat fixed routines may be attracted to a person who likes change and excitement. A very bold, outwardly directed personality may be attracted to a shy, inwardly directed person. A very assertive personality may be attracted to a more supportive or accommodating personality. An easygoing personality may be attracted to a more formal personality. A playful personality may be attracted to a more serious personality. No one personality is intrinsically more attractive than another, but as we become more discerning we find that we are automatically attracted to the people we like more and could be friends with.

LEVEL THREE FOR MEN: MENTAL ATTRACTION

By exercising his discernment and choosing only to date women he is attracted to physically and emotionally, a man begins to develop mental attraction. He is intrigued by a woman and wants to touch who she is and not just her body. He is not just attracted to her physically, nor does he just enjoy being friends with her. In level three, he is attracted to her character as well. He is fascinated by the way she thinks, the way she feels, and the way she conducts her life.

At level three, his attraction to some aspect of her character brings out in turn the best of his character. It could be any aspect of her character: her kindness, strength, and power; or her wisdom, clarity, and generosity; or her honesty, openness, and fairness; or her patience, courage, and persistence; or her self-sufficiency, competence, and gracefulness; or her compassion, love, and spirituality. There is no one particular attribute or combination of attributes that makes a woman attractive to all men.

Some men will be attracted to more mature character development, while others will be attracted to less mature development. It may be a woman's abundant and mature wisdom that makes her attractive to a man, or it could be her youthful, innocent desire to know more. It could be a woman's selfless generosity that makes her attractive, or it could be her desire to have more so she can share more. The degree to which a woman has developed aspects of her character does not interfere with making her attractive to a man. Neither more nor less is necessarily better. She is most attractive when she is herself and there is mental chemistry.

At level three, a man will begin to experience that a lot of women are interesting to him but only a few are outstanding. Only a few women will have the aspects of character to which he is most attracted. He will most successfully increase his discernment by getting to know and getting involved with only these women. Simply feeling physically attracted or friendly is no longer the primary requirement. Now a woman must also be very interesting to him.

LEVEL FOUR FOR MEN: SOUL ATTRACTION

Continuing to exercise his growing discernment by choosing to date only women who attract him on all three levels—physical, emotional, and mental—a man begins to realize his ability to feel soul attraction. When he reaches level four, his heart opens. Just as at level one he finds many women physically attractive, at level four he finds many women lovable as well.

To various degrees, he could fall in love with any of these women, but only one is the perfect soul mate for him. His love recognizes that this person, though imperfect, is perfect for him. His love allows him to see the good in his partner and motivates him to be supportive. As his love grows, he is able to discern whether this is the right person for him. This decision is not based on a list of conditions. The mind doesn't figure it out. The soul just knows.

Soul attraction is not based on recognizing and finding a list of special qualities and characteristics present in your partner. Instead, it is the recognition that you have what that person needs for his or her soul to grow and your partner has what you need. It is knowing that this is the person you are here to grow in love with, that this is the person you are here to share your heart and learn the lessons of life with. One way of saying it is, "I don't know why, but somehow we are supposed to be together. In my most clear and loving moments, this is what I know to be true."

To feel a soul connection with someone, our hearts must be open. To fall in love with someone is an indication that we feel someone could possibly be the one for us. It doesn't mean this is the one, but this could possibly be the one. At that point, it is up to us to move together through the five stages of dating until it becomes clear to us that this person is right or not right.

LEVEL ONE FOR WOMEN: MENTAL CHEMISTRY

Women also move through these four levels but, as we have already discussed, in a different order. Women are first attracted to men in their minds. A woman imagines what a man is like and is attracted to something in his character. It could be the smallest gesture of saying "Excuse me," or the way he knowingly smiles, or shyly asks her for a date. It could be the way he sings a song, writes a letter, communicates his ideas, walks his dog, holds a child, expresses consideration for others, or stands up for what he believes. It could be the kind of questions he asks, the success he has achieved, or the values he lives his life by. All of these are simply ways a man expresses his character. One or two of these expressions stimulate who she is.

At the lowest level of discernment for a woman, she is attracted to men by mental chemistry. There are a lot of interesting men, but to begin increasing her ability to discern the right man for her, she needs to date only those men she finds most interesting. Just as men with a low level of discernment long to be with women they see in magazines, women at their lowest level of discernment long to be with the men in romance novels. Just as for men, a woman's low level of discernment is innocent and a necessary foundation to grow upon.

LEVEL TWO FOR WOMEN: EMOTIONAL ATTRACTION

After some initial dating experiences with men, a woman starts to find that she likes some better than others. With this experience, she can now be more discerning in the men she chooses to date. At level one, she might go out with a guy because she didn't know if she liked his type, but he was interesting to her and interested in her. Now she has higher standards. When she senses that she doesn't like a man a lot, she decides not to date him. Eventually, as her discernment increases, she automatically feels attracted to men she likes, and even without knowing a man, she can already tell in advance that he is not her type and she will not date him. Not only will she be attracted to the right guys, but the right guys will be more attracted to her.

At this level a woman is attracted to a man's personality. She is generally open to experience all kinds of men with different personalities. Through trial and error she eventually discovers the kind of personality in a man with which she is most compatible and feels safe being herself. To a certain extent, the more we have learned to express freely who we are and to feel good about ourselves, the faster we move through the levels of discernment.

Some women are most attracted to a man who has a very shy approach, while others like a man who is very take-charge and assertive. Some women like men who are quieter, while some enjoy most a man who is very gregarious or funny. Some women are attracted to men who are very structured and deliberate, while others are attracted to men who are very spontaneous and fluid. There is no set way of being that makes a man attractive for every woman. Through her dating experiences a woman is able eventually to discern the kind of man she wants and not get involved with those she doesn't like as much.

LEVEL THREE FOR WOMEN: PHYSICAL ATTRACTION

By exercising her discernment and choosing to date only men to whom she feels both mentally and emotionally attracted, a woman begins to discover her physical attraction for a partner. She wants not just to be touched by his mind and heart, but to be touched physically. At this level, when a man holds her hand, puts his arm around her, or gives her a kiss, a lot of physical attraction is felt. Just as a man at level one longs to touch, a woman at level three longs to be touched.

At this level, when a woman already feels mental and emotional chemistry, she will begin to feel physical attraction. Only a few men at this stage will provide all three levels of chemistry. Many men may seem attractive to her, but only a few will also stimulate her mentally and emotionally. By holding to this standard in her relationships, she gives her discernment a chance to grow.

LEVEL FOUR FOR WOMEN: SOUL ATTRACTION

As a result of her growing discernment, a woman eventually develops her ability to experience soul attraction. She is able to fall in love with a man who has stimulated her on all four levels of attraction. She reaches level four, soul attraction, with her heart open. She will begin to see many men as lovable, but not necessarily the one for her.

To various degrees she could love these men, but she gradually learns to recognize which of these men is the perfect soul mate for her. Her open heart makes her capable of eventually seeing the good in her partner, even though he is neither perfect nor able to fulfill all her needs.

As her love grows, she is able to discern whether he is right for her, not because of his ability to be the perfect partner, but because in herself she feels an unconditional love that recognizes, "This is the person I am here to be with." This realization is not something that she has concluded on the basis of comparisons of what is available or what could be possible. Her soul just knows.

While the couple will still experience the normal challenges that any two people who don't understand each other would experience, there is a deep connection they keep coming back to that helps them overcome the inevitable conflicts, frustrations, and disappointments in any relationship.

THE BENEFITS OF SETTING STANDARDS

Through exercising our discernment and continuing to raise our standards, we make sure that we do not compromise ourselves and settle for less when we are ready for more. Choosing to date someone for reasons that do not resonate with our level of maturity will sabotage our ability to move through the five stages of dating. A mature man who continues to date any woman who seems physically attractive, friendly, or sexually responsive may never find real, lasting love. A mature woman who continues to date any man who seems interested in her looks but not her mind as well will continue to be disappointed.

Choosing to date someone we already know is not right for us is like shooting for the target and purposefully missing. Not only will this prevent us from hitting the target, but it is very confusing to our inner instincts. Until this pattern is corrected, we will tend to be attracted to the wrong types of partners. When we lower our standards, the wrong type is what we will attract and be attracted to.

When we choose to pursue someone we know with certainty is not right for us, we lose our momentum. It is like putting all your life savings in an investment that you are not sure about. You would never think, "Hmm, this investment is definitely not the best for me. I think I will put all my money here." It would be completely foolish. It would be better just to keep your money in a savings account.

In a similar way, it is much better not to date if you are not meeting people who match your standards. If you are at the lowest level of discernment, then dating anyone will help you grow in discernment. Once you have already developed your discernment, you lose something if you look back. For some time your ability to recognize the right person and your magnetic ability to be attractive to the right person will be diminished.

SUCCESS STORIES

After learning this, Roger experienced an enormous shift in his life. He had been dating for fun any woman he was attracted to. He knew that the women he was dating did not have the potential to be what he was looking for, but he continued anyway. With this new awareness he raised his standards. After a few months he began dating a woman who he thought had the potential. After another six months he proposed. Now he and his wife have been married several years and are very happy with two children.

Kent has a similar story, but he experienced an even more sudden transformation. After many counseling sessions, I was finally able to convince him that he was wasting his time and his life pursuing women just for sex. He would take out practically any woman, and pursue her until he achieved his goal. Kent was and is a fine person. He just didn't understand how he was compromising himself in this process. The very next day after he decided to stop flirting with and chasing just any woman, he met and fell in love with the woman of his dreams. They are now engaged to be married.

After taking my seminar for singles, Alexis decided to stop having relationships with men who were just physically attracted to her. Instead she became much more picky. She realized that her pattern was to immediately move into stage four of dating (intimacy) when a man was physically attracted. She would mistakenly assume that he felt all four levels of attraction for her and so she would respond to him as if he were about to marry her.

Within a month of her realization, she met Gus, who later became her husband. Although she fell in love right away, she wisely put her foot on the brake and went slowly. She was careful to move through each of the five stages, and now she is happily married. She is grateful for this insight and continues to share it by teaching Mars/Venus workshops for singles.

EVERY RELATIONSHIP IS A GIFT

Every relationship is a gift. It offers us the opportunity to prepare ourselves for finding and recognizing our soul mate. Each time you choose to move through the five stages of dating with a partner, you are increasing your ability to discern the right person for you. Each time, you gain the ability to shoot your arrow closer to the target. When a relationship ends, it is good to take some time to reflect on the gift and then begin again. When you feel grateful for something, then you are ready to move on.

Even divorce can give us the gift of discernment. If we take the time to be forgiving of our partner and forgiving of ourselves for our mistakes, then our next relationship can bring us closer to the mark. Through finding the gift or the good in each relationship, we will eventually make our dreams come true.

Cynthia was married four times before finding her soul mate. In each of her marriages, she thought she was with her soul mate. She so much wanted to find her soul mate that each time she fell in love, she would assume he was the one. Eventually she learned that love was not enough and that before assuming a man was her soul mate, she would take more time to get to know him. She is finally now married to her soul mate and is very happy.

Each time you choose to move through the stages of dating, you are in effect fine-tuning your ability to attract the right person for you. By working to make a relationship work at each stage and by ending relationships without resentment or guilt, you are paving the way toward a great relationship. Each one of these choices will increase your discernment.

REALIZING THE POTENTIAL OF A RELATIONSHIP

Correctly understanding the way men and women think and feel differently doesn't ensure that any relationship will move through all five stages, but it does allow us to correctly assess a relationship. Too many times, we reject each other not because we have found that a person is wrong for us, but because we believed something was wrong with that person. By ending relationships with a more loving and nonjudgmental attitude, we will continue to be attracted to the people who are closer to what we want. With this understanding we find that we become less picky and more open to the potential of a relationship.

> We reject each other not because we have found that a person is wrong for us, but because we think—mistakenly—there is something wrong with that person.

Even with a more accurate understanding of our differences we unknowingly sabotage the attraction in a relationship by switching roles. It is vital for the growth of romance and attraction that the man in a relationship maintain the role of pursuer, while the woman continues in the role of being pursued. When a man feels successful in pursuing her and a woman feels he could be the one for her, then their potential passion and attraction have a chance to build naturally. In Chapter 11 we will explore these roles more fully.

11

The Dynamics of Male and Female Desire

Women mistakenly follow the advice that if you want someone to be interested in you, you should be interested in him. This advice works for men who want a woman's interest, but it doesn't work the other way around. When a woman is really interested in a man, he tends to become more interested in himself. If she listens attentively, he will generally talk more. If she seeks to please his every need, he will gladly let her know what more she can do.

This man is not a hopeless case. He is simply from Mars. His major focus is just different from a woman's. One approach is not better than the other. A woman is most fulfilled when her needs are met, while a man is fulfilled primarily through being successful in fulfilling her. Understanding this fundamental difference can give both men and women the answers to many questions that come up while dating.

A man is like a magic genie. He comes out of his bottle with the opportunity to fulfill a woman's every wish. He goes back into his bottle, however, when he gets the message that he can't succeed in making her happy. Instinctively he is most interested in being successful. In relating to her, whatever will make her happiest makes him happy.

If he detects that her mission is to please him, he will also focus on how she can please him. He will automatically focus on what he wants and clearly let her know. He will give her ample opportunity to fulfill his wishes, wants, and needs. If she wants to pursue him, he will happily sit back and passively receive what she wants to give.

> If a man detects that a woman's
> mission is to please him, he will also
> focus on how she can please him.

This is not what will really make her happy. When he senses that she is not happy, she becomes less interesting to him and the attraction lessens. By making a few adjustments in her approach to dating, a woman can create the ideal opportunity for a man to become more interested in her. Even the right man, without an opportunity to become interested, will lose interest in a woman. He may stay interested, but his interest is only lukewarm. He keeps looking for other women, even when he is with her. There is a reason for this reaction. It has nothing to do with the man or how interesting the woman truly is. It has to do with how she responds to a man's interest.

ACTIVE AND RECEPTIVE INTEREST

There are basically two kinds of interest: active and receptive. Active interest is what we feel when we have a goal in mind: it motivates action to achieve a goal, thrives on achievement, and comes from a place of desire and confidence. Active interest wants to serve, while receptive interest wants to be served. Receptive interest is what we feel when we are openly considering the value of what is being offered: It is motivated to create opportunities to receive, thrives in response to support, and comes from a place of preference and worthiness.

These two kinds of interest are reciprocal in their effect on each other. When a man is very actively interested in a woman, his active interest will usually generate feelings of receptive interest in her. If a woman is receptively interested in a man, it will generate his active interest in her.

A woman's receptive interest in a man generates his active interest in her.

Let's look at a basic example. A man asks a woman for her number. He has his goal in mind and thus he is actively interested. A woman's response is naturally to consider the request. Her interest is receptive; she has no goal in mind, no hidden agenda, but instead reflects on whether she would like to talk further with this man. She notices how she feels about it and then decides whether to give out her number.

The man's confidence, which allows him to risk possible rejection to ask a woman for her number, generates in a woman the reassuring feeling that she is desirable. When she considers his request and gives him her number, his confidence is increased. Just as his active interest made her feel special, her receptive interest generated increasing confidence in him.

It makes a woman feel special when a man is willing to risk rejection to get to know her.

Some women will actually become interested in a man simply because he was interested enough to ask. Once again, his active interest generates within her a receptive interest in him. Even though many women feel free to offer their number to a man, they appreciate it much, much more if he asks. In essence, these women are saying that when a man is actively interested, they thrive.

In a similar way, when a woman is receptively interested in a man, he thrives. When she reacts to his advances, he feels more connected to her. When a man feels more connected, he is automatically more interested and motivated to get to know her. A woman's receptive interest is the fertile ground where the seed of a man's interest can grow.

> **When a woman reacts to a man's advances,
> he feels more connected to her.**

This insight about the two kinds of interest is essential because it explains to a woman what makes her more interesting to a man and it reveals to men the basic principle of how to sweep a woman off her feet.

BUILDING THE FIRE OF ROMANCE

A woman's receptive interest is like the kindling wood that is necessary for building the fire of romance, while a man's active interest is the match required to light the fire. Striking the match alone cannot possibly start the fire. A woman must provide the kindling. Slowly the heat builds so that the bigger logs have a chance to ignite.

> **A woman provides the kindling so
> the heat of romance can slowly build,
> eventually to ignite the bigger logs.**

If a woman doesn't provide the receptive interest, the fire will not have a chance to burn. Practically speaking, this means that when a woman is focused more on giving than receiving, when she cares more about pleasing him than about what would please her, a man will *not* become more interested in her.

This one pivotal insight is the opposite of what many woman think. A woman mistakenly assumes that if she is eager to please a man, he will be pleased and become more interested. Yes, he will be pleased, but he will not necessarily become more actively interested.

When a woman is actively interested in pursuing a man, it is flattering to a man and it will probably generate in him some receptive interest, but that is all. He will probably go with the flow as long as it feels good to him, but rarely does he become motivated to pursue her.

What makes a man more interested in a woman is when he feels really good in her presence. Remember, men are from Mars; they like feeling successful. When a man feels actively interested, it tends to bring out the best in him. When a man is actively engaged in achieving a goal, he feels best about himself. The way a woman makes him feel good is by creating opportunities for him to succeed in truly fulfilling her needs.

When a man really likes how he feels around a woman, he begins to like her more.

A woman can begin to understand this by imagining for a moment that she is a man. In one scenario, this man has worked really hard, has helped a lot of people, and makes a lot of money in the end. This money makes him very happy. In another scenario, the man doesn't work hard, he doesn't help anyone, but he too makes a lot of money. This money also makes him happy.

By putting yourself in his situation it is easy to sense how much better he feels about himself in the first case, when he worked hard and helped a lot of people. No matter what a man receives, he will feel better about it when he feels that he actively pursued it and achieved it. The better a man feels about himself, the more he is motivated to share himself and the more attracted he is to someone who makes him feel that way.

GIVING AND RECEIVING A MASSAGE

Giving and receiving a massage clearly points out the difference between active interest and receptive interest. When Philip is giving Marie a neck massage, he is actively interested in giving a wonderful massage. These are some of his thoughts and feelings when he is actively interested:

I wonder what she will like best?

What approach should I use to make her feel really good?

I think I will try doing this a little more softly.

I bet she would like this long gentle stroke.

Now I will move my hands down her back.

This will be very relaxing.

Oh, she has a lot of tension here.

I think I should do this move a little longer.

Oh, good—she released that tension.

I'll bet she is feeling much better now.

I wonder if there is anything else I can do for her.

I think she liked this a lot.

Each of these thoughts is an expression of Philip's active interest. If he is received as a success, then he will surely feel more connected and motivated to know her.

While Philip is feeling his active interest in pleasing Marie, Marie naturally responds with receptive interest. These are some of her thoughts and feelings:

I would love to have a massage.

Ah, this feels so good.

Umm, I like it when he touches me that way.

Wow, this is so nice.

Oh, don't stop; that feels so good.

This is really nice; I can just relax.

Hmm, I wonder what he is going to do next.

Oh, that was perfect.

I feel so much better.

I wonder what else he can do so well.

Marie's thoughts and feelings are all the expression of receptive interest. By remembering how a woman feels and thinks when she is having a massage, a woman can also connect with the kind of thoughts and feelings that make her most interesting to a man. It is often a revelation for a woman to discover that her receptive interest is the greatest gift she can give a man, just as a man's active interest is the greatest gift he can give her.

A WOMAN'S WORTH

Without an understanding of men, many women think they have to "do something" to earn a man's love and attention. These women do not understand the intrinsic value of simply being interested in and receptive to what a man has to offer. A woman does not recognize that being open and responsive to a man's "doing" is in itself giving back to the man.

A woman thrives when a man "does" for her. When a man is actively interested, she is most interested in him. Since this is her experience, she mistakenly assumes it is the same for a man, but it is not.

Most women don't realize their value to men. A man thrives when a woman is open and receptive to his interest and his attempts to interest, impress, and fulfill her. Her receptivity is her gift to him; he is grateful for the opportunity to know her, connect with her, and bask in her radiance. Without her to please, he is a man out of work. He needs a job. He needs the opportunity to succeed in a relationship with a woman. This is an enormous boost to his fulfillment in life.

DESIRE AND DYNAMIC TENSION

Desire, interest, and passion in a relationship come from dynamic tension. This dynamic tension is created, awakened, or "turned on" when a man gives and a woman receives graciously. When a man gives to a woman and is successful in pleasing her, then at some level he anticipates something in return. This anticipation creates excitement, interest, and enthusiasm. Quite automatically, he becomes challenged to become more involved.

Many women unknowingly diffuse this tension by quickly returning the gift. Instead of receiving the gift and letting the man savor the feeling of success, a woman will shift gears from being receptive to being actively interested in giving to him. She will begin planning how she will repay his gift. This shift will ultimately lessen his interest.

When a woman doesn't clearly know her worth or value to a man, then it can be hard for her to be receptive to his active interest. Instead of simply receiving, she feels she must keep giving back. She doesn't realize that by simply receiving, she is giving a gift. Not only is it not necessary for her to give back, but giving back can also prevent him from being more interested.

> **A woman mistakenly thinks that to be worthy
> of receiving what she really wants, she must
> keep giving back what she is receiving.**

The tendency to give back is just so automatic that a woman may not even know she is doing it. After all, on her planet it is just good manners to give back immediately. Let's use the example of the massage to explore some of the thoughts and feelings a woman might have when she is unable to receive. As you will see, initially she has the same feelings a receptive woman has, but quickly they turn into thoughts and feelings expressive of active interest. These are some of her thoughts and feelings:

> I would love a massage, but what will he expect from me? I wonder what he would like from me.

> Ooh, this feels good. I should give him a massage. I wonder what approach I should use on him.

Umm, I like when he touches me that way. I wonder how he likes to be touched. Maybe I should touch him this way.

Wow, this is so nice. I feel so bad that I haven't done anything for him. What should I do for him?

Oh, don't stop; that feels so good. But wait, I shouldn't be so selfish. What could I do to make him feel good? He is the one who experiences the most tension.

This is really nice. I can just relax. But I can't just relax—I should do something to make him feel better. He has had a long day; he doesn't need to be doing this now.

Hmm, I wonder what he is going to do next. I wonder what I should do so he will continue to like me.

Oh, that was perfect. I don't deserve this. I haven't done anything. What can I do so he will think I am perfect for him?

I feel so much better, but what can I do to repay him? I wonder if there is anything else I can do for him.

I wonder what else he can do so well. I wonder why he would want to be with me. I had better do something for him.

In each example, at first she is receptive, but then her mind is filled with thoughts of how she can please him, or what he might want, or what she should do to be worthy of his support. Instead of just relaxing and fully receiving the massage, this woman shifts from being receptively interested to being actively interested. Although it seems very loving, when a woman shifts to active interest, it can actually prevent a man from becoming fully interested in a woman; it can diffuse the dynamic tension that makes him desire her more.

THE POWER OF ATTITUDE

A man's interest in a woman can grow only when he feels actively interested. On the other hand, his interest will tend to decline slowly if he only feels receptively interested in her.

Likewise, when a man is actively interested in a woman, it gives her an opportunity to explore her true and authentic responses to his pursuit. This authenticity makes her more attractive to the right kind of guy for her. With this understanding, dating can be the ultimate opportunity to explore and access the potential of a relationship while having a good time.

If a woman pursues a man with active interest, it makes him receptively interested. Although he likes receiving her interest, warmth, and affection, it does not make him more interested in her. Receptive interest just does not bring out the best in a man. After a while he becomes interested in someone else, who does promise to bring out the best in him.

EXAMPLES OF ACTIVE AND RECEPTIVE INTEREST

When a man is actively interested in a woman, he is thinking about things like what he should do to impress her. When a woman is receptive, she gives a man the confidence to take the risks necessary to impress her. The more he takes risks to achieve his goal, the more invested he becomes. Her receptive interest actually empowers him.

If she begins to wonder if he is interested enough and then pursues him by trying to impress him, it can sabotage the potential of a date. Instead of making him more interested, it can make him less interested. Pursuing his interest has an effect that is the opposite of what she expects. If she makes the mistake of trying to impress him, then he will automatically relax and let her do the risking.

Certainly a man likes *not* having to take a risk: He likes being waited on; he likes a woman to be actively interested; but it doesn't cause him to like her more. A man's interest is engaged when he does it, when he earns it, when he achieves, when he wins her over. Men become actively interested when they are figuring out what to do, what to give, how to provide, how to achieve a goal, how to impress someone, and how to get the love, acceptance, and admiration they want.

To get a practical sense of active and receptive interest, let's explore the following examples. As you read through the table the difference will become increasingly clear. You may have to read it a few times to understand and to get a feel for the difference.

First we will explore examples of common thoughts and feelings a man might have when he is either actively or receptively interested in a woman. Next we will explore a woman's thoughts and feelings.

MAN IS ACTIVELY INTERESTED	MAN IS RECEPTIVELY INTERESTED
I wonder if she would be interested in me. I think she is interesting.	I wonder if I would like to spend time with her. She does seem interested in me. It might be fun.

MAN IS ACTIVELY INTERESTED	MAN IS RECEPTIVELY INTERESTED
I wonder if she would like me, I really like her. Let's see, how should I approach her?	I wonder if I would like to get to know her better. I don't know, but she seems to like me, so we'll see.
I wonder what I could offer her. I think I could make her really happy.	I wonder what she could offer me. She's beautiful. I certainly wouldn't mind finding out.
I wonder if I am good enough for her. Well, there's no harm in trying. I bet I could make her really happy. Here goes.	I wonder if she is good enough for me. She does turn me on. I bet she could make me really happy. You never know.
I wonder how I could get to meet her. When should I make my approach? What should I say? Okay, I'll simply introduce myself and be friendly.	I wonder if I should make it easy for her to meet me. She certainly is flirting with me. Well, there's no harm in just being friendly.
I wonder if she would go out with me. Well, she is worth it. I'm going to ask her if I can get her number. I'm not going to let her just walk out of my life without at least trying.	I wonder if I would want to go out with her. She sure seems to be interested in me. Maybe I should get her number and give her a call sometime.
I wonder how I could make her happy. I'll invite her to my favorite restaurant. I hope she likes it.	I bet she could make me happy. I certainly can't say no to this offer.

MAN IS ACTIVELY INTERESTED	MAN IS RECEPTIVELY INTERESTED
I wonder what she would like to do. Maybe I should look in the paper to see what's happening next week.	I wonder what I would like to do. I really don't care. I'll wait and ask her; anything is fine with me.
I wonder what she is feeling about me. I hope I made a good impression. Let's see, what else can I think of to do?	I wonder how I feel about her. I'm not sure if I should call her. I'll wait and see how I feel later.
I wonder how I could impress her. Let's make a plan. First we should have dinner and then have plenty of time to get to the movies by eight. She will have a great time.	I wonder if she is going to be good tonight. She looked great the other night. Let's see, what would I like to do? I am going to have a great time.
I wonder when I should make my move and kiss her. I don't want to seem too forward. Remember, go slowly. She seems to like me too. Well, it's now or never.	I wonder if she wants to kiss me. I sure hope she does. I'll bet she would be real good.

In reviewing the above table it also becomes clear that when a man is actively interested, he tends to be much more action-oriented, masculine, and directed. These qualities tend to make him much more attractive to women. While there is nothing wrong with being receptively interested, it just doesn't make a man irresistible to women. As we will see in the next table, it is receptive interest that makes a woman most attractive to a man.

<u>WOMAN IS ACTIVELY INTERESTED</u>	<u>WOMAN IS RECEPTIVELY INTERESTED</u>
I wonder if he would be interested in me. What should I do? How should I be with him?	I wonder if I am interested in him. He seems interesting. I think I would like to get to know him.
I wonder if he likes me. How should I approach him? I'll bet I could entice him.	I wonder if I would like to get to know him. He seems interesting. I can make some time for him.
I wonder what I could offer him. I'll bet I could really help him. He needs me.	I wonder what he could offer me. He's cute. I certainly would like to find out.
I wonder if I am good enough for him. I'll bet I could really please him; maybe then he would want me.	I wonder if he is good enough for me. I do like him. He does really want to spend time with me. Maybe he is the right guy.
I wonder how I could get to meet him. How should I get his attention? What should I ask him? Okay, I'll compliment him and then ask him a question.	I wonder how I could make it easy for him to meet me. I like him. I'll occasionally look his way so he can catch my eyes looking at him.
I wonder if he will ask me out. Well, he is a catch, and I am not letting him get away. I am going to get his number and give him a call. We could be right for each other.	I wonder if I would want to go out with him. I think he's interesting. Maybe I should let him have my number. He is charming. If he doesn't ask, I'll give him my number, in case he wants to give me a call.

WOMAN IS ACTIVELY INTERESTED	WOMAN IS RECEPTIVELY INTERESTED
I wonder how I could make him happy. I know just what to do to get his attention.	I wonder if he could make me happy. He may be the one. This is exciting.
I wonder what he would like to do. I'll look in the paper to see what he might like.	I wonder how I feel about what he suggests we do; it sounds like fun. This is exciting.
I wonder what he is feeling about me. I hope I look all right. I wonder if I said the right things.	I wonder how I feel about him. He seems really interesting. I like getting to know him.
I wonder how I could impress him. Let's see, what should I wear? I wonder how I should react when . . .	I wonder how he will make me feel tonight; I hope it's good. Let's see, what should I wear? What makes me feel good?
I wonder when I should make my move and kiss him. I want to make sure he is turned on to me.	I wonder if he wants to kiss me. I hope he does. I wonder how it will feel.

After reading this table of women's active or receptive interest, it becomes clear that when a woman is being receptive, her best and most feminine qualities have a chance to shine. There is nothing wrong with a woman being actively interested in a man, but she should remember that to be most attractive in the long run and for her to feel best about herself while dating, it is important to develop an attitude of receptive interest.

WOMEN GIVE WHAT WOMEN WANT

When a man receives from a woman, it opens him up to receive more, but when a woman receives from a man, it opens her up to give more. Without this insight about our different reactions, a woman will automatically give what she would want and assume that it will make a man most interested in her.

If a man was to listen attentively to her, she would definitely become more interested in him. If a man was to notice her needs and wishes and happily go out of his way to fulfill them, then she would be swept off her feet. Since this is her experience, she mistakenly assumes he will be swept off his feet when she does those things for him. As a result, she becomes actively interested in planning to do for him what she would love him to do for her. She thinks she is doing the right thing. When he doesn't respond the way she would, she mistakenly assumes that something is wrong with her or him.

> A woman gives what she
> would want and assumes it will make
> a man most interested in her.

The problem is that when a man is swept off his feet in this manner, he tends to take a nap. A man may like her attention and support very much, but it stops there. He likes how she makes him feel and in return he likes her as well. But when a woman brings out the best in a man, then he really likes how he feels and this motivates him to get to know her more. He becomes actively interested.

If a woman focuses on being increasingly receptive to a man's advances, then she holds the key to creating an opportunity for a relationship to flourish. It not only gives him the opportunity to experience his feelings for her but assists him in being the best he can be. In a similar manner, when a man is actively interested in a woman, it not only allows her to discover her true feelings for him but also allows her best self to come out and radiate.

12

Men Pursue and Women Flirt

To create the necessary attraction to move a dating couple through the five stages of dating, men and women must maintain complementary roles. To be most attractive, a man needs to do little things with an attitude of confidence and conviction. A woman needs to respond to the things he does in a receptive but not fully convinced manner. She needs to stay in a place of openness and not appear desperate or needy. A man should not get the idea that she is after him, but that she is open to finding out if she likes him.

> To move through the five stages of dating,
> men and women need to sustain
> complementary roles.

To create a relationship, a woman must be careful not to pursue a man but to be responsive to his pursuit. This kind of receptiveness and responsiveness is expressed through flirting. When a woman flirts with a man, she is simply interacting in a manner that expresses the feeling that maybe he could be the man to make her happy, maybe he could be that great guy she has been looking for her whole life, maybe he could be capable of fulfilling her needs, maybe he could be the one she would want to share a really special time with, or maybe he could just be interesting or fun.

Flirting is like shopping. When a woman shops she has fun checking out what she likes and does not like. She is not interested in proving herself to the salesperson. She freely tries things on and she can easily leave without buying anything. She has the freedom to look in other stores and return whenever she pleases. This is the perfect attitude for flirting. Flirting energy says, "I am looking and liking what I see. Maybe you could be the one to make me happy."

Pursuing is like going on a job interview. Sure, you may want to get a feel for the company, but you are primarily trying to impress the company so that it will hire you. While pursuing a woman, a man instinctively puts forth his best and most charming side for a woman to react to. Pursuing energy says, "I could be the one to make you happy. Check me out. Look at what I have done and what I can do." As long as he is doing the pursuing and she is responding in a receptive, playful, and pleased manner, then the attraction has a chance to build.

A woman's flirting responses to a man's pursuit are very exciting because a man is always looking for the opportunity to take credit for a woman's happiness. It compliments his ability to make a woman happy. Being successful in the pursuit is as much fun for him as it is fun for a woman to feel that someone she likes is trying to make her happy.

> **Flirting is very exciting to men because it compliments their ability to make a woman happy.**

Although almost anything a woman does with a receptive attitude is flirting, these are twelve examples of definite flirting signals that will enable a man to recognize that a woman is receptive to his approach and pursuit.

TWELVE WAYS WOMEN FLIRT

1. She may just smile and make eye contact for about three to five seconds in a way that says, "I might be interested," and then look away.

2. She might bat her eyelids in a way that says, "Well, I am waiting for someone like you."

3. She may tilt her head, as if to say, "I wonder if you are the right kind of guy for me."

4. She may get up and walk by the man, as if to say, "If you haven't noticed me, now you have a chance. Make your move."

5. She may look at him, catch his look, and then after three to five seconds look away to invite him to look her over. Then, after about ten seconds, she may look back with a smile that says, "If you are interested, introduce yourself. I don't bite."

6. She may brush up against him and then respond with a little sound like "Oh" that says, "Oh, I didn't mean to touch you . . . but I liked it."

7. She may casually touch his hand while talking, as if to acknowledge that she appreciates his understanding or attentiveness. She may then simply smile in a way that says, "I like feeling and connecting with you." Or she might raise her eyebrows as if to say, "Wow, that really felt good."

8. She may touch his leg above the knee or his shoulder as she makes a point as if to acknowledge that she feels safe, familiar, and comfortable with him. Then, after lifting her hand, she pauses as if to catch her breath because the unexpected spark of connection was so delightful that she momentarily forgot what she was saying.

9. She may be playfully argumentative in a discussion or even challenge his point of view in a manner that says, "We don't have to always agree, I like you anyway. I enjoy another point of view and I am stimulated by what you say."

10. She may ask him to carry something or help her with something. While he is helping, she may take a deep breath and relax on the exhale, as if to say, "It's so nice to be able to relax and be taken care of. This is really so nice."

11. She may ask him a question about something and then playfully revel in his brilliance, as if to say, "I like the way you think you are really helpful."

12. At the end of a date she may look him in the eyes, slightly tilt her head, smile, and then raise her chin slightly, as if to say, "I really had a good time and if you want to kiss me, I would like that too. Just do it."

All of these little expressions create the opportunity for him to feel her receptiveness to him. This is what draws a man in. He needs clear signs that if he pursues he will make progress. If a man does not get clear signals, the attraction may lessen because he doesn't anticipate being successful.

HOW MEN PURSUE

When a man pursues a woman, he is interacting in a manner that says he is interested in finding out if he is the one for her. His eyes, his voice, his attention, his interest, and his touch all say confidently, "I am interested in you and I bet I could be the one to make you happy, I could be that great guy you have been waiting for, I could fulfill your needs, I could do things to make you really happy, or I can be really interesting and fun." This kind of flirting is very exciting for women because women are looking for the occasional opportunity to relax and have someone care enough to take responsibility for their happiness and lead them where they would like to go.

> Women enjoy it most when a man takes the risk to impress her rather than waiting for her to do something to impress him.

In first getting to know a woman, you must be careful to connect for a while before you go for the number. You should first display your interest nonverbally, and get a clear response from her long before approaching her. If you can't get her attention, then you should have the waiter bring her a gift or hand her a little note. Let her read it away from you. If gradually she begins to flirt with an inviting smile, you should proceed.

Another approach is to meet one of her friends and to ask questions about her. It is much easier to introduce yourself to a friend. Then her friend will talk to her about you. If she looks your way, then her flirting has begun. You can then approach and simply introduce yourself.

THE BEST LINE IS THE EASIEST

Many men panic when it comes to figuring out an opening line. The best line is the easiest. Just introduce yourself; say "Hi, my name is John. What's your name?" After she answers, then you should be prepared to ask a few questions or make a few comments about what is going on around you or the weather. What is important is that you took the step, not what you say. Even if you are not coherent, she will be impressed because you took the risk to pursue her.

To get a Venusian to talk, the best question is, "Where are you from?" while the best question to get a Martian to talk is, "What do you do?" Men like to talk about what they do or have done, while women particularly like to talk about settings, relationships, and situations.

When you don't feel good at small talk or chitchat, you can still be very successful by continuing to be present, looking in her direction, and asking questions. You need to remember that if you are not good at chitchat, then the women you are attracted to will generally love picking up the slack and talking more.

WHY MEN BECOME TONGUE-TIED

It is perfectly normal for a man to become tongue-tied when he first meets a woman. This is another example of the way men and women are different. Men tend to use one part of the brain at a time, while women use many parts simultaneously. It is relatively easy for a woman to speak when she has strong feelings, but for a man, the stronger the feelings, the less he is able to think and speak. That is why when a man sees a woman to whom he is attracted, he can't easily figure out how to approach her until she leaves, or when he does meet her, he doesn't know what to say. Some men become even more nervous because they anticipate not knowing what to say.

For many men, it is a relief to find out that almost all men fumble the ball when approaching a woman. Women are used to it and they are not judgmental about it. They think it makes a man cute or charming. They are most flattered that he was willing to overcome his nerves and take the risk to meet them. The more inarticulate a man is, the more complimented a woman will feel. The more foolish he is willing to risk appearing, the more she feels he cares, and that is a big compliment.

A woman is impressed when a man is willing to try to meet her even though he doesn't have all the answers or isn't completely perfect and smooth. If he can't figure out what to say or ask, he can just stand there with his head slightly down and tilted to the side with a little smile, and a woman may fall in love with him. She may be thinking, "He is so charming. He doesn't have to be smooth and come up with funny lines and expressions to win a woman over. He just needs to take the risk to meet her and be a good listener."

Another important element in pursuing and flirting is the art of complimenting the opposite sex. In Chapter 13 we will explore in greater detail how to express our attraction to our date.

13

Acknowledge Men and Adore Women

Compliments are the best way to communicate our attraction and allow it to grow. If a man is attracted to a woman, he can let her know by giving compliments. Sometimes a man makes the mistake of complimenting a woman the way he would want to be complimented instead of the way they do it on Venus. Likewise, many women don't realize how to compliment a man successfully. The bottom line is that men want to be acknowledged, while women want to be adored.

On Mars they feel most complimented when the results of their decisions and actions are acknowledged and appreciated. A man on a date really likes it when a woman talks about what a good time she is having or how delicious the dinner was or what a great movie they saw. His reaction is then to feel very successful for having provided all that.

> On Mars they feel most liked and complimented
> when the results of their decisions and actions
> are acknowledged and appreciated.

When a woman says, "That was such a great movie," his response is the same as if he had written the movie. Since he provided the movie that pleased her, he feels she is pleased with him. In fact, he feels as if he directed it, wrote it, produced it, and even starred in it.

When a woman comments with enthusiasm about the food in a restaurant he has chosen, he feels thrilled. It is as if he had spent all day preparing that meal and she appreciated it. When she responds in a positive manner to the things he provides, and overlooks what isn't as wonderful, a man feels most complimented and appreciated.

When a woman says, "I am having such a great time tonight. I feel so good. The air is so clean and clear. The stars are so beautiful. The moon rising over the river is so romantic," a man is teleported into heaven. The more she appreciates the evening, the more successful he feels for having provided it. It is as though he has made the moon rise; he is so romantic; he has made the air fresh and clear. His affection for her increases because he feels so proud.

GIVING COMPLIMENTS ON VENUS

On Venus they are most touched when a compliment is personally directed. Certainly any compliment is fine, but the best compliments for women are more personal and direct. Men do not instinctively know this and miss the opportunity to connect with a woman by complimenting her in a more direct manner. Since men like to be acknowledged for what they do, a man may do the same for her and miss the chance to let her feel his attraction for her.

Instead of focusing on what a woman does or how she makes him feel, he should ideally focus on finding positive adjectives and nouns to describe her directly. It is fine to talk about what she has done, but it should always include a statement about her. That is how she can feel his affection the most and it is another way she gets to know him best.

A woman is most reassured in the way a man sees her and compliments her. A woman will feel most attracted to a man when he makes his compliments personal and direct, while a man will feel most attracted to a woman when her compliments are less direct and more about how she feels in response to what he has done, thought, decided, or provided. Let's explore this difference.

INDIRECT COMPLIMENTS (Best to Give Men)	DIRECT COMPLIMENTS (Best to Give Women)
I am having a wonderful time.	You are so wonderful.
I had so much fun.	You are so much fun.
That was a great movie.	You have great taste in movies.
This restaurant is fantastic.	You are a fantastic cook.
This band is great.	You are a great dancer.
This was such a perfect evening.	Your smile is so perfect.
I really enjoy talking with you.	You are so interesting.
I really like spending time with you.	You are so easy to be with.

<u>INDIRECT COMPLIMENTS</u> (Best to Give Men)	<u>DIRECT COMPLIMENTS</u> (Best to Give Women)
I have had such a delightful evening.	You are truly delightful.
I can't remember when I had such a good time.	You are such a pleasure to meet.
That really makes sense.	You are so smart.
Amazing—it only took you twenty minutes to do this.	Amazing—you are so efficient.
Wow, this is so impressive.	Wow, you are so impressive.
This is a great job.	You have done a great job.
I would never have thought to do that.	You are so brilliant.
Going to this movie was a great decision, *or* I am really glad we went to this movie.	You sure know how to pick great movies.

When a woman compliments a man in the indirect manner as suggested in the above table, it encourages him to continue pursuing her, it makes him feel more confident in his ability to win her over, and it makes him feel more successful and thus more interested in her. If she is not being direct in her compliments, she continues to leave a distance between them that he can cross in his pursuit of her.

When a man compliments a woman in a more direct manner as suggested, it reassures her that she is being cherished and respected. It connects her more directly to herself and how she feels about the man, and it directly softens her and opens her up to feeling more receptive and responsive. As she responds in a pleased manner to his compliments, he feels he is making progress in getting closer.

WOMEN LOVE PERSONAL COMPLIMENTS

A man will feel complimented if a woman loves his car, his stereo, or his favorite football team, but a woman feels complimented when she feels personally noticed and adored. Personal compliments are positive observations—things that a man notices about her when he is looking at her and relating to her.

For a woman to begin having deeper feelings for a man, his compliments need to become more personal. When he makes three or more personal compliments in a conversation, it is a clear sign that he is expressing and pursuing a personal attraction.

> **When he makes three or more personal compliments in a conversation, it is a clear sign that he is pursuing.**

Women will appreciate any sincere compliment, but when a man puts a little more thought into his words she will like it more. When a man takes a few extra moments to consider the right compliment for a woman, the compliment ripens. It conveys more of his best self and will stimulate more of her best self. The more special the adjective, the more special she feels. These are some examples of simple compliments versus more ripened compliments.

PLAIN COMPLIMENT	JUICY COMPLIMENT
That is a nice picture.	You are incredibly artistic.
You look good tonight.	You look magnificent tonight.

PLAIN COMPLIMENT	JUICY COMPLIMENT
You sing well.	You are such a gifted singer.
You have a good voice.	You have a divine voice.
You have a nice face.	You have an angelic face.
You have a nice smile.	You have such a radiant smile.
You look good.	You are so gorgeous.
You look nice.	You are so lovely.
You are smart.	Your brilliance is dazzling.
You have good taste.	Your taste is excellent.
You have nice eyes.	You have such a special sparkle in your eyes.
You look nice.	You look so beautiful.
That is a nice dress.	You look so exquisite in that dress.

Certainly it may sometimes be appropriate to use a simple and plain compliment, but the riper compliments become, the more receptive a woman begins to feel.

JUICING UP COMPLIMENTS FOR WOMEN

Even a plain compliment can be juiced up with any of these five simple words: *so, really, very, always,* and *such*. A man can easily transform any simple compliment to match his level of attraction, interest, enthusiasm, familiarity, and pride. Let's explore how these five easy words can juice up the most basic compliment, "You look nice."

1. You look *so* nice. (*attraction*)

2. You look *really* nice. (*interest*)

3. You look *very* nice. (*enthusiasm*)

4. You *always* look nice. (*familiarity*)

5. You have *such* a nice look. (*pride*)

To express more feeling in a compliment, he can just repeat any of these words or combine them like this:

1. You look *so, so* nice.

2. You *really* look *so* nice.

3. You look *very, very* nice.

4. You *always* look *so* nice.

5. You *really* have *such* a nice look.

JUICING UP COMPLIMENTS FOR MEN

Women can also use these five words to express more feeling in their indirect compliments to a man. Let's apply these five words to one of the most basic compliments that any man loves to hear, "I am happy we did this."

1. I am *so* happy we did this.

2. I am *really* happy we did this.

3. I am *very* happy we did this.

4. I am *always* happy to do this.

5. I am *so* happy; I had *such* a good time.

6. I am *so very* happy we did this.

7. I *really* am *so* happy we did this.

8. I am *very, very* happy we did this.

9. I *always* feel *so* happy when we do this.

10. I had *such* a *really* good time.

Another way a woman can indirectly compliment a man is to appreciate what he has provided. By appreciating the movie, the play, the singing, the food, the decorations, the service, the weather, and so on, she indirectly appreciates him, since he feels he provided it. If he brings flowers, then the way she compliments the flowers affects him most.

If a dating couple are not yet very close, then the easiest way for him to experience her receptivity and responsiveness is for her to acknowledge and appreciate what he has provided. If she is the right person for him to pursue, this experience generates in him a greater desire to get close to her.

When a woman appreciates the flowers a man brings, he ends up feeling more than just complimented. When she says, "I love these flowers," he not only ends up feeling complimented but gets a glimpse of how it might feel to be loved by her. In this way he has the freedom to get closer or back out.

Let's look at how she might ripen up the simplest of compliments, "I love these flowers."

1. These flowers are *so* nice; I love them.

2. These flowers are *really* nice; I love them.

3. These flowers are *very* nice; I love them.

4. Flowers are *always so* nice; I love them.

5. These are *such* nice flowers; I love them.

6. These flowers are *very* nice; I love them *so* much.

7. These flowers are *really* so nice; I love them.

8. Flowers are *so* nice; I *really* love them.

9. These flowers are *such* a nice gift; I love them *very* much.

10. These flowers are *really* nice.

THE BEST COMPLIMENTS ON VENUS

A woman particularly appreciates a compliment when it focuses on something she put a lot of herself into. Take sunglasses, for example. A woman generally puts a lot of energy into picking the right glasses for herself. If a man notices those glasses and sincerely likes them or thinks they look good on her, then he will score big by complimenting her on her choice of sunglasses.

By complimenting something special in this way, he makes her feel more special. However, not all personal compliments are appropriate. Women can appreciate personal compliments as long as they are G-rated. As you begin to advance through the different stages of dating, they can become more personal.

Personal compliments go over big on Venus, but still they need to be done in a friendly, casual tone with no heavy feelings, expectations, or strings attached. They are best given in the same casual tone and manner as one would say, "It was such a great day today" or "I'm sure glad it didn't rain again" or "I'm so glad the elections are over. I get so tired of watching political advertisements."

The best compliments regard something special either about her person or about something on which she has spent a lot of time, thought, energy, or creativity. These are a few examples:

SOMETHING SPECIAL ABOUT HER: I really like your smile, your face, your blue eyes (or whatever color), your accent, the color of your hair, the thickness of your hair, the shine of your hair, your hands, your smile, your shiny teeth, your suntan, your soft skin, and so on.

SOMETHING SHE HAS PUT TIME INTO: I really like that you are involved with this group; I think it's great that you volunteer for this program; you are really very generous with your time to help this way; and so on.

SOMETHING SHE HAS PUT A LOT OF THOUGHT INTO: I really like the way you do your hair; I love the way you have arranged your apartment; you really have a great sense of color; and so on.

SOMETHING SHE HAS PUT A LOT OF ENERGY INTO DOING OR BUYING: You look so great in that hat; you are really a great tennis player; you are in such great shape; you look so healthy; you look so beautiful in that jacket; and so on.

SOMETHING SHE PUT A LOT OF CREATIVITY INTO: You are a great dancer; you have such rhythm; you write beautifully; you have such a sense of style in the way you dress; and so on.

SOMETHING SHE IS PROUD OF OR FEELS COMPETENT ABOUT: You are really a very talented designer; you are a brilliant organizer; you are so committed to work; you are such a responsible and loving mother to your kids; you do such a good job around here; and so on.

FOLLOW A COMPLIMENT WITH A QUESTION

After giving a personal compliment, it is usually good to follow it with a question. Ultimately a man can best get to know a woman if he asks questions and she talks. The more he gets her to talk and share, the more opportunity there is for her to discover how much she is attracted to him. Asking a question after making a compliment also helps a woman to open up to receive the compliment. From this more receptive place, she can begin to share herself by answering his question. These are some examples:

"I really like your red hair. Do you get a lot of compliments about it?"

"That's a pretty necklace. Have you had it long?" or, "Where did you get it?"

"I really like your accent. Where did you grow up?" or, "How long have you lived here?"

"You sure look great tonight. Did you just get here?"

"I really like your smile. Did you have a good day?"

"You have such pretty eyes. Did you get them from your mother or father?"

"I noticed you from across the room and wanted to meet you. Where are you from?"

"You are really smart. How did you know that?" or, "Where did (or do) you go to school?"

"I really like your sunglasses. You have a lot of style. Where did you get them?"

"You look so healthy and radiant. How much do you work out?"

"I really like your earrings. Where did you get them?"

"I really like your shoes; they match your belt perfectly. Are they comfortable?"

"You have a great suntan. Where did you get it?"

In each of these compliments, by finishing it with a question a man gives the clear message that he continues to be attracted to her. Her responsiveness to his compliments and questions then fuels his ability to pursue her. When a man combines compliments with questions, a woman gets the reassurance she needs to continue to open up. By acknowledging a man's competence and ability to make her happy, she gives him the confidence to continue pursuing her.

With this deeper understanding of how to express our attraction to the opposite sex, we can relate and respond to our partners in a way that brings out the best in them. As a result, the whole dating process can become much more enjoyable. When frustration, disappointment, worry, and embarrassment on a date are minimized, then we are able to experience and assess more accurately the potential of a relationship. Through a series of positive dating experiences, a solid foundation is created to help us recognize when a dating partner is someone special.

14

Men Advertise and Women Share

The complaint most frequently expressed by women who are dating is that men talk so much about themselves. Either the man goes on and on talking about what he does, what he can do, and what he has done, or, after the woman does get a chance to talk, he'll quickly respond with what he thinks she could do, should do, or shouldn't do. He confidently assumes that his expertise and competence are impressing her, while in reality she is being turned off—feeling ignored, left out, or unimportant to him. As a result, she may mistakenly conclude, "Another man who thinks only about himself." As we explore men in greater depth, we will see why this conclusion is not entirely correct and what women can do to create a two-way conversation.

When I tell men about this complaint, they are generally amazed. They say, "If she doesn't like me to talk about myself, then why does she ask so many questions? Whenever there is a quiet moment she begins asking questions. Why do we have to talk all the time anyway? I am fine just being together, watching a movie together, driving somewhere together, listening to music, or doing anything together. I don't have to talk all the time. I thought she wanted me to talk. Isn't that what women are always saying, 'Men don't talk enough; they don't communicate'?"

These two issues, like so many of the issues we will explore together, can finally be resolved by first understanding how men and women approach dating and relationships. With this new perspective, suddenly we have the information and insight necessary to begin finding the answers to the questions that come up while dating. To understand each other better, let's once again pretend that men are from Mars and women are from Venus. Let's go back in time and observe life on Mars and Venus before we came together on Earth.

LIFE ON MARS

Martians are primarily work-oriented. They value themselves on the basis of their ability to achieve results and success at work. Every Martian instinctively knows that his success is based on three things: his competence, his ability to let others know how competent he is, and the opportunity to serve. Everything in his life is geared toward becoming more effective, letting others know how competent he is, and then being of service. Mars is covered with billboards advertising a host of facts and figures describing what Martians can do, promise to do, and have done. Martians are definitely into advertising and marketing.

> A man's life is geared toward becoming more effective, letting others know how competent he is, and then being of service.

At celebrations on Mars, a military man dresses up by putting on his uniform, which indicates to all who he is, what he can do, and what he promises to do. He then puts on all his medals and awards to let others know his achievements, what he has done. This is not an egocentric man, but a person who is very proud of who he is and what he has accomplished; this is a man whose life is dedicated to saving the lives of others at the risk of losing his own. His dress reflects that expression of who he is.

A businessman does the same. On special occasions he demonstrates that he is competent by driving a fine car or wearing an expensive suit with well-polished shoes. What does this say? It says he is successful; other people have experienced his competence and have rewarded him well. If they have trusted him, then you can too. This man can take care not only of himself but of others. Men of all occupations on Mars find ways to identify their expertise and advertise themselves.

Certainly not all men do this the same way, but they all do market themselves. Different men have a variety of ways and uniforms to display their expertise, values, and success, but in the end, whether he is wearing a black tux and shiny shoes or blue jeans and white running shoes, he is in some way advertising that he is a "can do" guy, someone you can trust and depend on.

Once a man feels he has something to offer, some service to provide, then he uses every opportunity to market himself or what he has to offer. This tendency is definitely present when he dates a woman. His main objective is to let her know that he is the one for her. He is the one who could make her happy. He has what she is looking for. And so he talks to let her know. In short, he uses communication as a medium to advertise his services. Talking about himself is one of the best ways a man knows to sell himself and to show he cares.

> **A man uses communication as a medium to advertise his services.**

A man does not instinctively understand what a turnoff it is for him to dominate a conversation by talking about himself on a date. To a woman it appears as if he cares only about number one, himself. He doesn't realize that instead of talking about himself, she wants him to ask questions and be interested in getting to know her. To her, the sign that he cares would be his full interest in her; his taking time to ask questions, listen, and respond attentively.

> **Instead of talking about himself, a woman wants a man to ask questions and be interested in getting to know her.**

For a man, the first few dates are like a job interview. He is selling the woman on the idea that he would be great for her. He is showing her his stuff to win her over. No one has ever explained to him that on Venus, the best thing he could do is to get her to talk about herself, her feelings, her likes and dislikes, and her life.

DATING IS LIKE A JOB INTERVIEW

On Mars, it would be offensive and foolish to go for a job interview and begin interviewing the interviewer. Interviewers are warned about overly aggressive job candidates who try to take over and control an interview by asking a lot of questions about the company.

A successful Martian would be turned off if someone in the world of work approached him for a job and then immediately turned around, asking him about his feelings, goals, and plans. Before an employer is willing to talk about himself, first he wants to know if the job candidate is qualified for the job. Who's hiring whom is a very important part of the equation.

For a man, asking a lot of questions on a date would be like going to a very successful company for a job interview and asking about its plans for the future or how it first got started. Not only would that be insulting, but he wouldn't get the job.

During the first few dates a man is presenting his résumé: "Here I am; this is what I have done and can do. Ask me anything." This is his Martian way of opening up and sharing himself. To her, however, when he talks about himself, it is as if he is not interested in her, as if he doesn't want to get to know her. From his perspective it is just the opposite; the reason he is talking about himself is that he wants to get to know her. He is sharing himself, waiting for her to open up and share with him. She, however, is waiting for him to show some interest and ask her questions.

> The first few dates for a man are like presenting his résumé: "Here I am; this is what I have done and can do. Ask me anything."

Martians pursue a job only if they want it. A man doesn't go to the trouble of trying out or proving himself for just anybody. Putting yourself out there to possibly be rejected or fail is not fun. If he is asking her out and then proceeding to talk about himself, it is because deep inside he cares a lot, enough to try to impress her and risk failure. To understand this different perspective can free a woman to correctly interpret a man's apparent self-centeredness and recognize it more as a compliment than an insult. Although it is not exactly what she wants, at least he is interested in winning her over.

A man generally has no idea that something so useful on his planet, like advertising, could be so counterproductive with a woman. He doesn't know that manners on Venus are very different.

LIFE ON VENUS

Venusians have different ways to show they care. Just as Martians are work-oriented, Venusians are relationship-oriented. They value love, communication, and intimacy. Certainly Venusians also work hard and have many other interests, but they find their greatest fulfillment through relationships and their greatest unhappiness from the lack of loving relationships.

Every Venusian instinctively knows that her ability to find fulfillment is based on three things: the ability to give love, the demonstration of her ability to have loving relationships, and the opportunity to receive love. Every decision in her life flows in the direction of creating loving relationships to give and receive love.

Demonstrating her ability to be loving is more important to a Venusian than advertising her competence in the work world. Particularly when a woman goes on a date, she is more interested and impressed by a man's ability to have a relationship with her than by his expertise at work. However, this does not mean that a man does not need to have some expertise or competence.

A confident and competent man is very attractive to a woman, but what makes her more interested in him is his ability to give and receive in a relationship. When a woman has a conversation her objective is to share. A man makes the best impression by asking questions and listening. Sharing in her thoughts and feelings is the way to win a woman over.

> **A confident and competent man is very attractive to a woman, but what makes her more interested in him is his ability to ask questions and listen.**

On Venus, the way to demonstrate consideration and caring for another person is to ask lots of questions and be careful not to dominate the conversation. When two women get together to talk, one starts out by asking questions and listening with interest. After some time they switch roles. This is the unspoken guideline for sharing on Venus.

Even if one of the women talks for a long time, the other woman does not mind because she instinctively knows that her friend will give her the chance to talk. Her time will come. This switching of roles occurs when the person talking stops talking and starts asking questions. Then the listener gets a chance to talk. This, however, works only because both Venusians understand the ritual.

With a Martian it doesn't automatically work. She asks questions and he answers. But he doesn't know that after she asks him questions he is supposed to ask her questions. When she seems really interested in him, he doesn't realize that this is a signal that he is supposed to show he is really interested in her by asking questions.

> **When a woman asks a lot of questions, that is a secret Venusian signal that he should stop talking and ask her questions.**

When a guy does all the talking, he thinks he is doing all the work and doesn't even consider in his wildest dreams that she has been waiting for him to demonstrate his interest in her. While this may seem to some men like much ado about nothing, asking questions and listening are the bottom line of how to get to a woman's heart. Making this tiny adjustment can make a world of difference for any man wanting to win a woman over.

WHAT WOMEN CAN DO

Women commonly ask me what they can do if a man just talks about himself. The answer here is very simple, but most women would never think to do it because on Venus what I am going to suggest would be very rude . . . but sometimes when you are with a Martian it's fine to do as the Martians do and just interrupt.

> **When a man talks too much, do as the Martians do and just interrupt.**

What a woman can do to stop a man from talking so much is to simply stop asking questions and join in the conversation. She should not wait for him to ask questions or wait to be invited; instead, she should just listen for a few moments or minutes and then start in.

While this sounds easy, to make this shift can be very difficult for some women. There are four basic reasons a woman asks so many questions instead of just joining in the conversation: she believes it is polite, she believes it will make him more interested in her, it feels better if he asks, and she has tried interrupting and it didn't work. Let's explore each of these beliefs in greater detail.

1. It Is Polite to Listen

On Venus it is rude to just interrupt. If a Venusian wants to talk, she should first ask questions, show interest, and wait for her turn. While this is fine on Venus, it is very different on Mars. Martians expect and want you to join and participate. They don't mind a friendly interruption. It actually makes the whole process much easier for them. Interrupting and joining in will also make you more attractive to them.

2. He Will Become More Interested in Her

If a woman politely listens and asks questions, she thinks that after a while a man will just become more interested in her, but in actuality he will probably become more interested in himself. Most women already know that a man tends to do one thing at a time, but still they don't realize that if they continue to ask questions a man will do one thing, keep talking. If the woman focuses on him, then he will focus on himself. If she is concerned with pleasing him, then he will be concerned with pleasing himself. If she is concerned with his needs, then he will be more concerned with his needs. He will not even be aware that she is feeling neglected. If she keeps asking questions, he will just assume she has nothing to say.

Certainly if she truly enjoys and appreciates what he is saying, then that will make him more interested in her, but for that interest to be lasting, he needs the opportunity to know her. For him to become interested in her beyond the initial physical attraction, she needs to open up and share herself. If she just asks questions about him, then he will become more interested in himself and not her.

> **When a man talks, he tends to become
> more interested in what he is saying
> than in the listener.**

A woman makes the mistake of thinking a man will be more interested in her if she asks him a lot of questions about himself, because when a man asks a lot of questions to open a woman up it makes her more interested in him. But this is not the case for men. The more a man gets to know a woman, the more interested he can become. When a man does all the talking, he tends to become more interested in what he is saying than in his date.

3. It Feels Better If He Asks

It just doesn't feel very romantic if a woman has to compete to get a word into a conversation. Even though men may have a hard time understanding this feminine experience, it is very true.

A woman feels more special if a man shows his interest by being eager to ask questions. If she has to interrupt to be heard, then it feels as though she is not as special. No matter how much she learns about Martians and where they are coming from, a woman feels that if a man is truly interested, then he will ask her questions. When he asks questions, it reassures her that she is special and worthy of love. It is evidence that this man cares about her. It just isn't as romantic if she has to interrupt.

In a perfect world, a man has read this book fifty times and remembers to ask a woman questions, but we don't live in a perfect world. Until that day it is wise for a woman to master the art of politely interrupting. To do this, it is helpful for women to remember that it's not that he doesn't care enough to ask questions; it's that he is from Mars and doesn't instinctively know how important it is to show he cares by asking questions. He thinks he is showing how much he cares by answering her questions.

4. Interrupting Did Not Work in the Past

Another reason it can be hard for women to interrupt is that by the time they do interrupt they are so angry. While a woman is listening, she may begin to resent that he doesn't even care what she thinks. She may feel humiliated or offended that she is being ignored or excluded. By the time she does interrupt, the tone of her voice indicates to a man that he has done something wrong.

To him this doesn't make sense and seems unfair, because from his side he has been innocently open to her joining in at any time. He feels unjustly attacked or blamed for something he did not do. As a result, he may become defensive and resistant to what she has to say. Naturally, if this has occurred in the past, a woman will have some reservations about trying it again. With an understanding of how men are different, however, a woman can eventually learn to interrupt.

THE FIRST STEP

In learning to interrupt, the first step for a woman is to remember that men and women approach dating differently. A man's automatic way of showing interest is to advertise. If he is not taking the time to listen, it is probably because he is advertising. This means he is interested and very receptive to being interrupted. Even if he seems interested only in hearing his own voice, he is still very receptive to her joining in the conversation. This is hard for a woman to remember because on her planet, a Venusian demonstrates her interest by directly asking questions.

It is not just women who misinterpret; men also take things the wrong way. When a woman doesn't join in a conversation, a man either assumes that she has nothing to say or gets the message that he hasn't yet earned her acceptance, and so he keeps talking. In either case she ends up feeling neglected and annoyed by his self-centeredness. He unknowingly turns her off so that she eventually doesn't want to talk to him.

By understanding what is easiest for men and women and correctly interpreting the signals, we can relax on a date and do what is most natural. Generally a man will feel relieved when a woman joins in and carries a conversation. It takes the pressure off of him and lets him relax and get to know her. Men are happiest when a woman opens up and shares, while women enjoy carrying the conversation as long as they feel a man is interested.

Once we get to understand each other, we are really a perfect fit. A man likes to listen and a woman likes to talk. If she can correctly interpret his behavior, then she can do what she enjoys best and he can do what he enjoys best. Without the correct interpretations, however, she listens when she would rather be talking and he keeps talking when he would rather listen and get to know her. Dating doesn't have to be a struggle; it can be easy and fun. It is all a matter of how we interpret each other.

TIPS FOR INTERRUPTING GRACEFULLY

Even with this understanding, it is still awkward in the beginning for a woman to interrupt a man. To be graceful on her planet is to listen and wait to be asked. To interrupt just doesn't feel natural to a woman, because it isn't natural. But it's like learning anything new. At first it is awkward to speak a new language, throw a ball, roller-skate, drive a car, type, or ski. In the beginning it seems unnatural or difficult, but after a little practice it becomes not only automatic but second nature. Although it is not really natural, it can become our second nature and *seem* natural. With some instruction, this process can be much easier. These are some tips for interrupting gracefully.

1. Don't Say, "Can I Say Something?"

It makes you appear out of sync and insecure and breaks the flow of conversation. A man expects a woman to just join in a conversation. He mistakenly assumes that if she is not talking, she has nothing to say. In a similar fashion, she assumes that if he is not asking for her point of view, then he is not interested.

The secret for interrupting is to do it assuming that he wants to hear what you have to say. This assumption is generally true, and even if he wasn't interested, it gives him the opportunity to become interested. When men have conversations, they don't spend time thinking how to invite the other men into the conversation. The very fact that they are talking to another man is evidence that the other is invited to speak whenever he likes or whenever there is a pause.

Instead of asking permission to join a conversation, a woman ideally can just start in with a phrase like "That reminds me of a time when I . . . ," or simply a phrase like "I think . . ." or "I like . . . ," and then take her turn. These simple statements work particularly well. The less words the better. Just join in.

2. Don't Say, "Are You Ever Going to Take a Breath?"

Here the message is that he is doing something wrong. This can be hurtful, particularly if he is trying to win you over. Instead, say, "That's very interesting. I think . . ."

Whenever a woman tells a man, "That's very interesting," he feels heard and is then happy to relax and listen. A graceful interruption allows a man to save face and doesn't directly point out that he has been talking too long.

3. Don't Say, "Do You Even Care What I Think?"

This makes you seem unnecessarily needy and resentful, and it doesn't express your most loving self. Instead, be playful. If you feel that your point of view is being excluded, then be playfully assertive, saying something like "Whoa (as if talking to a friendly horse), hold it, I think . . ."

Men appreciate this assertiveness if it is done with a playful tone, definitely not a mistrusting or hurt tone.

4. Don't Say, "You Don't Understand . . . I Feel . . ."

This is the most annoying comment a woman can make to a man. And yet it is her most instinctive and automatic response. Certainly on Venus it is not intended to be offensive. To another Venusian, it is easily understood, and her response will generally be, "Oh, I'm sorry (as in Excuse me, I didn't mean to bump you), tell me again." But a Martian's response is generally the opposite. He will become defensive. If she thinks he doesn't understand, then that is a signal that she must think he is incompetent. Martians know that they must appear competent whenever possible or they will not be successful. They automatically become defensive. Instead of listening, the man wants to explain that he does understand. Ironically and tragically, the more he cares, the more defensive he will become. His new objective is now to explain to her that he does understand. As a result, once again, he is doing the talking and she is doing the listening.

All this mess can be avoided if she can practice saying it differently. All she has to say instead of "You don't understand" is "Let me try to say this differently." This one little shift will change everything. Now he will listen even more intently. He still clearly gets the message that she didn't feel heard, but he doesn't feel the need to defend himself.

To get a feel for this, I suggest that a woman practice out loud right now (or as soon as it is appropriate) saying these two phrases. Feel how he might feel in reaction to the first phrase, "You don't understand," and then feel how he might react to the suggested phrase, "Let me try saying this differently." The difference is enormous. The same message is conveyed, but in the first case it seems like an attack and in the second it is a simple request, like "Would you pass the butter?"

5. Don't Say, "Excuse Me, but Do You Mind If I Say Something?"

This approach makes a woman appear powerless and wimpy. It also can be interpreted as unnecessarily negative; as if she is implying that he is not allowing her to say anything.

This is the kind of statement you expect from someone who is eavesdropping outside a conversation and wants to suggest something. It implies that the man is not being inclusive, when he feels he has been open to her input all along. Instead, assert yourself gracefully, assuming that what you have to say will be welcome: "That's right, I think . . ." or "I never thought of it that way, I thought . . ."

6. Don't Say, "Are You Even Interested in What I Think?"

This sounds like a criticism and may unnecessarily turn him off. Remember, he *is* interested in what the woman thinks, but he is waiting for her to interrupt when she has something to say.

Instead, say, "That is very interesting. I think . . ." and then go on to express your opinion. Acknowledging that what a man is saying is interesting before sharing your point of view will make him more interested in what you say. While this seems obvious to men, it is not to women. Women tend to think that if they are interested listeners and ask lots of questions, then the man will stop talking and be interested in what they think.

Women make the mistake of assuming that a man is not interested if he doesn't ask questions. The truth is: If he is talking, it is a sign that he is interested in winning her over. If she then gracefully interrupts, it allows him to become interested in what she has to say and in her. The more she joins in the conversation, the more interested he will become.

7. Don't Say, "Let's Talk About . . ."

While this is a fine way to change subjects, it is not a good way to get him to stop talking. His response would generally be, "Okay," and then he would continue to talk about the new subject.

Whenever a woman wants to change the subject, it is generous on her part to take a moment to acknowledge that what the man has said has been valued or appreciated in some way. Men need to feel as if they at least contributed something useful, if not of interest. She could say, "Hmm, I would never have thought of that," and then just change the subject. There is no need to say, "Now let's talk about . . ."

After making some comment to acknowledge him, just change the subject.

8. Don't Say, "Well, I Disagree. I Think . . ."

Sometimes women feel the only way to be heard is to bluntly disagree. Sure, it is okay to disagree, but don't express your disagreement as a way to interrupt. Instead, say something like "I have another take on this . . ." or "I have another way of looking at that . . ."

These statements are gracious, and they make a man not only open to what a woman has to say but intrigued. It is as if she is saying, "I think what you are saying has merit and I have something different to say about it." Rather than getting defensive about his point of view, he is intrigued to hear what else can be said.

A man is turned on by a woman who is able to express her point of view graciously. A woman should not receptively agree with a man just to appear nice and sweet. That is a surefire way to kill attraction.

9. Don't Say, "Would You Like to Hear What I Think?" or "Would You Like to Know How I Feel?"

All of these kinds of statements make a woman appear to have low self-esteem. Although on Venus these may be considerate ways to interrupt, on Mars they make you appear insecure and insignificant. It is hard for a man to respect a woman if she cannot respect herself.

Instead, she could simply say, "I think . . ." or "I feel . . ." The best technique for interrupting is always to just step right into a conversation as if it is your turn and you have not been overlooked.

10. Don't Say, "May I Ask You a Question?"

A woman should not wait to get a man's permission before expressing her opinion. Not only does it put her in a weak and powerless position, but it also makes it very hard for him to listen.

Many times a woman will say something like, "May I ask you a question? I once had this experience . . ." She then goes on to talk about what she wants to say. This is very frustrating to the man because the whole time he is listening, he is trying to figure out your question and prepare an intelligent answer. If you want to talk, definitely don't disguise it as a question.

Instead, just interrupt with a comment like, "That makes sense. I remember an experience I once had . . ." This is a much more graceful segue and it makes it much easier for him to listen. A man loves to hear that he makes sense, and then he will love to hear what you have to say. Remember that whenever you ask a man questions, he will move into the mode of talking and solving problems. If you want to be heard, don't ask him questions.

Not only does interrupting give you a chance to be heard, but men like it. It is a sign that you are feeling self-assured, that you trust that he cares to listen, that you accept his style of just talking when you want to, that you are connecting to him and willing to join with him in conversation, that you are receptive to what he says, and that you are responsive.

I suggest that you now review the above statements and see how they could easily be misunderstood by a Martian to make you appear closed, resistant, resentful, critical, insecure, insignificant, unworthy, unresponsive, and mistrusting. While certainly these are not accurate descriptions, take a few minutes to reflect on how you may appear this way to an unsuspecting Martian.

WHY MEN DON'T LIKE BEING QUESTIONED

Most women are surprised to hear that men don't like being questioned. Certainly a few questions are fine, but a man prefers it if a woman carries the conversation. As we have explored, when he diligently answers her questions, the last thing he imagines is that she is feeling neglected. He feels he is doing his best to carry the conversation. She asks questions and he answers them. What more could he do to make things better?

When a woman asks lots of questions, she assumes that she is being loving and supportive. Asking questions for her is the best way of demonstrating that she can be loving. It is also a way for her to test a man's ability to have a relationship. If he doesn't understand Venusian manners, however, and ask questions back, she may get turned off before getting to know him.

Just as a man can unknowingly turn a woman off by not asking questions, a woman can unknowingly turn a man off by asking too many questions. Quite often men will express their annoyance about women who ask too many questions. Even if a man is really attracted to a woman, this annoyance can be enough to turn him off. He may not even know why he is turned off, but many times it is simply a woman asking too many questions.

Sometimes, however, it is not as simple as just annoying a man by asking questions. There is another aspect. When a woman begins to open up to a man, she will naturally begin to share the events and issues of her day. When she talks about problems, a man mistakenly assumes that she is asking him what to do about them. So even when a woman isn't asking for his advice, a man may think she is and then proceed to give her some advice.

> **When a woman talks about problems, a man mistakenly assumes that she is asking him what to do about them.**

Whether she really is asking a question or he is mistakenly thinking she is asking him to suggest an answer to her problem, a woman needs to understand what turns a man off. It is not just asking a question that is a turnoff; it is how she responds to his answers that makes the difference. If he gets the message that she appreciates his answer, then he will become more interested in her, but if he gets the message that his answer is not enough, then he will eventually become annoyed.

With so much confusion between men and women, it is amazing that they ever get together and stay together. It is no wonder there is so much divorce once people do fall in love. Without an understanding of our differences, these very little issues eventually escalate into the enormous tensions that give rise to divorce.

When dating couples learn to master these basic communication skills, they can experience the success, intimacy, and fulfillment in their relationship that not only encourage them to move through the five stages of dating but also ensure that they continue to grow in love for a lifetime. In Chapter we will explore some simple ways to apply this new understanding of how men and women think, feel, and communicate differently.

15

Why Men Don't Call

Quite often a man will ask a woman for her number or take her out on a date and then not call. The woman then becomes perplexed and wonders, What went wrong? Is it something I said or did? Does he like someone else better? Will I ever hear from him again? Should I accept other dates? What if he calls while I'm in the shower? Women become annoyed when a man doesn't call. Most men have no idea why it is so important for a woman to receive that call.

**Even when things go really well on a date,
a man may still not call.**

There is an explanation. After understanding it, many women are enormously relieved. It is a great comfort finally to understand men and correctly interpret some of their behaviors that at first seem so confusing. With an under-

standing of how men approach dating, not only can a woman correctly interpret a man's behaviors but she can interact in a way that ensures her getting what she needs.

First of all, quite often it is the case that a man really enjoyed going on a date, but he still doesn't call the next day. His not calling does not mean he doesn't care. When a man doesn't call the next day, it is often because he is following another set of instincts.

WHY WOMEN APPRECIATE A CALL

A woman instinctively expects a call because on Venus the way you show someone you really care is to give some reassurance. A call letting her know you had a good time, in a tone of voice conveying that you have warm and friendly feelings, will generally do the trick. Venusians instinctively call each other after spending some time together.

> While it may be obvious on Venus,
> a man needs to learn the importance of
> calling to give a reassuring message.

For women, staying in contact is a way to show you really care. When two women friends meet again after not having talked in months or years, one of the first things they do is apologize for not staying in touch. Yet this is not the case between two guys. When two male buddies have not talked in months or years, they are just happy to see each other. They don't even think about apologizing for not staying in touch. When they get back together, it is as if one day has passed. Yet when women get back together, they need to get reacquainted before they feel really close.

This same principle is true between married men and

women. A man may go out of town for a week. When he gets back, the first thing he wants to do is have sex, but his wife may not feel the same way. Her feeling is "How can you just want to have sex? We haven't even talked for days. Don't you even care about how I feel?" She may feel a need to get reacquainted before becoming intimate again.

A man doesn't instinctively understand Venusian manners. In many cases, as we will continue to see, he is clueless. He is just following his innocent and automatic instincts, and actually thinks that by not calling he is ensuring the success of the relationship. His instincts motivate him to wait a while before calling to avoid appearing needy or desperate. He senses that if he is too excited or interested, it may compromise his value to her.

THE WISDOM OF WAITING TO CALL

On Mars, they are primarily work-oriented. As we have already explored, dating to a Martian is like a job interview. Everyone who has ever applied for a job knows that the worst thing you can do after a job interview is call right away to see if you got the job. Instead, you patiently wait for someone to call you to let you know whether you got it. If you appear too anxious, then you weaken your position.

A man instinctively doesn't reveal his excitement, assuming that if he appears needy it will weaken his position.

Instinctively a man knows not to show how much he cares or how much he needs someone. Martians pride themselves on being confident, independent, and autonomous. This principle works in the business world, but it misses in the world of intimate relationships with Venusians. When a man finally does call after a date, the woman, having waited, wondering if he was going to call, is at the very least annoyed with him. Her tone of voice clearly lets him know that he has not pleased her. From there the relationship spirals downward.

HOW WOMEN REACT WHEN A MAN DOESN'T CALL

These are some common comments by women about men who didn't call back soon after a date:

- "When I called him, I couldn't believe that he seemed so unapologetic."

- "I can't believe that when he called he didn't even say he was sorry."

- "He acted as if no time at all had passed."

- "He was so insensitive; he acted as though nothing was wrong."

- "I can't believe that he just called me out of the blue, months later, as if everything would be fine."

- "I called him the next morning and he asked why I had called. I was so furious. I never talked to him again."

- "When he finally called a week later, I was so hurt. I had to let him know how I felt, but he just didn't get it."

- "He said he was sorry for not calling, but he didn't mean it. When I was distant, he didn't even ask how I felt."

- "I couldn't believe that he didn't call me. I called him and told him he should get to know me."

In each of these examples, the woman is particularly annoyed by normal and automatic Martian behavior. Without an understanding of how women are different, men will continue to sabotage relationships unknowingly by not calling and women will continue to sabotage relationships by being upset with the men when they do call.

When a man finally does call, a woman is either directly combative or indirectly withholding. The radiant woman he first met is no longer so warm, self-assured, and responsive. She now appears mistrusting and rejecting, all characteristics that make most men head for the hills.

Instead of having a nice warm conversation when they talk again after a date, they both find their attraction diminishing because of the woman's reactive feelings. He feels interrogated by her and that he is being treated unfairly, while she feels neglected and mistreated.

When a man calls and is met with a rejecting or mistrusting attitude, it is definitely not very encouraging to him. Just as she wants a call to reassure her, he is looking for any encouraging messages that he can be successful in pleasing her.

> A woman wants a call to reassure her, while a
> man is looking for any encouraging messages
> that he can be successful in pleasing her.

It is easy to see that by not understanding the different emotional needs of men and women during dating, we may unknowingly turn off the other sex.

WHEN A MAN IS NEEDY

The truth is that if a man does appear needy, it will be a turnoff to women. If he were to call the next day feeling insecure and needing some reassurance, many women would be turned off. Women are most attracted to a man who is confident. Many men do instinctively know this. What men don't know is what a turn-on it is to a woman when a man calls the next day after a date to let her know that he had a good time. When he can communicate a feeling that he definitely likes her and wants to spend more time together, it is music to her ears. This kind of confidence not only makes him very attractive to her but also gives her the reassurance she needs and greatly appreciates.

> Most men don't realize how much a woman
> will appreciate him if he calls after a date.

When a man starts to understand that women are from Venus, then it starts to make sense. When he learns what works, he does it. Most men just don't have a clue what a gift it would be if they were to give strong reassuring messages after a date. By giving a woman the reassurance she needs, the man frees her simply to enjoy the relationship and not wonder if things are going well.

THREE GOOD REASONS FOR A MAN TO CALL

1. Call to Let Her Talk About the Date
Even If You Don't Have a Lot to Say

Since many men don't have a lot to say after a date, they are not automatically motivated to call. It feels a little foolish to call when you have nothing to say. Call her even if you don't feel like talking or you have very little to say. You can at least ask her questions.

Give her a chance to talk about the date. As she talks, it will remind you of what happened and how you felt. You may find you do have something to say. Ask her what she liked about the movie or dinner. When you let her talk about it, she will be able to appreciate you more. By listening to her talk about the date, you will get more points than you got from actually taking her on the date. If you call first before she calls you, then you get bonus points.

When you call, if you get her answering machine, let her know you had a great time and then ask her to call you and give her times when you will be available.

2. Call to See If the Attraction Is More or Less

Men commonly make the mistake of thinking the attraction is less than it is. After a date, it is a good practice to date a woman again just to see what happens with the attraction. If you are not going to date her again, at least give her a call and talk to see how you feel when talking to her. Sometimes the way she reacts to a call may win you over and rekindle feelings that you may have forgotten. Calling a woman after a date does not mean that you have to ask her out again. It is fine to be unsure. If she makes the mistake of asking, just say you're busy this week.

Although many of us make snap judgments on a first date, for some of us they are not always right. Generally, if the attraction is still there after a date, then it is not only good but fun to pursue it. Remember, taking a woman out a few times does not mean you are leading her on. It is leading her on only if you are sure she is not the right person for you and you behave as if she could be.

As we have discussed, when you are feeling uncertain, it is important to continue pursuing a relationship until the attraction dissipates or increases. If you pursue a relationship to its completion, then your future ability to discern and be attracted to the right person for you will increase. This practice is particularly important for people who repeatedly find themselves attracted to people who disappoint them. Each time you are able to follow your feelings of attraction and then, after you get to know the person that person goes away, you are actually preparing yourself to be attracted to the right one.

3. Call as a Courtesy and an Expression of Good Manners

Even if you are not sure that you want to pursue the relationship, it is still important to call. Let her know you had a good time. On her planet it is just good manners. It doesn't mean you want to marry her. She will appreciate it, and so will the next man who pursues her.

Just as men like to be encouraged by knowing that a woman had a good time, a woman needs to feel reassured that she is worthy of being loved. By calling and letting her know you had a good time, it makes her feel good. Each time you go out of your way to respect a woman's need, it makes you more attractive to all women.

Even if you don't go out on a date, but just ask a woman for her number, make sure you call. Otherwise you are just another jerk making it worse for other men. If you ask a woman for her number, at least give her a call.

> **When a man asks a woman for her number,
> the least he can do is give her a call.**

Quite commonly a man doesn't call back when he is not planning to pursue a relationship because he figures that calling a woman to reject her could be construed as presumptuous. He assumes that it would be insulting in some way to call. He would feel arrogant to presume that she liked him and would want him to pursue the relationship.

For many men, dating is like the process of buying a house. If you are looking for your dream home, each time you visit a house on the market, you don't call back and say you are not interested. It is expected that if you don't make an offer you are not interested. No one particularly cares what you think about the house unless you go back several times and make an offer.

In a similar way, if a man has actively pursued a relationship with several dates, then generally most men will feel the need to end the relationship officially with a call. Yet because some men don't know how to end relationships gracefully, they still don't call.

A man may think that by not calling he is sparing a woman the experience of being directly rejected. One male friend of mine was completely surprised when years later a woman remembered him with a lot of annoyance because he hadn't called her back after a couple of dates.

> **Commonly a man thinks by not calling he is ending the relationship gracefully.**

A man tends to give what he would like to receive. If a woman doesn't want to go out with him, he generally doesn't want her to call and tell him directly. He makes a few calls and she generally says she is busy or she is seeing someone else, and so he gives up. He doesn't go around complaining to other guys that she didn't call him back. And yet women do feel neglected and disrespected when a man doesn't call, particularly when he says he will or if he didn't clearly close out the relationship on their last date.

This is why women are annoyed. If it is a great date, he

doesn't call; if he is not sure, he doesn't call; and if he wants to end it, he doesn't call. No wonder dating can be so frustrating and disappointing.

Another reason a man generally won't call is that he doesn't want to burn any bridges. He incorrectly imagines that by not calling and officially rejecting her, if he changes his mind in the future she will be receptive to his asking her out. When a man is uncertain, his approach may be to do nothing and say nothing that could be used against him. His experience is that women remember everything. What he doesn't realize is that they also remember when he doesn't call.

> Some men postpone calling because they are not sure and they don't want to burn any bridges.

Sometimes when a man is not sure he will just postpone. He likes to think things over a lot before he gets involved. He doesn't want to lead a woman on or disappoint her. The irony here is that not calling sometimes has the effect of stringing her along and upsetting her much more. Just a call to acknowledge her existence would make a world of difference.

Sometimes a man knows clearly that he doesn't want to date a woman again, but he doesn't want to face having to reject her or hurt her. Men like to please women, not disappoint them. Most men just don't know how to call and say, "I had a good time; thanks and good luck." For a man it seems really awkward to say, "Have a good life," or "I don't think I will want to take you out again." Particularly when she asks, "Why?"

> For a man it seems really awkward to call back just to say, "Have a good life!"

Just the thought of her asking, "Why don't you want to get to know me?" is upsetting. He doesn't know how to deal with a question like that. Instinctively he knows it is completely inappropriate to give a list of reasons why you don't like someone. If she really needs the feedback, a friend should let her know. It is not his job, particularly if he doesn't want to pursue the relationship.

A man generally doesn't know that if she asks why, he can still be polite and say something like, "I don't think I am the right person for you," and just keep repeating that as his answer if she keeps asking the question. That is polite and it is good enough. If you don't have anything good to say, then don't say anything. To be completely accurate, when you don't want to pursue someone, one simple answer will do: "I don't feel enough chemistry to pursue a relationship."

You either feel or don't feel enough chemistry to pursue a relationship. It is not about the other person at all. Some people like mangoes and some don't. Whether you like mangoes has nothing to do with the intrinsic value of mangoes; it has to do with you. There is nothing wrong with you or with the mango if you don't like mangoes.

In stage one (attraction), when you are not interested in pursuing a woman, the easiest and sometimes the best way to let her know is to call back and leave a message on her answering machine when you know she is at work. This is a great solution and most women will greatly appreciate at least getting the call instead of being ignored and wondering if you are going to call.

In stage two (uncertainty), when you are not sure you are interested in pursuing a relationship, it is also acceptable to leave a message. In this case you simply acknowledge the truth, that you had a good time and you will get back to her in a few weeks.

In stage three, when you have been in an exclusive relationship, it is definitely not acceptable. A breakup needs to be direct. No matter how painful or difficult, she needs the opportunity to react and be heard. She deserves it and will appreciate being heard.

TEN POLITE WAYS TO CALL BACK

Even when a man is motivated to call back, he doesn't because he just doesn't know what to say. Whether you are not sure you are interested or you are definitely not interested, these are some polite ways to say the truth and be positive.

1. Time Will Tell

"It was really nice meeting you. I had a good time with you at the party. I'll see you around."

This lets her know that you are not interested in pursuing her at this time, but that you are not burning any bridges either.

2. Good Luck

"Thanks so much for going out with me. It was a pleasure to meet you. I had a nice time. Good luck and I hope you do well at school (or with that project, etc.)."

This is a graceful and considerate way of letting her know that you will not be pursuing the relationship, without having to mention the relationship word. Men just don't feel comfortable saying, "I am not going to pursue this relationship." This approach also does not prevent you from calling her up again if you want to date her again.

Instead of saying "Have a good life," it is good to personalize your statement, wishing her good luck with something personal like a trip she is planning, a family situation, or a challenge at work. These are some more examples:

"Good luck, and I hope your new business does well."

"Good luck, and I hope you have a safe journey to visit your brother."

"Good luck, and I hope you successfully resolve that mess with your landlord."

"Good luck, and remember to drink lots of water for your cold."

"Good luck, and have a great time on your vacation."

"Good luck, and I hope you find the keys to your garage."

3. Postponement

"I had a great time yesterday. I have a lot of pressure at work (or I have a really busy schedule) and I need to focus on that right now. I probably won't be calling for a few weeks. I'll be looking forward to seeing you again."

When you are busy at work and don't have the time or energy for dating, a friendly call to let her know will be greatly appreciated. Remember, she doesn't have any idea why you are not calling. Women greatly appreciate being reassured that all is well.

4. Getting Involved with Someone Else

"I'm really glad I got to know you. I've decided that I want to get involved with someone else, and so I won't be calling. Thank you for being so much fun; I really enjoyed the time we spent together."

This approach should be used only if it is true and if you have dated a woman more than three times. And even then, it should not be used the day after a date. It might be shocking for her to hear that you decided to get involved with another woman after spending time with her. Although this happens a lot, it seems too quick to her and may make her feel that you really didn't care about her.

Even if after a date a man has decided to see someone else, he should at least give himself a few days to decide for sure. In the meantime, he should give her a call after the date and just let her know he had a good time. Then, after waiting a few days or a week, he should call and let her know he has decided to get involved with someone else.

When you decide to get involved with someone else, never say why. It is hurtful to describe why another person is more desirable to you. It is enough to say you decided. If she wants to know why, simply let her know it is just a feeling in your heart that says you are not the right guy for her.

Don't say how great the other woman is with statements like, "Oh, she's perfect for me; she is so beautiful," or "She is so wonderful." Nor is it polite to compare by saying things like, "She has more time for me," or "She doesn't experience big mood swings." This kind of brutal honesty is hurtful and not easily forgotten. Even if she says she really wants to know, it is still not appropriate and is uncalled for.

5. Not Ready

"Thank you for a wonderful date. I realized I am still dealing with a past relationship, and I don't think I am ready to be dating a lot. I hope you don't mind if I call sometime in a few months. This really isn't the right time for me."

This is particularly useful when you are trying to figure out if you want to have an exclusive relationship with someone. Once you think you might want an exclusive relationship, it is important to start one and see if you like it. It is hard to decide if you definitely want to be exclusive with one woman while you are continuing to see other women.

> **Once you think you want an exclusive relationship, it is important to start one and see if you like it.**

6. Not Available

"I had a really good time with you. But I realized that I am not really available right now. I need to take some time for myself. So I won't be calling for a while. "

There is nothing wrong with realizing that you are not into dating. If this is the case, make sure you let her know; otherwise she will wonder what went wrong.

7. Ready to Move On

"I really liked spending time with you, but I think I am ready to move on. I wanted to let you know it was nothing you said or did. I just realized I needed a change. Thanks and I hope you find the right guy for you."

Sometimes we are not ready for an exclusive relationship. At a certain point, if we are not ready, then no matter how good a relationship is we may need to move on. If this is the case, it is important to let her know.

8. Wrong Timing

"I really enjoyed being with you. I don't think the timing is right. You are in the process of ending a relationship. I'll give you a call in a few months. I hope things work out for you."

Or, "Thanks for a wonderful time. I realized that I am still in the process of ending my last relationship and it wouldn't be fair to you. Maybe I'll call in a few months when things get resolved with my last relationship."

Rebound relationships are fine as long as you and your partner are not expecting an exclusive relationship. Keep in mind that when people have just ended a relationship, to a certain extent they are empty and seeking to be filled up. Their discernment is generally at an all-time low. Thirsty or hungry people are generally not very picky about what they eat, but once they are well fed, it is time to be picky again.

9. Not Sure

"I had a great time the other night. I wanted you to know I'm not sure if I want a relationship right now. So I probably will not be calling for a while."

When you are in stage two and you are uncertain about a woman, it is considerate and good manners just to let her know what is happening. It is okay to be uncertain, but it is not okay just to ignore her and go on as if she didn't exist.

If she starts asking you a lot of questions—"How do you feel about me?" "Is there someone else?" "Did I do something?" "Is there a problem?"—you don't have to talk a lot. Instead, answer her questions with questions. Get her to talk and then listen. Listening to her feelings will actually help you move through the stage of uncertainty more quickly.

If she asks, "How do you feel about me?" answer briefly, "I like you very much." Then ask her, "How do you feel about me?" and then listen.

If she asks, "Is there someone else?" then say briefly, "Well, like I said, I am unsure right now." Then ask her, "Is there someone other than me?" and then listen.

If she asks, "Did I do something wrong or upsetting to you?" answer briefly, "I am not sure." Then ask her, "Have I done something to upset you?" and then listen.

If she asks, "Is there a problem that I don't know about?" answer briefly, "I am not sure." Then ask her, "Is there a problem that I don't know about?" and then listen.

Remember, when you are in the second stage, you just don't realize it is a time to think things over. Get different experiences. Don't burn any bridges or attempt to build any. It is a time for a man to back away as much as he feels the need to before deciding if he wants to move forward to the third stage, exclusivity, or back to stage one, following his attractions.

10. Not Right for Each Other

"I think it's clear we are not right for each other, but I wanted to call and at least say thanks and wish you happiness."

In the first two stages, both men and women must feel free to experiment and move on. Until you are in an exclusive relationship, it is not appropriate to have any expectations that a person should continue in a relationship. If a man or woman does have these kind of expectations, it is generally a major turnoff.

Dating in stages one and two is a time to experiment. One is not under any obligations at all. There is no guilt in wanting to move on. Sometimes the easiest way is just to say, "I don't think we are right for each other," and move on.

This tenth approach, however, is generally most applicable for someone in stage three who wants to break up. He has taken the time to get to know someone and feels they are not right for each other.

All of the ten approaches above make it a little easier to move from relationship to relationship until you find the most special one for you. These same approaches can also be used by women to say no politely to a man's approaches or requests for a date. Women, however, can just say, "I am not interested in that kind of relationship with you. I would rather just be friends." That is all the explanation a man needs.

> To close out a relationship, a woman
> can just say, "I am not interested in that
> kind of relationship with you. I would
> rather just be friends."

This approach is very safe for a woman to use because in most cases, she (unlike most men) does want to be friends. Even if she doesn't really want to be involved much as a friend, she knows that when she says she just wants to be friends, he won't be calling.

THE BENEFITS OF MOVING ON

Although it is only good manners to call and close out a relationship, there are other benefits as well. The way we close a relationship determines the kind of person we will be attracted to next time.

If we must become indifferent to our feelings to end a relationship, or if we feel some kind of guilt, then we will tend to repeat patterns. When we end a relationship with good feelings, we will take another step closer to the partner of our dreams.

If you can't easily end relationships in stages one and two, then it will be much harder to move through the next stages. Once again, remember that the attraction stage is a time to discover your likes and dislikes and to get to know the kind of person you are and what you want. Being able to say no to someone because he or she is not the right person for you strengthens your resolve to find the right person.

Saying no also helps you adjust and make more accurate your ability to be attracted and turned on to the kind of partner with whom you would want to pursue a long-term relationship. This same principle is equally true for women and men. The very act of saying no to a relationship that is not right for you fine-tunes your ability to be attracted to the person who *is* right for you.

16
To Call or Not to Call

Women today are looking for a new kind of relationship, not the kind their mothers and fathers may have had. They want intimate communication and lasting romance. To achieve this end, new skills are definitely required. A woman today needs to be not only soft and feminine but also assertive.

Many successful women have learned to be assertive in the work world, but still wonder why they are single. They haven't yet learned the art of being assertive *and* feminine. For most women, this is not easy because they have no role models. Either they saw their fathers being assertive and their mothers being accommodating or it was the other way around: Their mothers were dominant and their fathers were yielding and passive.

> **Most women have not yet learned the art of
> being assertive *and* feminine.**

For our parents' generation, it was taboo for a woman to call a man. That was considered too pushy and not feminine. Women were warned by their mothers, Don't be too easy, too available, too accommodating, or he will not respect you. Well, they were not making this up. It was true then and it still is.

Whenever a woman pursues a man more than he is pursuing her, he will pursue her less. Why should he risk failure when she is happy to pursue him? Automatically, he will relax more and become more passive about the relationship. Instead of thinking what she may want, he begins thinking more about what he wants. This turnaround is very confusing for a woman because her assertive approach is successful in the working world but backfires on a date.

> **When a woman pursues a man, automatically
> he will relax more and become more passive
> about the relationship.**

These women are just not aware that men need to be successful in their pursuit in order to discover whether they really care for a woman. Certainly a woman who pursues men does sometimes succeed in getting a man, but often the consequence is not what she had hoped. When they get married and she wants to relax and simply be herself, he loses interest.

In some cases, once they settle down and she stops pursuing him, he finally gets the opportunity to feel his desire to please her and pursue. In this case his interest in her finally gets a chance to rise. This is not always the case, though; more often he just loses interest.

This tendency also shows up in dating. Quite often a woman will decide to end a relationship and then the man suddenly becomes more interested. She then blames him for this, because she doesn't understand her part in sabotaging the relationship. She mistakenly assumes that he is not right for her because he wants her more now that she decides to respect herself and stop pursuing him. His renewed interest can actually be a great sign.

> Quite often a woman will decide to
> end a relationship and then the man
> suddenly becomes more interested.

A seed cannot sprout unless it is given the right conditions. Similarly, a man's attraction and interest in a woman cannot grow if she is too assertive and aggressive. When a woman stops pursuing a man, she gives him the opportunity to find within himself the desire to pursue. In early stages of dating, his ability to be interested in her is like a burning candle: Too much interest and pursuit from her side can easily snuff it out.

The five stages of dating ensure that you don't have to take unnecessary chances. Before marrying your partner, you will have experienced that he or she fully knows you, likes you, loves you, *and* is still attracted to you. Your partner is interested in you without your having to play any games or try to be more than you are. Having said all this, there are still ways for women to call men without sabotaging the potential of a relationship.

This issue of whether a woman should call or not, particularly in stages one and two of dating, can be critical in determining the outcome of a relationship. A deeper understanding of the way men and women think and feel differently can create many new options for a woman to be assertive *and* feminine.

A WOMAN'S OPTIONS

When a man takes longer than a woman would expect to call back, a woman is generally upset for two reasons. The first reason is that she doesn't instinctively understand that he is from Mars and that he doesn't understand Venusian manners. The second reason she is upset is that she has waited days for his call, feeling powerless. She wants to call but she doesn't.

Everyone tells her she shouldn't call, and instinctively there is a part of her that doesn't want to call, but another part wants to call. In a perfect world, it would feel better to her if he called her. When he calls, it makes her feel special. If she has to call and ask questions to be reassured, no matter what he says, it is still not as nice as if he were to call on his own.

But all is not so hopeless. With an understanding of men, there are other options. To make the time pass more quickly she has two options, and both are good suggestions.

Option One: Fill Up Your Time

The first option is fill your life up with activities and relationships so that you are not just waiting by the phone. There is no greater mistake than to stop your life for a man. A man is most interested and attracted to a woman whose life is full, but who happily makes some room for him. He is less attracted if she needs him to fill up her life and schedule. He is most attracted when she needs him to share the fullness of her life.

To a certain extent, a woman should think of romantic relationships as a special dessert and let other relationships with friends and family be the main meal to fill her up. When she finds herself anxiously waiting for a man's call, it is a sign she needs to focus on finding fulfillment through her other relationships.

Needing a man for everything will ultimately sabotage a relationship with him. No man can satisfy all of a woman's needs. He may think he can, but he can't, and it is a big mistake to expect him to. The pressure it eventually puts on him will push him away.

Option Two: Give Him a Call

The second option is to give him a call. For many women this approach has never worked, and as a result they just don't call. Some women continue to call, although it does not help the relationship. They just assume that it wouldn't have worked anyway and move on. With an understanding of how men are different, it is possible to call a man and have a great conversation, get the reassurance you may like to hear, and support the unfolding of the relationship. To call a man after a date it can be helpful to follow these guidelines.

SEVEN GUIDELINES FOR CALLING A MAN AFTER A DATE

1. Don't Call If You Are Upset with Him

It is generally a mistake to call a man and be upset with him for not calling. Many women do call and tell him how upset they feel. When the man doesn't get it, that's the end of the relationship. Unfortunately, this prevents the natural unfolding and development of the relationship.

It is a mistake to call a man and be upset with him for not calling.

If you are upset, then definitely don't call a man. Talk to a girlfriend if you need to share your feelings. After airing your feelings, you will probably feel much better, particularly if you remember that men are from Mars and they have different instincts. Remember, the reason a man doesn't call is that his instincts are different.

2. Don't Ask Questions

Just as women complain when men do not call back, men complain about women who want to talk about the relationship.

Unless a man is entering the commitment stage of dating, he generally doesn't like to talk about the relationship or define it. Men just want to live in the moment and see where things go. They want to let it develop, like planting a seed. It doesn't work to keep digging it up each day to see if it is sprouting.

> Just as women complain when men do not
> call back, men complain about women who
> want to talk about the relationship.

There is a way for a woman to get the reassurance she may be needing. Instead of calling to ask for it, try calling to give him what he may be needing. Just as a woman greatly appreciates a man's call to reassure her that he is interested and had a good time, a man greatly appreciates being encouraged by messages that he was successful in making her happy.

Don't call to ask questions, but instead call to share a few good feelings. If he does not feel pressured to make any reassuring statement, then his natural appreciation for her good feelings will be reassuring enough. These are some examples of questions that you do not want to ask.

Five Questions Not to Ask a Man After a First Date

Are you seeing anyone else?

This implies that he should not be seeing anyone else. In the attraction stage of a relationship, it is perfectly fine to be seeing others. If he is seeing someone and he has to lie, this will definitely prevent him from eventually finding true feelings for you. It is inappropriate in stage one to feel pressured to see only one person.

Do you want to spend more time with me?

This is too pushy. It makes him feel as if you are too needy and demanding. Already he feels sucked into a relationship, and he is not necessarily ready for that. Remember, this is stage one. In stage three, we naturally begin to think about commitment and a possible future together.

Did you have a good time? Do you like me? (Both imply: *Would you like to get together again?*)

This weakens a woman's position. It implies that you feel insecure and hope that you have pleased him. There is also a feeling of obligation implied; that is, if you have pleased him, then he should please you. A man needs to feel clearly that he is not obligated in any way to pursue the relationship. There are no strings attached in stage one.

How much time do you have available for a relationship? (or, *Are you busy this week?* or, *What are you going to do next weekend?*)

What do you expect him to say? "Yes, I have plenty of time because my life is empty and I have no friends"? Just as this would make him appear unlovable and undesirable, to ask him this question actually makes you appear just as undesirable and unloved. In stage one, any indication that you are planning a future together is premature and can push him away. This question is just as untimely as asking if he wants to get married soon and have kids. He will let you know when he is ready.

When would you like to get together again?

This is way too pushy. You might as well ask him to get out his calendar to schedule a date.

3. Make Positive Comments

Instead of asking questions, the secret of calling a man is to make positive comments. Let him know how you feel; don't ask him how he feels. Let him know that you had a good time; don't ask him how he felt. Avoid asking questions like the plague.

Instead of asking questions, use F.Y.I.O.—"for your information only"—statements. These comments do not make or even imply any request for information regarding his feelings or intentions. These are some examples:

Statements that Men Love to Hear

"I really loved that movie, it was great! The scene . . ."

"I had such a good time the other night. The food at Greens restaurant was definitely the best . . ."

"That show was so great. I got the CD. It was so dramatic. My favorite song . . ."

"I had so much fun at the fair. I can't believe I had never been before. I told my sister about that giant Ferris wheel . . ."

"That soup we had was really fantastic. I can't figure out what they put in it. I think it was baked eggplant and garlic . . ."

"I love Chinese food. I'm so glad you picked Jennie Low's. I felt so good afterward . . ."

"Thanks for building those shelves in my garage. They look so great. I put all my old albums out there . . ."

"I am so glad you decided to stop and get a dessert. It was so good . . ."

"I remembered today what you said last night and realized that it made a lot of sense. I think I am going to . . ."

"I had such a good time last night."

The direct way to a man's heart is through complimenting and appreciating the things he provided. When a man experiences a positive response to the things he does or provides for her, he is more inclined to feel attracted. This is how a man's affection for a woman grows.

4. Talk About What Happened, Not About Him

"I really liked the movie we saw. It was great . . ." (and then talk about what you liked about the movie).

He feels, "She liked the movie. She is fun to do things with. I like her." Talking about what happened goes directly to his heart.

Don't say, "I really liked spending time with you." The implied message is the question, "Did you like spending time with me? Do you want to spend more time with me?" He may now feel some obligation to spend time together so that you will not feel rejected. Instead of focusing on his success, he is now thinking about how he may fail you.

> **Men are attracted to success. When a man feels he is a success in fulfilling a woman, he is more attracted to her.**

Talking about the movie frees him to connect with you without feeling any pressure to spend more time together. When you say you liked the movie, he can join in. When you say you liked him, then the only way for him to connect is to be arrogant and agree that many women like him or to connect by saying he likes you too. To come out and say he likes you may be too much at this early stage of the relationship. The less pressure he feels to spend time together frees him to desire to spend more time together.

5. Let Him Know the Positive Responses You Had and Leave Out the Negative

In stage one of a relationship, let him just see the supportive and positive side of your personality. When you talk about the date, let him know primarily your positive responses and leave out the negative. Otherwise, he might mistakenly begin to think that you are a difficult woman to please. What allows a man to grow in attraction and form an emotional bond of affection is feeling that he can be successful in making you happy.

> ### A man forms an emotional bond of affection as he succeeds in making a woman happy.

A woman is generally unaware of this Martian sensitivity. If the movie isn't any good, she may feel, "Well, all is not lost; at least we can talk about how bad it was." Regardless of whether the movie is good or bad, she looks forward to talking about it.

Venusians experience the bond of affection growing as they feel heard and understood. After a lousy experience on a date, a women will actually look forward to talking about it in great detail. She generally has little awareness of how it makes him feel.

6. Don't Give Advice on Anything, but Instead Ask for Advice

Even if a woman thinks a man would greatly benefit from her advice on a particular matter, she must be very careful not to offer any unsolicited advice. Even if he asks, she should still be careful. Men like to feel that they can offer a woman some expertise. Men need to feel that they have something to offer. When a woman brings more to him than he feels he can bring to her, it has the same effect as when a woman pursues a man.

Men also don't like it when a woman quotes another expert. This is another way women give advice. They quote other people or experts to make their point. This can be an immediate turnoff. It is fine if the man is asking for advice, but for a woman to quote someone when he is not asking is even worse than if she were to offer direct advice.

Men and women come to relationships for different reasons. A man is most interested in a relationship when he feels he has something to offer and share. When he feels good about himself and his work, then he wants to share that with a woman. The more competent a man feels in the presence of a woman, the more attracted he will be to her.

To increase the opportunity for a man to feel attracted to a woman, if she feels she would like his advice on something, then by all means she should ask. Whenever a man gets to feel useful to a woman, he will feel more proud of himself and like her more. The more interested a woman is in what a man can offer her, the more interested he becomes in her.

When she does ask for his advice, her response is very important. If she disagrees with his advice or doesn't like it, she must be careful to allow him to save face. He needs to at least get the message that she appreciated his attempt to help. Another man would instinctively know how to do this, but a woman will not.

Without an understanding of our differences, a woman commonly turns a man off by pointing out what she doesn't like about his advice. Particularly when she doesn't want to use the advice, she will think it is polite to explain in great detail why she disagrees with it. In the end he feels frustrated, as if he has wasted his time.

If a woman disagrees with his advice or doesn't value it enough to use it, then these are some comments that will allow him to save face. These are the kind of comments any man would give to another out of respect:

> "That's a good idea. I would have never thought of that. Thanks. That's very helpful."

> "That's very interesting. Thanks. That makes it easier for me to figure out what to do."

"I certainly had not looked at it from that point of view. This will be very helpful for me in figuring out what to do. Thanks."

"This is so helpful. I didn't realize . . . I think I am closer now to making a decision."

"That's a great point. It really helps me finally to figure out what to do."

"That sure makes sense. I'm glad I talked to you. Hearing different points of view sure helps to clarify things. Thanks."

7. Don't Offer to Help Him in Any Way, but Instead Ask for His Help

The more a man succeeds in helping a woman, the more attracted he will be to her. A woman also experiences a greater attraction to a man when he is helpful to her. She then mistakenly turns this around and assumes that if she is helpful to him, he will be more attracted to her. This is not true.

Certainly a man will appreciate a woman's help if he has asked for it, but offering help can easily backfire and make a man feel mothered and smothered. If a man wants help he will generally ask for it. When a woman offers to help it can easily make her appear too eager to win his affections, or it can come across as an insult.

On Mars, they don't offer unsolicited help. To offer to help a man carry a box implies that he doesn't have the strength to do it himself. To help a man solve a problem implies that he doesn't have the competence to do it himself. Men are very picky about receiving help because they really like proving that they can do things alone, if they can. If they can't, then it is fine to ask for help, and they will.

> To offer to help a man solve a problem
> implies that he doesn't have the
> competence to do it himself.

When talking to a man in person or on the phone, it is important to remember not to offer advice, and not to suggest that he get help for something. This can be a real turnoff. He is not stupid. He knows he can get advice.

I remember once when I was trying to fix the toilet, my wife sensed my frustration and came in hoping to help. After a while, she said, "I bet if you called the plumber, he would know what to do." In her mind, she was just letting me know that I didn't have to fix it. While she was just being polite on her planet, it was an insult on Mars. I certainly already knew that I could call a plumber. I didn't need her to tell me that. The best thing she could have done would have been just to ignore my frustration and go about her business.

When a woman calls a man back, she must be very clear about this. If she calls to offer help, she loses him. If she calls to get help, he will feel complimented.

HOW TO ASK A MAN OUT

With this in-depth understanding of men, it becomes clear why it works best for the man to ask the woman out. There are some ways that a woman can ask a man out without being too aggressive about it or running the risk of becoming the pursuer.

Instead of asking him out on a romantic date, she can ask him to help her with something or accompany her somewhere. As long as she is genuinely asking him for something that would make her life more comfortable and fulfilled, then it is fine to ask. Ideally, the request should be practical and not romantic. These are some examples:

"Would you please help me pick out a barbecue grill this weekend?"

"Would you please help me move some boxes in my garage?"

"Would you please help me change the lights in my backyard?"

"Would you please help me go shopping for a car?"

"Would you please read this article I am writing and tell me what you think?"

"Would you please pick me up after I drop my car off to get it fixed?"

"Would you help me fix the light fixture in my attic? It's not working."

"I have been sick with a cold. Would you please pick up take-out dinner for me? I don't think I should be going out tonight."

"Would you please come with me to pick up a package at the airport?"

"Would you please help me feed my horses today? My brother got sick."

"Would you help me take my dog to the vet? He got really sick. I don't want to go alone."

"Would you please help me buy a new computer?"

"Would you please help me buy a new stereo?"

"Would you please help me figure out my VCR?"

"Would you please help me rearrange my
furniture?"

In each of these examples, the man has the opportunity to be a friend, but more important, the woman has been able to create a fertile opportunity for him to experience being helpful to her and thus become more attracted to her. In Chapter 17, we will explore more deeply the dynamics of what makes a man more interested in a woman.

17

Men Love a Woman with a Smile

Something undefined gets turned on in a woman when a certain man looks at her in a certain way. Likewise, something just awakens in a man when a woman smiles or laughs in a certain way or simply brushes up against him. That undefined something can be explained: a man gets turned on when a woman's radiance makes him feel more like a man; a woman gets turned on when a man's attention makes her feel more like a woman.

Ultimately, a man is most attracted to a woman when she makes him feel masculine. In a similar manner, a woman is most attracted to a man when his presence makes her feel feminine. The greatest power a man or woman can gain to create attraction is the ability to awaken in another more of who the other is.

When a woman makes a man feel masculine, his body is filled with the fire of desire to get close, and he becomes purposeful. He feels inspired to be better, and he is motivated to fulfill her needs: He wants to be with her, to get to know her, and, in some magical manner, his life suddenly has more meaning. He is excited by the thought of winning her over and encouraged by a feeling in his gut that says confidently, I could make her happy. As he is magnetically drawn to her, she brings out the best in him.

> **A man is excited by the thought of winning a woman over and encouraged by a feeling in his gut that says confidently, I could make her happy.**

When a man makes a woman feel feminine, her mind is stimulated and intrigued; she feels warm, tender, and vulnerable inside; her heart begins to open as she remembers that she is special; she is excited by the thought of being seen, heard, and desired; and she is reassured by the possibility of getting what she wants and needs. As she is magnetically drawn to him, his active interest brings out the best in her.

> **A woman is excited by the thought of being seen, heard, and desired and reassured by the possibility of getting what she wants and needs.**

It is this feeling of being inspired to be our best that can make dating and relationships so fulfilling. For many, these good feelings are hit and miss. Sometimes they are there and sometimes not. By understanding the dynamics of what makes men and woman attracted to each other, dating can not only begin to fulfill our need for intimacy but can also help us discover and express the best parts of who we are.

What allows a woman to bring out the best in a man can

be summarized in one expression: feminine radiance. When a woman expresses her feminine radiance she is generally embodying the three basic characteristics of femininity: she is self-assured, receptive, and responsive. It is these three qualities that make a man most attracted to her.

What allows a man to bring out the best in a woman is his masculine presence. When a man expresses his masculine presence he is generally embodying the three basic characteristics of masculinity: he is confident, purposeful, and responsible. It is these three qualities that make a woman most attracted to him. With an awareness of these different characteristics, we can begin to understand why some dates work and others don't. With this insight we can gain the power to attract the right person for us.

WHEN WOMEN ARE FROM MARS

After reading my book *Men Are from Mars, Women Are from Venus,* some women realized that they too were from Mars and that this was the primary reason they were not attracting the right guy. When I described how men think and feel, it was also the way they thought and felt. Certainly there was a part of them that related to the Venusian side of themselves, but it was not a big part of their lives.

This role reversal is very common, particularly with women who are very active and committed to their careers. At a certain point, they want to be married, but they continue to get involved with "guys who don't commit." The irony is that many of those same guys who don't commit will turn around and get married right away to someone else. As we will see, it is not necessarily who we are that makes or breaks a relationship, but how we express and communicate who we are.

When a woman comes from her Martian side, she can certainly make a man feel good, but she can never really bring out the best in him. It is only when she takes the time and has the awareness to develop and express her attributes from Venus that she can bring out the Martian in him. This is not automatic, because women today are pressured to be like men during the day at work. Depending on how stressful their job is, it can be very difficult to shift back to having feminine feelings and characteristics.

Even when women think they are from Mars, they are still from Venus. They still have all the feminine characteristics within them. With a little attention to what those attributes are, they can and will come to life. Through getting in touch with her feminine feelings and characteristics *and* with some practice using Venusian approaches to dating, a woman will automatically become more attractive to the right men for her.

STRONG AND ASSERTIVE WOMEN

Strong, independent, assertive, and successful women often have difficulty finding the right man and then sustaining a relationship, primarily because the very characteristics that make them successful at work can make them unsuccessful in relationships. When a woman can actively pursue a goal in the workplace she will succeed, but when she actively pursues a man (and she may date many men), something will always be missing. And what is missing is what can emerge only when a man feels he is doing the pursuing.

Although there is nothing intrinsically wrong with a woman expressing her Martian attributes, it will backfire if she doesn't also get a chance to sometimes be feminine. Finding a balance of Martian and Venusian in her life is essential. Particularly when a woman has to be Martian at work, it is even more important than ever to come home to a relationship that makes her feel more feminine.

While dating and finding a fulfilling relationship can be more difficult for these women, all successful women have an incredible ability for self-correction. All a woman needs is the complete awareness and understanding of the problem, and then she immediately sets out to fix it. In this case nothing in her is really broken, but something is being neglected. By clearly identifying the three Venusian attributes and nurturing their development through dating, she can change the tide and begin enjoying success in both areas of her life, work and relationships. A strong and assertive woman can be very attractive, but she must learn to express her power in a feminine way.

Whether a woman is more Martian or Venusian, by becoming aware of the three Venusian attributes and applying the dating strategies for each, she will achieve the same result. Not only will she begin to bring out the best in men, but she will like herself more and have a better time.

Sometimes when women hear these new approaches to dating, they feel they have done everything wrong. Instead of focusing on the failures, remember that now you have the opportunity to change the patterns of dating that you may be repeating over and over. Unless you identify what didn't work and what you can do about it, the chance of change is nil. Even if some of these ideas are challenging to the foundation of how you have always related to men, give them a chance and experience that they work.

THE FIRST ATTRIBUTE: SELF-ASSURANCE

The first attribute that makes a woman most attractive is self-assurance. Most women have noticed some special women who have men wrapped around their fingers. They wonder how the special woman does it: That man will do anything she wants.

These special women always exude an air of grace and trust. They are self-assured. They respect themselves and assume others will respect them. A self-assured woman trusts that others care and that they want to support her. She does not feel alone. She feels supported by friends and family and by men. In her mind, almost all men are likable until proven otherwise.

When she is not respected, she doesn't take it so personally, but moves on. She realizes that she still deserves what she needs and gracefully tries another approach to get it. If that fails, she quickly looks elsewhere for support. She doesn't expect perfection and is open to finding new ways of getting more of what she wants.

Some women are naturally self-assured. They are born with this attitude, just as some singers are born with an incredible voice. For most, this attitude needs to be developed and cultivated. It is already inside a woman; it just needs the opportunity to come out and be exercised. By becoming aware of how it looks and feels, a woman can begin to find it and give expression to this part of herself.

Self-assurance is an attitude that assumes you will always get what you need and that at this moment you are in the process of getting it. It is different from confidence. Confidence assumes that you can do what you set out to do, even if you have to do it all by yourself without any help. Self-assurance assumes that others are available and want to help and you don't have to do it all by yourself. When a woman is too confident and independent, it is sometimes a sign that she is not assured at all that others are there for her, and so she has to do it all herself. With this new awareness, she can begin to open up to others for their support and not isolate herself.

> ### Self-assurance assumes you will always get what you need and you are now in the process of getting it.

When women see another woman with a lot of self-assurance, they just assume that she feels this way because she is able to get the support of a man. While there is some truth to this, it is really the other way around. When a woman is self-assured, then the support comes her way. When a woman behaves and interacts with a man assuming that she will get the respect she deserves, that she can get the support she needs, and that she is already worthy of that support, then automatically she brings out the best in him.

> ### When a woman is self-assured, then the support comes her way.

As a woman grows in self-assurance, she will not be attracted to men who cannot respond to her in the ways she deserves. It is not that men suddenly become perfect for her, or that she finds a perfect man; it is more that she is able to bring out the best in a man.

Why Men Stay Interested

When a man is actively interested it is because he is in the process of getting what he wants. He is in the successful pursuit of making a woman happy, and this also makes him happy. As he succeeds, he anticipates getting more in return, and this makes her even more interesting. What turns a man on is the message that he could be the one to make a woman happy. As long as he is making progress, he is happy. When a woman is self-assured that she will get what she wants, then that is the perfect complement to the man who wants to succeed in a relationship.

Not only does her attitude of self-assurance make her more attractive, but it sustains his interest in her. Most women don't realize that it is not so much what men get now that keeps them interested, but the possibility of what they will eventually get. When a woman is self-assured she fuels a man's confidence and his anticipation of success.

> **It is not so much what men get now that keeps them interested but the possibility of what they will eventually get.**

Without this understanding of our differences, a woman mistakenly assumes that she must in some way earn a man's affections. Instead of being self-assured that she is already worthy of what he gives, she begins to feel an urge to please him and win his love. Whenever a woman tries to win a Martian's love, she will lose. It is for him to win her love and for her to give him the opportunity. This understanding of Martian temperament in itself frees women to be more self-assured.

A woman mistakenly assumes that when she is pleasing to a man, eager to satisfy his needs first, he will then be more motivated to please her. This woman may have an air of confidence because she knows she can please him, but it is not self-assurance. Trying to please a man will never earn his lasting affections. The opposite is true. When a man succeeds in pleasing a woman, then and only then is he more motivated to please her.

Why Men Become So Charming

This helps explain what makes a man on a date most charming and interested in a woman. When a woman is attracted to a man, he gets the message that he could be the one to make her happy. He seems to be making her very happy, and this brings out the best in him. If, however, she begins to feel obligated to return the favor and focuses on making him happy, much of the charm disappears.

Often women complain that they go out with a man and have a great time and then the next day he becomes a complete jerk. One day he is interested and the next he is distant and uninterested in them. They complain, "He got what he wanted and was out of here." It is no wonder that women mistrust men and feel used. These women do not understand their part of the problem. When a woman gives more than she is getting, or gives all of herself before she receives all that she wants, she is setting herself up to be disappointed. When a woman shifts from feeling self-assured to trying to satisfy a man's wants, he may continue to see her but it is never the same. He becomes less and less interested in her.

> When a woman shifts from feeling
> self-assured to earning a man's affection,
> she becomes less attractive.

This does not mean a woman should not give of herself or seek to satisfy a man's needs and wishes as well. As long as she is centered, secure in the feeling that she is getting what she wants, then it is fine for her to give what feels right to her. If he wants more and she wants to wait, only if she respects her own needs first can he begin to respect them. She will make it easier for herself and for him when she is self-assured, so that he will respect her wishes with regard to her needs, her schedule, her preferences, and her beliefs and considerations regarding physical and emotional intimacy.

In most cases, when a woman shifts to trying to earn a man's love and attention, she doesn't even have a clue as to how she may be preventing a man from becoming genuinely and actively interested in her. When a man pulls away, a woman commonly blames him and doesn't realize how she can be part of the equation.

> When a man pulls away, a woman
> blames him and doesn't realize how
> she can be part of the equation.

Certainly a man likes it when a woman reacts as if he is everything she wants, as if just being with him makes her happy, as if she is getting everything she needs and he is perfect for her just the way he is. This kind of response is very seductive. When she responds to him as if he has fulfilled all her needs and in truth he really hasn't, then the next day, as she begins to feel what she is not yet getting, he begins to lose interest and doesn't even know why.

What Makes a Man Listen

A woman's attitude has the power either to turn a man on or to turn him off. For example, a man will most respect and want to hear what a woman has to say when she speaks in a manner that first assumes he is interested. The very act of assuming a man will be interested makes him more interested. Even if he wasn't that interested in the subject matter, he will become interested, because he is interested in her. It is all in her approach.

> A man will most respect and want to hear
> what a woman has to say when she speaks
> in a manner that assumes he wants to hear
> what she has to say.

If her attitude says she feels assured that he will be interested, then he will want to hear her and know her. It is this attitude of being self-assured that draws a man's interest. A woman needs to remember that she is the jewel and he is providing the setting for her to shine. As long as he gets credit for making her shine, he is happy to be the provider of support in the relationship. This attitude that she is already worthy of attention makes her more desirable and intriguing to him.

Men are interested in being successful. The opportunity to provide fulfillment to a woman is very interesting to any man. Certainly a man is interested in being fulfilled as well, but it is being successful in fulfilling a woman that makes him feel most fulfilled in a relationship. A man is always interested in what will make him successful.

When a Man Is the Jewel

A woman's position is compromised when she behaves as if the man is the jewel and she would like the position of providing the setting. Automatically the romance and attraction will lessen. Certainly, a man likes feeling he is the jewel when a woman seeks to please him, but ultimately he likes much more the experience of winning her over. When a woman shares herself with self-assurance that she is the jewel, a man responds by wanting to win her over.

A woman's desire to please a man is clearly a demonstration of love, but at the same time a woman must know that if she denies herself to please him, it makes her less attractive. No matter how happy she makes him, if she is editing herself, holding herself back, and not expressing her true self, he will eventually lose touch with his feelings of attraction for her.

What Men Love and What Is Boring

A man loves it when a woman feels free to be herself in his presence. From his perspective, her difference from him makes her very attractive. Through being authentic, she can let her feminine radiance shine and he is drawn to her like a moth to the flame. He is turned on by her ease and comfort with herself and her freedom of expression. When she can be herself in his presence, that is a message to him that he doesn't have to change himself to be with her.

When a woman feels she has to become something other than her true self to be lovable, then she becomes less attractive. Not only does it restrict her true radiance, but it gives a message that he is also expected to change in order to be acceptable.

THE SECOND ATTRIBUTE: RECEPTIVITY

The second attribute that makes a woman most attractive is receptivity. Some woman are just able to flow through dating situations, while others get rigid and stuck. This fluidity and flexibility to flow around obstacles may be mistakenly viewed as being too accommodating, but when it comes from receptiveness, it is very different.

When a woman is accommodating, she could be giving up herself or what she wants in order to please a man. This trait is not bad, but if she does it too much she runs the risk of giving up too much of herself and then resenting her partner when he is not giving her what she wants. A receptive woman is able to receive what she gets and not resent getting less. As soon as she is expecting more and resenting getting less, she is no longer being receptive.

***

A receptive woman is able to receive what she gets and not resent getting less.

***

Receptivity is being able to receive whatever can be received in a circumstance. It is the ability to benefit or find something good in every situation. Even if she can't find it, being receptive means she is open to finding it.

For example, when a man doesn't call, she is still open to the possibility that he is from Mars and he just forgot. An unreceptive woman would feel, "Well, that is just an excuse and I don't buy it. If I am going to get involved with a man, then he'd better call me back." When a woman is receptive and things are not exactly what she wants, she is receptive to the possibility that things will get better. She does not close up.

Receptivity means being able to say yes and no at the same time. She is open to receiving what she wants, likes, or appreciates, but she can also at the same time be very closed to what she doesn't want.

For example, a woman can be very receptive to kissing a man but be closed to anything more. When a woman says no to a man's sexual advances for more, she just needs to do it in a manner that is also receptive to his kissing her. He will continue to be attracted to her. He just needs to feel that one day more is possible.

When a Woman Wants to Wait to Have Sex

Some women are closed to the process of dating because they feel under pressure to be fully sexual before they are ready. They don't even want to date because men expect so much. Men expect it because it seems as if everyone else is getting it. On television it is everywhere. And there are many women who freely give it. As a result, other women don't realize that there are alternatives.

When a woman becomes sexual before she is ready, then she has stopped being receptive and becomes accommodating. Instead of allowing a man to please her, she tries to please him. In this way she compromises her position. If she is not open at all, a man may become frustrated as well. There is a middle ground here. Let's look at an example.

David was very attracted to Suzanne. After dating for several months they had moved into stage three, exclusivity. David was used to having sex with the women he dated and he was not monogamous. He was thirty-five and had been married before. After learning about the five stages of dating, he agreed to shift his way of dating and become more discerning about the women he dated. Then he met Suzanne.

Suzanne was thirty-two and had also been married before. She was so special that David quickly decided to be exclusive. He told her how much he loved her and wanted to make love with her. She was very clear that she didn't want to have sex right away. He then asked about kissing and being physically affectionate. She said, "I would like to do that, but I don't want to have to be pushing you away all the time. So I would rather do nothing."

He said, "What if I promise that I will only go to first and second base?" She said that would be fine, but the deal was up if he tried to steal third. He agreed.

David was very happy for a while and so was Suzanne.

She also wanted to be physically affectionate but just didn't want to go all the way. As long as he was respectful of that she was fine. They were having a great time in their relationship and they were falling more deeply in love.

David again asked her if she would make love with him. Suzanne said she was not ready. She also didn't like his bringing it up while they were being sexual. He said, "If I don't ask, then how will I know when you are ready?" She said, "Let's just do this for the next month and then we'll talk about it again."

This continued for three months and then David proposed. They were engaged for about three months and then they got married. While they were engaged, David got to third base, but they waited till their marriage night to go all the way. David said it was really hard to wait, but it sure made him respect Suzanne. Their wedding night was very special—definitely a night to remember. Now they have been married for several years and they still have a very loving and passionate sex life.

Suzanne was able to maintain being receptive to David while also saying no to what she wasn't ready for. By gracefully standing up for what felt right to her, she remained most attractive to him. She just needed to feel free to be physically affectionate without having to go any further than she wanted.

When a Woman Gives Too Much

When a woman gives more in the relationship, she is no longer receptive to what a man has to offer; instead, she begins to expect more from the man. This makes her very unattractive.

Let's look at another example:

Deann got involved with Carlos. They were both in their mid-twenties. After a few dates, they were being physical and Carlos wanted to go all the way. Deann asked him if this meant he was going to see only her. In the heat of passion Carlos said yes.

The next day everything changed. Deann suddenly had a host of expectations. Some of these were:

She expected him to call her every day.

She expected him to love her and no one else.

She expected him to see only her.

She expected him to spend more time with her.

She expected him to be more interested in what she had to say.

She expected him to do romantic things for her.

She expected him to spend less time with his friends and more time with her.

All of these expectations came up the morning after she had sex with him. The next day Carlos also changed. He began to doubt if he really wanted to be that involved. Suddenly other women were looking very fine and he felt he wasn't ready to settle down.

In their relationship, they had moved to stage four (intimacy) and skipped stages two and three, uncertainty and exclusiveness. Carlos immediately moved back into uncertainty and decided not to proceed. It was almost predictable.

Carlos and Deann may have had a chance, but because they were not ready to be so intimate, Carlos immediately backed out of the relationship and Deann was hurt. Once she had given more than she was getting, her chances of moving through the five stages with Carlos disappeared.

When Expectations Are a Turnoff

A man thrives when he feels that he does not have to give, but that he chooses to give. He wants to give because he cares and it makes a woman so happy, not because he owes her. Expectations are a turnoff.

When a man feels he has to give because a woman has given so much to him, then it is no longer fun to give. It is like working to pay off your debts. A woman loses her sense of receptivity when she expects more than a man has been giving.

It is fine to expect a man's support if he has been giving it consistently over time, but this kind of expectation is different. It is based on past experience of what to expect, not just her assumption that he will support her because he owes her.

Receptive Communication

When a woman is receptive to a man it doesn't mean that she necessarily agrees with him. As long as a woman conveys that she is not threatened by a man or what he has to say, he doesn't care if she completely disagrees with him.

As a matter of fact, men like it a lot when a woman can playfully disagree. If he is talking about the Republicans and she is a Democrat and responds by completely disagreeing with him, he doesn't mind at all. It is all in the way she disagrees.

> Men love it when a woman can both disagree
> and express an attitude that she still likes him
> and trusts him to be a good guy.

To him she is saying, "I trust you can handle my having a different point of view. I accept you the way you are; you don't have to be just like me and I still like you. I appreciate having this conversation with you; it is stimulating to have a difference of opinion." This message is music to his ears.

Receptivity Embraces the Differences

Accepting a man while disagreeing with him makes him feel free to be different. Men instinctively know that in many ways they are not like women. When a woman deals with their differences in a positive manner it frees him to be different. He feels free when he does not have to be like her to be liked and loved by her.

In return, he will become very interested and give her the respect she deserves, acknowledging that she is unique and different. Having a positive and open attitude about our differences causes men and women to be more attractive to each other.

Men are generally very open to women's being different. A man closes down to a woman's different way of looking at things only when he feels unfairly attacked or blamed. When a man does not feel blamed or judged for being different, then he is much more receptive to her way of being and is happy to find a middle ground.

THE THIRD ATTRIBUTE: RESPONSIVENESS

The third attribute that makes a woman most attractive is responsiveness. A man loves a woman with a smile. A man loves to feel he can make a difference. A man is most interested in pursuing a woman when he gets clear messages that he can make her happy. It actually gives a man energy to anticipate being successful in making her happy.

The secret to being responsive is to be authentic. If a man does not truly delight, impress, or please a woman and she responds with artificial delight, admiration, or fulfillment, he will know she is faking it and eventually feel manipulated. He will sense that she is trying to please him by being pleased.

> A woman's responsiveness is most attractive
> when it is authentic and not exaggerated.

Certainly she is aware that her pleasure makes him happy, but she must be careful not to pretend. It is okay to hold back negative responses in the first three stages of dating. Just as a man needs to put his best foot forward to impress a woman, she needs to put forth her most positively responsive self.

It is fine to share negative responses if the man is also sharing negative responses, but she still should be careful. A man judges his success in a relationship by the positive responses that he gets.

> It is not so much what a woman does
> for a man that makes him happy,
> but the way she responds.

When she is not pleased she can simply give a zero response. The absence of a positive response will be a clear message to a man that he didn't succeed. If a movie he takes her to is not very good, she doesn't need to share her negative responses, but she can instead seem unresponsive and change the subject to something more positive. Each time a woman chooses to find and express her positive responses to a man's attempts to fulfill her, then he feels encouraged to pursue her.

Retelling an Adventure

I was once sitting in a hot tub on a cruise when a young dating couple got in. After I asked about their journey on the island of Mykonos, she proceeded to tell me and everyone else in great detail their adventure.

She said, "My boyfriend, Bill, decided we should rent mopeds, and as soon as we got out of town, mine broke down. We were stranded most of the day. He really got upset and lost it. Finally we got back and spent the rest of the day at the beach."

I watched him shrink in embarrassment as she told this story. The other women in the hot tub asked more questions, and not one of the women realized that this story had totally embarrassed her date. As more people came and went she continued to tell the same story. Well, it was no surprise to me that he quickly got out and later they were not talking to each other. He was embarrassed and steaming mad.

As I listened to the story, I realized how she could have told it a little differently and he would have been proud. There was no negative intent on her part, it was just her not understanding Martian sensitivities.

She could have said, "We had an incredible adventure. Mykonos is such a beautiful island. Bill decided to rent mopeds. I thought it was such a great idea. He arranged the whole thing and got a great deal. Unfortunately, when we reached the outskirts of the city my moped broke down. I thought we were stranded. I didn't know what to do. Bill was great. He assured me that everything would be fine and proceeded to flag down every car that passed. Finally, he got us back safely and we had a lovely day at the beach. They have the most beautiful beaches and the water is so clear."

All of the above was also true and accurately expressed how she felt. It was just a matter of consciously focusing on what he did that was positive and not on the negative aspects. Let's look at another example of how a woman unknowingly turns off a man.

Standing Outside the Movie Theater

Once while entering a movie theater on a date with my wife, I overheard a conversation between a dating couple in their sixties. It was clear that it was one of their early dates. I could see him sincerely trying to please her. Although I heard only the last part of the conversation, I knew what had happened before.

They had just come out of a movie that he thought for sure she would have liked, but for some reason she hated the movie. As she expressed her dislike of the movie, I watched him crumble. His whole posture wilted down.

As I passed by I heard him say, "Well, what would you like to do now?" and her response was, "I would like to stand here and tell every person what an awful movie that was. I can't believe they made that movie. It was just terrible. No one should have to see it."

Now, this woman was not trying to put her date down. She didn't even have a clue as to how he was taking her words. He was feeling not only put down but completely flattened. If she had understood his needs at that time, then it would have been an easy choice for her to postpone sharing her frustrations over the movie.

Many women don't realize what a pleasure it is for a man to feel successful at pleasing or fulfilling a woman. It gives him such a lift. When anything on a date makes a woman happy, he will take credit. When she likes the movie, on an emotional level it is as if he had written the movie script and starred in it. When she likes the soup at the restaurant, it is as if he had cooked it. When she compliments the movie or the soup, he feels complimented. A woman's pleasure on a date can light up a man's life in the same way that his consideration of her needs and feelings lights up her life.

Unfortunately, there is a flip side to this dynamic. When a woman criticizes the movie, he takes it personally in various degrees. It is his movie script she is rejecting. When she talks about how bad the service is in a restaurant, he may feel as if she is complaining about him. Without even knowing it, a woman can completely derail a man's romantic feelings. By focusing on sharing positive feelings on a date, a woman can ensure the natural development and unfolding of attraction in a relationship.

When a woman says, "I had such a good time the other night. That band was great. . . ." she should purposely leave out telling him how frustrated she was that she had to wait thirty minutes to use the rest room or how much she hated the guy who was smoking in front of her. By focusing on the positive and leaving out the negative, she may have a little less conversation, but he will stay interested. She can then share the negative goodies with her girlfriends: They will understand and be happy to hear her stories and then tell her their own.

MAKING THE CHOICE TO RESPOND

It is crucial that a man experience repeatedly that he can make and is making a difference in a woman's life. Men always thrive in a relationship when they feel needed and appreciated. When a woman can respond to the little things he does, then his affection, attraction, and interest have a chance to grow.

As a woman learns to respond to men with each of these

three attributes of femininity—being self-assured, receptive, and responsive—she is able to be most attractive to men. Not only will a man find her more attractive, but by consciously making the choice to express herself in this manner, she will be happier as well. In Chapter 18 we will explore the three attributes of masculinity that make a man most attractive to a woman.

18

Women Love a Man with a Plan

Every man has the power to bring out the best in a woman, but only a few men realize it. If a man could see himself through a woman's eyes, he would experience that which makes him irresistible to her. He would clearly see the attributes he already has that really turn a woman on. It is almost impossible for a man to see himself this way. He doesn't recognize that what a woman wants most, he already has.

It is easy to conclude that a man is most attractive to a woman because he has a great personality or because he is very talented, handsome, friendly, funny, witty, strong, entertaining, rich, successful, wise, or interesting. Regardless of any of these traits, what makes a man most attractive to a woman is his ability to make *her* feel like a woman.

When a man makes a woman feel feminine, her femininity is actually awakened, switched on, or, as we commonly say, turned on. When a woman is turned on by a man's presence, it brings out the best in her and as a result she is attracted to him. To the degree that a man makes a woman feel feminine, then to that degree she is turned on by his unique talents, traits, interests, or characteristics.

> **If a man doesn't turn a woman on, it doesn't matter how funny, rich, or successful he is.**

What allows a man to bring out the best in a woman can be summarized in one expression: masculine presence. When a man clearly expresses this aspect of who he already is, a woman is mysteriously attracted. She is most attracted to him when he is confident, purposeful, and responsible. These three attributes make a woman feel more self-assured, receptive, and responsive to him.

With an awareness of these three attributes, a man can harness his power to win a woman over and successfully progress through the five stages of dating. With this new insight, he can begin to understand why some dates work and others don't. With an awareness of this power within, he can begin to exercise it on every date. As he gets stronger he will gain the ability to know the right partner for him and sweep her off her feet.

THE FIRST ATTRIBUTE: CONFIDENCE

The first attribute that makes a man most attractive is confidence. A woman can sense when a man is confident. She automatically begins to relax and feel assured that she will get what she needs. When a man does not feel confident, a woman begins to worry. Her feminine side, which wants to relax and receive, panics, and her masculine side rises up to protect her and make sure she gets what she needs.

Confidence in a man makes a woman breathe deeper, relax, and open up to receive the support he has to offer.

Confidence does not mean that a man has to be perfect, nor does he have to have all the answers. Confidence is a can-do attitude. He knows that no matter what happens, there is always a solution. Even if he doesn't have the answer, he is confident that he can, and will, find one.

When a man has a can-do attitude, even if he doesn't have all the answers, a woman can breathe deeper, relax, and open up.

With confidence, a man gains the objectivity to stand back and look for what can be done. At distressing times, he remains cool, calm, and collected. When a man gets angry and says mean things, he is definitely not coming from his confidence. Instead, he is feeling threatened and threatens back.

A confident man contains his feelings until he has figured out what to do. He may not know the outcome, but he senses that no matter what happens, he can always find the next step to improve a situation. He feels that no matter how bad things get, he can eventually figure out what can be done, or find someone who knows what can be done, and then do it. A confident attitude reassures a woman that everything will be all right.

A Man with a Plan

When a man is confident he is able to come up with a plan. Women love a man with a plan. A woman doesn't like it when a man is too dependent on her for direction. Although women give men a lot of directions and suggestions, they wish they didn't have to. A woman is happy to do some of the planning, but she wants the man to lead the way confidently.

A woman enjoys a date most when a man has a plan and he feels confident about it. He knows what time it is, where he is, where he is going, how long it is going to take, what he will do when they get there, and that he has the money he needs. He is confident that all will go well and as planned. If things don't work out as planned, he has a backup plan.

A confident man's backup plan is that he will assess the situation and make the best of it. He will forge his way into unknown territory and have an adventure. He will do his best and things will turn out fine.

When Men Lose Confidence

Confidence is natural to men, but they can easily lose it when they don't understand something. A man loses confidence on a date because he doesn't understand women. When a woman seems upset by something, he may not understand what to do. Instead of taking charge and finding a solution, he too quickly surrenders to asking her what she would like. Then she feels she has to come up with the plan.

It is fine for a woman to help with the plan, but she must not feel that she is fully responsible. It is so easy for a man to think, "Well, I really don't care what happens. As long as she is happy I will be fine. I'll just do what she says." He doesn't realize that what makes her happiest is not having to figure out what makes her happy.

Before asking her what to do, he needs first to consider various options and ask her what she thinks and then be open to what she suggests. When he thinks of options, she doesn't have to feel the whole responsibility of what their plan is. Even if he doesn't know what to do and can't even come up with other options, just the act of trying to come up with something before asking her will make a big difference.

After thinking for a while he could even say, "I've been thinking about what to do and I really don't know. What do you think?" After listening to her, instead of just saying okay, he should think about what she suggests to see if he could improve it and then conclude, "Okay, let's do this . . ." Like the quarterback on a football team or the director at a camp, he then sets the game plan. This explains why women love quarterbacks and camp directors.

Applying Mars/Venus Dating Skills

When a woman is disappointed or displeased with a man, or if some element of his plan unravels, he can easily become overly defensive. When she doesn't like his plan, he feels that she doesn't like him. When he is confident that he has what it takes to make a woman happy, then he doesn't get defensive or upset with her when she is disappointed. Instead he applies his Mars/Venus dating skills and then changes his plan.

With an understanding of women he can learn to listen without trying to solve the problem. As he listens without trying to help her see the situation differently, she gets a chance to feel that he cares about her feelings and is trying to be understanding. When he is sincerely interested, understanding, and sympathetic, then no matter what the disappointment, she will feel better and he will become more attractive to her.

> By being a sympathetic listener, a man can transform even a disappointing date into an intimate and rewarding experience for the woman.

By understanding the way women think and feel, a man has a huge advantage over most men out there dating. Most men will ruin a date by trying to talk a woman out of being upset or disappointed. They don't realize the power of listening to win a woman over. They don't realize the importance of little things and not necessarily big things to impress her most. The more a man learns about women, the more confident he will feel on a date. This confidence makes him very attractive.

Dates become disasters not because of what happens but because of how the man handles a woman's feelings in reaction to disappointments. A man can get too attached to his plan and forget that the real gift he gives a woman is his sincere interest in making her happy. When circumstances don't do it, then he can really score big by being caring, understanding, and respectful of her reaction to what has happened.

THE SECOND ATTRIBUTE: PURPOSEFULNESS

A man with a purpose is most attractive to a woman. When he has a plan, a dream, a direction, a vision, an interest, or a concern, he is very attractive. It doesn't matter how great or grand the plan or purpose is. He is attractive to the degree that he feels passionate about achieving his purpose. He then becomes even more attractive when he focuses his purposefulness on her. When he becomes focused on making her happy, then she is swept off her feet.

This does not mean that he gives up his other goals and wants only to make her happy. That is a turnoff. A woman knows that she cannot fulfill all his needs. She doesn't want him to stop his life for her. That would put too much pressure on her and their relationship.

A woman does not want a man to give up his goals in life in order to make her happy.

A man needs to have a sense of purpose separate from his relationship. He needs to have a direction first, and then he is ready to create a relationship to support him in making his dreams come true. He feels a need for a woman to share the rewards and benefits of achieving his goal. The opportunity to share his success with a woman gives meaning to his life.

As long as a man has a goal and has not given up, he has a future. Women love a man with a future. When a man is passionate about his work, his interests, his goals, and his future, he is very attractive. When he is self-directed and self-motivated, a woman feels very relaxed and comfortable with him. Rather than feeling she needs to take care of him, she feels he has the energy and motivation to take care of her sometimes, and for her this is good.

A Man's Purpose in a Relationship

In a relationship a man's purpose is to provide support for the woman and receive her love in return. As long as he stays "on purpose" a relationship has a chance to grow. When he starts to focus only on what he is getting in return, he gets "off purpose" and the woman begins to close down.

Romantic rituals help a man to stay on purpose. In most of the traditional romantic rituals, the man provides and the woman graciously receives. These rituals are important because they give him the repeated experience that he can succeed in his purpose very easily. All he has to do is plan a date, make a few calls, spend a little money, and open doors, and he is suddenly a great guy. She appreciates him and he feels good.

When a woman graciously receives his support without feeling obligated to give in return, it uplifts her as well. Romantic rituals are there to make her feel special and remind her to receive and not give so much. In this process, he gets the opportunity once again to taste the nectar of being selfless and giving unconditionally.

> Romantic rituals are there to make
> a woman feel special and remind her
> to receive and not give so much.

When men are stressed, they can forget their purpose. They can work so hard that they forget that they are doing it to provide for the people they love and care about. They start caring more about work than the opportunity to be in a caring relationship. By taking time to be romantic, a man gets an opportunity to experience and remember why he is doing it all. When he feels a woman's love, he remembers, "Oh, this is why I do it." Her receptivity to his support allows him to feel more committed to his purpose.

For a man to stay on purpose in his relationships, he needs to remember why he is having a relationship anyway. The purpose of having relationships has changed. We no longer need each other to survive. Relationships that are based on survival do not survive anymore. Both men and women want something more than the security of a partner working for the good of the family. We may want that as well, but today we want even more. We want emotional fulfillment. We want romance. We want intimacy. And we want to find a deep and lasting love.

> Relationships that are based on survival
> do not survive anymore.

Romantic rituals remind men that to receive the love they want, they have to continue doing little things for a woman. A man should not expect it just to happen. He doesn't expect his business to flourish without hard work, nor should he expect romance to be different. By remembering that his purpose is greater than the old way of having relationships, he is then motivated to learn more and find new ways of relating.

THE THIRD ATTRIBUTE: RESPONSIBILITY

When a man does what he says he will do, he automatically expresses a sense of responsibility; he radiates a sense of confidence that he will do what he sets out to do. It doesn't even matter if a woman has met him before or has experienced his being responsible. She will assume him to be confident and purposeful. She will be drawn to him like a bee to honey.

When a woman is attracted to a successful or influential man, what she is really attracted to is the responsible side of him that made him successful. The long hours required and the extra push to make something happen cause him to emanate a sense of responsibility. Even if he is not responsible in all areas of his life, his ability to be passionately purposeful and responsible to what is most important to him will always show.

When a man is responsible, it says he cares, and that is what women are most hungry for. When a woman dates a man, she needs to feel not that he is just wanting to take from her, but that he wants to find a meaningful relationship. The more he cares, the more she can trust him. One way a man can express this caring in dating is by taking care of the little things. Each time he does, it reassures her that with him she does not have to be "on" all the time. His sense of responsibility allows her to relax.

Why a Man Needs to Be "On"

Certainly men shouldn't have to be "on" all the time either. But when a man is dating a woman, particularly in the first three stages, he needs to be "on," just as he does when he goes to work. That is what makes a person a professional. A professional man is someone who competently does his job whether he feels like it or not. He does it regardless of his mood. He is reliable and responsible.

On a date, a man is there for a woman regardless of how he feels. When he needs downtime, he should do that at home by himself or with his friends.

> In the first three stages of dating, a man can get his partner's love when he is "on," and when he is feeling down, he should be on his own.

There is no greater way to kill romance than for a man to tell a woman all his problems. In an instant, she will start feeling responsible for him and start feeling maternal. Certainly in the fourth stage of dating (intimacy), he can let down his sense of being responsible and share more of his vulnerable side, but definitely not until the couple has many months of experiencing clearly that he can be responsible for himself and for her.

> Before sharing his vulnerable side, a man should clearly demonstrate that he can be responsible for himself and for her.

This may start to sound unfair, as if the man is supposed to be "on" and the woman doesn't have to be. The truth is, men love it when a woman lets go of being so responsible, because then her receptive and responsive feminine side can be turned on.

Jason's Objections

At first Jason objected to this idea. He said, "Wait a minute, I like a woman to be responsible too. I don't want to do everything." Jason had not yet experienced the pleasure of being successful on a date. He grew up in a family with lots of girls and without a father. He had experienced being taken care of by women all his life. He had never seen or tasted the satisfaction and empowerment that occurs when a man is successful in being responsible for himself. He also didn't have the confidence that he could make a woman happy, because his father had not been able to make his mother happy.

His mother and sisters were not responsive or receptive to his plans but instead were busy directing him, improving him, and sometimes being critical of him when he was like his father. He was just being a boy, but he didn't get the support that would allow him to feel good about himself. As a result, later in life, he was happy not to risk failing again and to let the woman be responsible. He felt much more comfortable letting the woman be the responsible one. Jason was very playful, funny, and entertaining, but at forty-seven he was still unable to make a commitment to get married.

By consciously choosing to be more responsible, Jason eventually learned to like being responsible and having the power to make a woman happy. Within six months, he was able to find the woman of his dreams and get married.

When a Man Can Relax

In stage four, as couples become more intimate, it is important that sometimes the man relax and the woman take over, but this should be the exception and not the rule. When the woman is feeling down, the man needs to have the strength to pull himself up and be there for her. If he can't be there for her, then he should at least not expect her to be there for him. He needs to take the time he needs to pull himself up and then come back and be there for her.

When a Man Takes Charge

A woman loves it when a man takes charge to follow through and do something without putting it back in her lap. This is very important to her because most women already have a tendency to be overly responsible. The more complex and stressful their lives become, the more overwhelmed and exhausted they become.

A woman begins to feel responsible for doing everything for everyone. Her way of getting relief is to share these feelings with someone she loves. If she can share, something happens inside her and she doesn't feel so responsible. It is as if she sees all possible problems and, unless she tells someone, she feels it is all up to her.

> By sharing, a woman is able to release the burden of feeling solely responsible.

When she can share those feelings with a friend who is also responsible and he can stay relaxed and present, she begins to relax and come back to the present moment. When a man can hear a woman's feelings without minimizing them or trying to fix them, she can let go of feeling so responsible and feel good again. Even though he is not taking on her problems, the more responsible he is, the more it has the effect of relaxing and nurturing her.

When she feels that she is being heard, then she knows that if he can do anything to be of assistance he will do what he can. Most important, she has been able to talk about it. For her, that is the most important part of a man's support.

DATING CAN BE FUN

A man scores big when he does little things for a woman with a caring, understanding, and respectful attitude. By putting these new Mars/Venus dating techniques into practice, a man immediately begins building the strength to be confident, purposeful, and responsible. These qualities not only make him most attractive to a woman but will bring out the best in her. Even if he hasn't yet found his soul mate, the whole process of dating will be easier, fun, and uplifting.

19

Why Some Women Remain Single

Many women remain single even when they want to get married. They wonder, "Why am I still single? Why can't I find a man who will commit?" This frustration has nothing to do with looks, personality, level of success, or the availability of men. It does involve their style of approach.

These women mistakenly approach their relationships with men the way they want men to approach them. They are repelled by the thought of a needy man, so they are very careful to not need a man. When asked if they need a man, they are proud to acknowledge that they don't. In some cases it is as if they are disgusted to say the word "need" out loud. These are some of their responses:

HOW SINGLE WOMEN RESPOND TO THE QUESTION "DO YOU NEED A MAN?"

"No, I don't need a man. But I would *like* a man in my life."

"No, I don't need a man. But I *want* a man in my life."

"No, I don't need a man. I can take care of myself. I just want to be with a man because I choose to, not because I need him."

"No, I don't need a man. I don't need another father."

"No, I am not desperate. I just want to have a loving relationship."

"No, I have been there and done that. I just want a partner to share with."

"No, what do I need a man for? I can completely support myself. I just want a companion."

"No, I don't need a man. I just want romance and intimacy."

"No, I am happy now. I just want someone to go to weddings, parties, and the movies with."

"No, not really. I just don't want to be lonely anymore."

Although these responses seem very reasonable and positive, they reflect an attitude that clearly doesn't attract men, or at least doesn't attract men who will become motivated to make a commitment. These women are surprised to hear that their self-reliant attitude does not make them attractive.

They have spent years becoming self-sufficient, believing this would make them more attractive, and then suddenly they are being told to start needing men again. When they first hear that men need to feel needed and men are most attracted to a woman who needs what he has to offer, they become confused.

To clarify this confusion and put it all together, a woman needs to understand within herself why she may need a man and then learn how to express this vulnerability in a healthy way.

WHY A WOMAN NEEDS A MAN

Modern women have become so responsible for themselves that it is no longer obvious why they need a man. In the old days, it was clear that a woman needed a man's protection and physical support. A woman felt comfortable declaring to herself, her friends, and the world that she needed a man. Today, she can take care of herself. She feels awkward needing a man because she doesn't need him for the same things.

To pave the way to get married, a woman needs to first determine what she needs a man for. The more self-sufficient a woman becomes, the more she hungers for the nurturing support of a man's romantic affections, friendship, and companionship. Women today experience a deep longing to feel the intimate passion that only good communication and romance can provide.

Instead of needing a man primarily for survival and security, a woman needs a man for emotional comfort and nurturing.

The more a woman does *not* need a man in the traditional ways, the more she needs his romantic attention and affection. Even when a woman chooses primarily to be a mother and is dependent on a man for physical support, she still needs a man's romantic affection. The whole thinking of women in the last thirty years has changed dramatically. Romance is at a premium.

WHAT A WOMAN NEEDS

When a man opens the car door for a woman, he is not doing it because she can't. He knows she is quite capable of opening the door herself. He does it to show her he cares. He does it to say, "I understand how much you give, and tonight let me give to you." He does it to say, "You are special. Let me show you how special you are to me."

When she gets this message again and again on a date, she begins to relax and glow. She feels happier and more fulfilled. Why does she feel so fulfilled? Because a deep hunger or need is being met. It feels good, it feels nurturing, because it is. It is exactly what she needs and he is happy to do it. After a long day at home or at work, taking care of the needs of others, a woman has many needs. This is a list of what modern women need.

A WOMAN'S NEEDS

She needs the attention of someone who cares about her.

She needs the help of someone who wants to take care of her needs.

She needs time when she is not considering what everyone else wants but when someone is considering her wishes.

She needs someone who understands what she likes and makes a plan so that she doesn't even have to think.

She needs someone to anticipate her needs, wants, and wishes and to offer to help without her having to ask.

She needs someone to notice her, love her, and adore her.

She needs someone to miss her and desire her.

She needs to love freely and trust that she will be loved in return.

She needs someone who cares about her well-being to understand what she is going through and recognize the validity of her feelings.

She needs someone she can confide in who is trustworthy and will not turn on her or break her confidence by revealing her secrets.

She needs someone who regards her as special.

She needs someone to help her in her life so she doesn't feel she is doing it all by herself.

She needs someone to feel passionate intimacy with.

She not only needs these things but needs to have them fulfilled by someone with whom she feels a natural chemistry on all levels: physical, emotional, mental, and spiritual. While these needs are not requirements for her survival, like eating, drinking, breathing, and shelter, they are required to help her feel a higher degree of emotional fulfillment.

When the lower needs for survival are met, then the higher needs for love and intimacy become more important. For example, if you're really hungry, then getting fed is all you're concerned about. Once you have plenty of food, your other needs become important as well. When a woman can provide for herself she begins to strongly feel her higher needs to find fulfillment.

> **When the lower needs for survival are met, then the higher needs for love and intimacy become more important.**

To experience increasing fulfillment, a woman does not have to have all of her needs met at once. The whole process of dating is a gradual process of satisfying her needs a little more at a time. To be satisfied, she just needs to feel hope that one day her emotional needs will be met. In a similar manner, a man doesn't have to have all his sexual needs met right away; he just needs the hope that they are moving in that direction.

When a man moves into a woman's world and expresses his support, she appreciates his willingness to help as much as the help itself. On an emotional level, she suddenly feels she is not as alone in the world. When a man does something concrete and tangible for a woman, not only does the woman feel supported, but the man gets to feel successful.

THE WISDOM OF DATING RITUALS

The wisdom of dating rituals is to define the roles of man as giver and woman as receiver. Dating rituals are designed to assist a woman in relaxing and letting a man take care of her needs. They reinforce this most important pattern: the man doing things to fulfill the woman's needs and the woman graciously receiving. The result is that a man becomes more confident, purposeful, and responsible, while a woman becomes more self-assured, receptive, and responsive. Dating rituals assist us in bringing out the best in our partners on a date, which in turn brings out the best in ourselves as well.

Without understanding this wisdom, some men and women feel uncomfortable with dating rituals. They feel that they are demeaning to women and imply that women are helpless. They are concerned that by encouraging these rituals they are reinforcing the incorrect notion that women are helpless. Nothing could be further from the truth.

WHY MEN GIVE

When a man opens the door for a woman, it does not mean that she is so weak that she can't do it. Instead, it means that she is special and he wants to make her evening as comfortable as possible. When a special guest visits your home, you graciously open the door and roll out the red carpet. This does not imply in any way that the guest is helpless and incompetent.

When a man pays for a woman's meal, it does not mean that he makes more than she makes, or that she can't afford to pay for it. Instead, it means that it is his pleasure to provide for her. She gives to so many people all day long, so he wants to give to her that evening. It is *his* pleasure to give.

If they are in an exclusive relationship, it does not mean that he pays all the time. But when he takes her on a special date, he pays. It is nice for her to offer to pay sometimes but wise for him not to accept the offer most of the time.

People who feel that romantic rituals reinforce the role of women as helpless, needy, and dependent on men do not understand the true spirit of a man's providing something for a woman. They mistakenly conclude that if a woman receives a man's support, she is then obligated to provide him with sexual favors.

This mistaken conclusion is arrived at when a woman doesn't readily understand that by receiving a man's gift, she has already given him a gift.

> **A man's gift is to be responsible for a woman's fulfillment, while a woman's gift is to be responsive and receptive to his gift.**

To understand these dynamics, it is very important to understand how women and men experience emotional fulfillment in different ways. What makes women feel good is not always the same as what makes men feel good. We can most dramatically discover what makes us feel good by exploring what make us feel bad or unfulfilled. By exploring the different causes of depression in men and women, we can clearly see how different our needs are.

THE DIFFERENT CAUSES OF DEPRESSION

The major cause of depression in women is feeling isolated. When women are most unhappy, it is when they feel that they have to do it all and there is no one there for them. This sense of having to be completely responsible for themselves and others becomes a source of depression.

> **The major cause of depression in women is feeling isolated.**

Ironically, for men it is the opposite. When a man feels he is responsible for himself, then he feels good about himself. When he feels he can provide for another, he feels even better about himself. The more others need him, the better he feels.

Men like to feel they are being helpful and of service. In a sense, men like to be used. As long as a man feels fairly rewarded, he is most fulfilled when he is being used. When a man is responsible and giving and is appreciated and rewarded, he is happiest. Women, on the other hand, become depressed when they are used too much.

As long as a man feels fairly rewarded, he likes being used.

The major cause of depression in men is feeling not needed. A man out of work or with nothing to do becomes increasingly depressed. A man becomes depressed when he experiences that what he has to offer is not needed. This is why appreciation is so important to men. When a man feels needed, then his confidence and sense of purpose increase. Automatically he feels more responsible.

When a man feels needed, it can bring out the best in him. A woman doesn't instinctively understand how important this is to a man. Certainly a woman wants to feel appreciated, but what she doesn't understand is that men don't feel needed unless they are appreciated for what they do. Without appreciation, a man loses touch with his purposefulness.

When a man doesn't feel that he can successfully provide for himself or another, he will become depressed. With insight into the source of a man's depression, it is easier to understand why a man needs a woman. Here is a list of some of a man's needs.

A MAN'S NEEDS

He needs someone who notices his efforts and appreciates what he provides.

He needs someone to share what he has accomplished.

He needs someone to give him the opportunity to fulfill her needs.

He needs someone to accept him just the way he is.

He needs someone to bring him out of himself.

He needs someone to trust him and depend on him for what he can provide.

He needs someone to inspire him to be the best he can be.

He needs someone who likes him very much.

He needs someone who is pleased with him and responsive to him.

He needs someone who is receptive to his plans and suggestions.

He needs someone who admires him for what he has done or tried to do.

He needs someone who will forgive his mistakes.

He needs someone who appreciates and acknowledges his best qualities, like patience, strength, generosity, kindness, dedication, loyalty, assertiveness, compassion, courage, wisdom, humor, and playfulness.

In simple terms, a man needs a job and a woman needs someone to hire. We have different needs but we perfectly complement each other. We are a perfect fit. This difference gives us insight into what is most important for men and women and reveals why romantic rituals are so important. Romantic rituals allow men to experience being needed, while they give women the opportunity to let go of feeling so responsible to give.

WHEN WOMEN GIVE TOO MUCH

When a woman gives of herself, even if she is appreciated and rewarded fairly, she will not get what she primarily needs. There are many successful women who are taking medication or in counseling for depression. The source of their depression is not that they don't feel needed, but that they don't get what they need.

There is nothing wrong with women who give a lot. Giving is an expression of love, and it is always good. The problem comes up when women cannot get back the support they need and deserve. When women give more than they are getting, they become increasingly unfulfilled.

WHEN WOMEN ARE TOO RESPONSIBLE

When women are too responsible, they are also less attractive to men. In the old days, a woman was in many ways helpless to provide for herself. She clearly needed a man. This helplessness actually made her very attractive to men, and gave a man the confidence to pursue her and the sense of purpose and responsibility to provide for her and be supportive.

But times have changed and women are not helpless. They

do not need men the way they used to. With more advanced education and job opportunities, women are more responsible for themselves. While this is good, it creates new problems. Sometimes the more successful and responsible a woman is, the less inviting to a man she may become.

> **The more successful a woman is, the less inviting to a man she may become.**

This doesn't have to be the case. By recognizing that she can still need a man in her life without having to be helpless, she can be successful in attracting the right man for her. For a woman to feel good about herself and also attract a man, it is not enough to just need a man; she must become adept in feeling and expressing her needs.

HOW TO NEED A MAN WITHOUT BEING NEEDY

Savvy women have realized that being needy is definitely a turnoff. Unfortunately, many times they throw out the baby with the bathwater. To avoid feeling or appearing needy or desperate in any way, these women deny or rationalize away any feelings of needing a man. In their minds, they can want a man, they can like to have a relationship, they can choose to be with a man, but it is not acceptable to need a man.

By taking a moment to see herself through the eyes of a man, a woman can begin to understand that there is another option. A woman can still need a man and not be needy or desperate.

> **From a man's point of view, there is a world of difference between a needy woman and a woman who needs him.**

When a woman is needy, she is not just feeling her need; instead, she feels that she needs more than a man is offering. As a result, she gets upset with him or she reacts in a manner that indicates she will be upset with him. When she signals that she needs more instead of appreciating his contribution, he gets the message that it is not enough. It is not her needing more that turns him off. It is her lack of appreciation for what he is offering that makes her "needy."

> **Needing more is not a turnoff,
> but not appreciating is.**

To need a man does not mean to need more from him. By focusing on appreciating what a man offers, a woman can avoid being needy. By cultivating the attitudes of self-assurance, receptiveness, and responsiveness, a woman can need more and yet appreciate what a man has to offer.

A woman does not have to be helpless to ask a man for help, nor does she have to be hopeless to need his support. She can need more and graciously receive whatever he gives. It is always flattering to a man when he feels needed.

From a man's perspective, a woman is most attractive when she is aware of her needs *and* she feels self-assured that her needs will be fulfilled. Just as a man is most attractive when he is confident that he will achieve his goal, a woman is most attractive when she is assured that she will get the support she needs.

With this attitude of self-assurance, a woman does not have to deny her need for a man just because he has not yet appeared in her life. Her self-assurance that she can and will get what she needs makes her most attractive and prevents her from feeling needy or desperate. When a woman cultivates the three attributes of femininity—self-assurance, receptiveness, and responsiveness—she gains the ability to need a man without becoming needy.

GIVING MEN THE RIGHT MESSAGE

By being self-assured instead of demanding more from a man, a woman gives the message that she trusts that she will eventually get her needs met. This openness makes a man much more interested. When a woman is receptive to what he is offering, a man gets the message that he may be accepted and not rejected. By being responsive to his attempts to please her, a woman allows a man to feel appreciated. He gets the message that he could be even more successful. These three attributes ensure that she is not giving the wrong message about her needs.

When a woman expresses the best of her feminine side by being self-assured, receptive, and responsive, it brings out the best of a man's masculine side. The more a man senses that a woman needs what he has to offer, the more interested he becomes. Quite automatically he feels more confident, purposeful, and responsible.

He is confident because her self-assurance sends a message that there is a job opening. He is purposeful because her receptive smile sends the message that he could get the job to make her happy. She has a need and he has the solution. Her responsiveness encourages him to feel he could be successful in fulfilling her needs. This encouragement makes him feel more responsible to fulfill her needs.

HOW WOMEN SABOTAGE THE DATING PROCESS

When a woman denies feeling her needs for a man, she sabotages the dating process. Her sincere attempts to find a lasting and loving relationship end each time in disappointment. By making this shift and feeling her needs for a man in a healthy way, she opens a door for the right man to walk in. By feeling her needs in a healthy way, she is able to appreciate and to accept men much more.

Needing a man can be compared to any other healthy need. For example, if you are a little hungry then you might *like* to eat, but it is not a very big deal. When you are more hungry, you *want* to eat and it tastes better. If you haven't eaten in five or six hours and you feel a healthy hunger, it is because you *need* to eat. When you need to eat, the food tastes so very delicious and satisfying.

Likewise, when a woman feels her healthy need for a man, he can sense that she will be responsive, receptive, and self-assured. This makes her best qualities shine. If he is the right man for her, or at least closer to the right guy, then he will be attracted to her. By clearly feeling her needs for a man, she becomes a magnet capable of attracting the right man for her. In Chapter 20, we will explore where she will find him.

20

Where to Find Your Soul Mate

People who are happily married often say they met their soul mate when they weren't really looking. Their paths crossed as if by accident, when and where they least expected it. They just "happened" to meet at a party, on a trip, on a walk, at a church class, at a convention, or at work. They associate their success in finding a mate with chance, fate, divine intervention, or just luck.

They feel lucky because they weren't even looking. They feel it was by chance because they met their partners in a place where they wouldn't have expected to find them. And they felt it was fate or divine intervention because their meeting was accidental, with no conscious intention.

This doesn't mean you have to wait for your lucky day or for an accident to occur in order to meet your mate. There are very clear reasons why these couples found their mates. Since they were not aware of those reasons, they assume it was just fate, luck, or chance. But definite conditions had been satisfied before they could meet and recognize their perfect partners. By understanding those conditions and deliberately creating them, you can speed up the process of finding your partner.

GOD HELPS THOSE WHO HELP THEMSELVES

People attribute finding their soul mates solely to chance, fate, luck, magic, good fortune, or God's grace because they don't realize how it is actually done. Certainly everything really great is done with God's help, but God helps those who help themselves. Every day, without knowing what they are doing, individuals happen to do the right thing to find a soul mate. They put themselves in the right place at the right time, and then it can miraculously happen.

Even when the fruit is ripe, we still need to find it and pick it. In a similar way, to find our soul mates we need to be ready, but we also need to be in the right place. Whether intentionally or unintentionally, these people put themselves in environments that allowed them to meet a potential partner with whom they felt immediate chemistry.

> Whether intentionally or unintentionally,
> we put ourselves in the right place to meet a
> potential partner with whom we can feel
> immediate chemistry.

By understanding the different elements that create chemistry, we can discover the best places to meet a potential soul mate. There are certain places where you will definitely meet people who will be attracted to you and vice versa. Most people just don't realize what makes for healthy chemistry.

THE FIRST ELEMENT OF CHEMISTRY: DIFFERENT INTERESTS

By studying the lives of soul mates, you can begin to see that there are certain elements that are almost always present. When the chemistry of healthy attraction is experienced, certain predictable conditions are being met. The first and most important element is different interests.

Happily married soul mates always have different interests. Certainly they have many shared interests, but quite often they have many more different interests. Generally, it is only after a few years of living together that they discover their many different interests. They don't realize it in the beginning.

> **Soul mates have many shared interests, but quite often they have many more different interests.**

When couples fall in love, they don't go around saying, "I met the most incredible person. She is so different from me." Instead they tend to say the opposite. They say, "Oh, I met this incredible person; we have so many things in common." They say this because they haven't yet discovered how different their interests are. Without this understanding, single people can easily miss opportunities to meet their soul mate.

The insight that different interests create chemistry explains why it is sometimes so hard to find a soul mate. Our soul mate will have different interests and will work and spend time in places we rarely visit. The only way we can meet someone with different interests is by accident. By recognizing this truth and actively seeking out situations where people have different interests, we dramatically increase our chances of experiencing more chemistry and meeting the right person. Let's explore a few examples.

To find your soul mate, make sure you go to places wh[...]
the people are definitely interested in things that you are [...]
interested in at all. If you don't like to dance, then take da[...]
ing lessons, go out dancing, or go to a dance competition[...]
you don't like to eat out, then start eating out more.

If you aren't very religious, start going to church.

Almost always in a marriage, one partner likes the eveni[...]
and the other likes the morning. To find your partn[...]
change your schedule occasionally. If you like to go to b[...]
early, then start going places at night. If you like to sle[...]
late, then start getting up and taking brisk morning wall[...]
You will meet so many more people. One of them may [...]
your soul mate, or one of them may introduce you to yo[...]
soul mate.

If you don't like sports, then start going to local games a[...]
sporting activities. If you don't like going to school, th[...]
take a few classes at night. If you don't like to read, sta[...]
hanging out at a bookstore or library. If you normally dri[...]
places, then walk more if possible. If you bring your lunch [...]
work, try eating out occasionally. If you eat out a lot, tr[...]
shopping at the supermarket. If you eat a lot of junk foo[...]
try shopping at a health-food store or green market.

If you don't like to read very much, start hanging out at a bookstore or library.

When you expand your territory in this way, your chance[...]
of meeting your soul mate go up dramatically. With this new[...]
insight, finding a partner who shares chemistry with you[...]
becomes a much easier task.

Kim's Chance Meeting

Kim is a single mother who works in a restaurant. She said, "I had to reschedule my regular weekly massage. While I was waiting in the reception room at the health center, I met my future husband, Peter. It was just by chance that I met him. Peter is a contractor and he was there to bid on a job. It really is amazing that we love each other so much. We are so different. He loves to create change and build things, while I like antiques and stability. He is a Republican and I am a Democrat. He likes to stay home at night and I like to eat out. . . ."

Their interests were so different that Kim would never have found Peter if they hadn't met by accident in the reception room. Because Peter stayed home at night, he would have missed meeting Kim, who worked nights at a restaurant.

With the Help of Friends

Mark is a policeman. He said, "I met my wife, Vicky, through my friend Chuck. They first went together for three years. Chuck used to talk about her all the time. When they split up, I gave her a call and we started going out. I am grateful to Chuck for introducing us and we are still great friends.

"If it hadn't been for Chuck, I don't think we would have ever met. I like sports and she doesn't. The only reason I met her is that Chuck invited me to his birthday party. We met playing cards.

"Even then there were a few sparks flying between Vicky and me. But she wasn't available. I remember thinking Chuck was a very lucky guy. Now I feel like I am the lucky guy. Vicky and I have a wonderful marriage and three great kids. Chuck married someone else."

When a man is like Mark, who doesn't like parties, his

chances of meeting his soul mate go up when he starts going to more birthday parties, dances, and weddings. Likewise, when a woman is like Vicky, who doen't like sports, her chances of meeting her soul mate go up when she goes to sporting events, activities, and celebrations.

Daphne's Lucky Project

Daphne, an interior decorator, said, "I met my husband, Carl, at work on a remodeling project. My client wanted a hot tub. Someone gave me his number to consult with. Well, Carl knew just what I needed. I knew by the way he handled the project that this was the kind of man I could rely on. He was the man to do the job and he was also the man for me. We immediately liked each other. It was just by luck that we met; I would never have gone shopping for a hot tub for myself and he lived in another county."

If not for her client's desire for a hot tub, Daphne would never have found her husband. She was not even interested in hot tubs. Carl was a real outdoorsy, rugged kind of guy. He rarely went shopping and certainly was not into interior design. Their paths would never have crossed.

Without Daphne's lucky project, the only way Carl could have found Daphne would have been to spend more time at shopping malls. By taking a little time to check out interior design stores, his chances of meeting Daphne would have increased. He might have actually met her or someone who would eventually lead him to her or her to him.

Daphne might have met Carl by moving out of her comfort zone and going camping, joining a nature club, or going on some group adventure like river rafting or a skiing trip. She could easily have met him or someone who would eventually have led him to her or her to him.

Different Interests Create Chemistry

Single people mistakenly assume that their soul mate will share their interests. As a result, they look for partners with similar interests. They don't realize that there are hundreds, even thousands, of places to find their soul mate.

Certainly, it is possible to find a soul mate in a place where we share an interest, but it is also just as possible to find a soul mate in a place where people are interested in things that we are not.

> To find your soul mate, go to places where the people have interests different from yours.

If you have been to the places that appeal to you and you have not found your soul mate, try looking in the places where people have interests different from yours. Even if you don't immediately find your soul mate, you will at least begin to experience more chemistry with the opposite sex. You will become more desirable, and this will motivate you to keep looking.

Try New Things

Whenever you go somewhere new, a new part of you h chance to come out. That is one of the reasons we attracted to people with different interests. We are s lated in their presence. They are so different from u something new inside us gets stimulated. When som the same as you, you are not necessarily stimulated just wanted to be with ourselves, we wouldn't need a at all. Trying new things actually gives you more en makes you more attractive.

THE SECOND ELEMENT OF CHEMISTRY: COMPLEMENTARY NEEDS

The second element is complementary needs. Soul mates basically have something that their partners need. When a man has what a woman needs, then she feels chemistry. For men, it is the other way around. When a woman needs what a man has to offer, he feels chemistry. This mutual dependence creates healthy emotional chemistry.

Emotional chemistry frees us from being limited by our unrealistic pictures of what our ideal partner will look like or be like. When a man is able to experience the thrill of feeling needed by a woman, he is no longer caught in pictures and expectations of what his ideal partner should look like. He is released from judging her physical appearance when he enjoys the pleasure of making little romantic gestures and feeling her responses.

When a woman experiences a man treating her in a special way, she is free from fixating on how her ideal partner should look. By experiencing the chemistry that results from being receptive to a man's approach, she is free to follow her heart and not get caught up in unrealistic expectations of perfection.

Places Where a Woman Needs a Man

With this insight, a woman can wisely look for her soul mate in places where she would be most receptive and responsive to what a man has to offer. If you need help setting up your computer, then by going to a computer fair, where you actually need what the men there have to offer, you may meet the man for you. Particularly if you are not even interested in computers, your chances increase even more.

> **If you need help setting up your computer,
> then by going to a computer fair, you may
> meet the right man.**

By asking for directions when you are lost or on a trip, you become more receptive to appreciating what a man can give you. If you take a trail ride or go on an adventure tour, there are many times when you would need a man's help. By attending any class to learn something, you are creating the ideal opportunity for a guy to be helpful. Attending any sporting event that you know very little about makes you more receptive to receiving a man's help in understanding the game. Men love to be experts. Whenever you go to places where a man's expertise can be helpful, there will be more chemistry.

> **By attending any class to learn something,
> you are creating the ideal opportunity for
> a guy to be helpful.**

If she goes to a dance, a woman definitely needs and appreciates a partner to dance with. When women dance with women, it puts a man out of a job. A man feels a greater risk of being rejected when he doesn't feel needed. Ideally, you can go dancing with couples who are friends. With your girlfriend's permission, you can dance with your friend's boyfriend or husband. When an interested man sees that you are dancing with a man you are not involved with, he will be encouraged to ask you to dance. People naturally get on a train when it is just about to leave. Likewise when a woman is already dancing with someone it makes a man want to ask her to dance even more.

Places Where a Man Feels Needed

With this insight a man can wisely meet the woman of his dreams in a place where she will feel most receptive to what he has to offer. By doing volunteer work in a community, he may find the perfect woman for him. By helping out with parades, he will meet many women. When a woman has a chance to experience the benefit of a man with a plan, she begins to feel her chemistry with him. Whenever a situation arises where leadership is required, you should jump at that opportunity. Even if your soul mate is not there, someone may be watching who will eventually introduce you to her.

> **Whenever a situation arises where leadership is required, you should jump at that opportunity.**

By baby-sitting for a friend and strolling with the baby at different times in the park, you will attract women like bees to honey. Women will immediately begin to think, This man is really caring; he is responsible; he helps take care of a baby. If you are not really that caring, you should not fake it just to get a woman. The point of these suggestions is not to create temporary attraction but to find a woman for whom you feel lasting attraction. When you show your responsible side, the woman for you has the chance to feel her attraction for you.

> **By baby-sitting for a friend and strolling with the baby in the park, a man will attract women like bees to honey.**

You do not need to worry that she will feel you are taken. She will come up and talk about the baby. She will ask lots of questions about the baby to give you many opportunities to explain that it is not yours. When she finds out you are available, she will be really thrilled. If you don't know anyone with a baby, then you can borrow someone's dog and walk it at different times in the park.

You can most effectively find a partner in places where women are dependent on you for a certain kind of support. Whenever there is a crisis in the community, a fire, flood, earthquake, storm, tornado, or hurricane, these are the best times for you to go out, be of service, and find a wife.

When a man wears a uniform, it helps a woman feel her chemistry. A uniform symbolizes that a man has a certain purpose in which he is confident and responsible. When you wear your uniform, it demonstrates that you are proud of what you do and that you love your work. These are big pluses. On your day off, whenever you can get away with it, you should wear your uniform.

> Women love a man in a uniform,
> and a man should wear one whenever
> he can get away with it.

By putting himself in situations where he is needed by women, children, and the elderly, a man can bring out the best in a woman. When she expresses a sense of grace and receptiveness in response to his efforts, he can feel the potential chemistry between them.

Sometimes he cannot feel the chemistry unless he first actually does something that stimulates a response in her. Her response makes him feel that by providing for her needs, he can get the trust, acceptance, and appreciation that he needs in order to thrive in a relationship.

Likewise, when a man expresses a sense of confidence, purposefulness, and responsibility in his actions, a woman feels the chemistry she has for him. His efforts convince her that she could get the caring consideration, understanding, and respect that she needs in a relationship. Let's explore an example of how emotional chemistry can be triggered.

Harry, an acting teacher, said, "I first met my wife, Trudy, in one of my classes. She was a great student. I felt so attracted to her when I first looked at her that I could barely teach the class. When I thought about asking her out, I couldn't even breathe, much less think of what to say. Eventually I summoned up my courage and offered to help her read scripts after class. It was a memorable moment. The sparks were flying.

"The next week I assigned romantic scripts to act out. After class, she asked me if I would read scripts with her again. I was a bumbling idiot when I tried to talk with Trudy, but I could read a script. Although someone else wrote the script, when I read it Trudy was won over. To this day I still thank Shakespeare. We both smiled that day and we have been smiling ever since. Even to this day, I help her work on her scripts. I love having a skill that she clearly appreciates."

THE THIRD ELEMENT OF CHEMISTRY: MATURITY

The third element is maturity. Soul mates basically have similar levels of maturity. In most cases, as we continue to grow older we gain a certain depth in our lives. We will automatically feel a chemistry with someone who reflects our level of maturity or depth. This maturity does not necessarily have to do with age, but it is a big factor.

One of the ways to experience this chemistry is to visit places where you are assured of meeting people your age. School reunions are great for this. Even if you don't meet someone right away, by reconnecting to these people you may get their support in finding someone. Many of their friends will be your age.

We cannot fully recognize a soul mate until we are ready. We need to know ourselves first before we can recognize the right person for us. Each time we gain experience of the higher stages of dating, our maturity and discernment increase.

After ending a long-term relationship, or a marriage, one of the best ways to find a soul mate is to revisit previous partners with whom you have felt chemistry. After taking several months to grieve the loss of a relationship, when you are feeling more complete and autonomous, then take some time to get reacquainted with all past partners who are available.

Just call to get reacquainted and see if sparks begin to fly. Many people grow and mature in a relationship so that when they move on, they find they are ready for a relationship that didn't work in the past. Let's look at an example.

Getting Reacquainted

Tricia, a bookkeeper, said, "I had finally completed a two-year relationship and was looking forward to spending a quiet weekend in prayer, meditation, and catching up on my reading. I felt I had had enough of men for a while and I said, This weekend is for my relationship with God."

Then, out of the blue, Tommy, an old boyfriend, called. They hadn't talked in four years. They had dated for more than a year, but after a while they just went their separate ways. Tricia had always felt a special chemistry with Tommy and was very sad when he got involved with someone else.

During his call he said he had been married and divorced in a two-year period and that for the last year he had been single again. He had called just to catch up. In their phone conversation, after hearing her voice, he realized that he had made a mistake in leaving her. He told her, "It is so great to talk with you after all these years. I am feeling so much love in my heart for you. It's as though the angels in heaven are singing."

With one phone call he realized that he was ready to have a committed relationship with her. He was ready to move into stage three because he had grown to the place where he knew what he wanted and immediately felt chemistry on all levels: physical, emotional, mental, and spiritual. He wanted to give their relationship a chance. He had matured so much in his last relationship that he immediately knew she was the one for him.

Tricia told him that her weekend was reserved for God. Instead of taking that as a no, Tommy got excited and said, "That's it; that's why I must have called. I am the answer to your prayers." They both laughed. Tommy was so insistent on coming that Tricia finally agreed. He drove six hours to be with her. He even got a speeding ticket.

They stayed up all night talking. After one month they became engaged, and within six months they were married. Tommy and Tricia had loved each other before, but it just hadn't been the right time. With the wisdom that only experience can provide, they now realized they were soul mates.

Maturity Means Greater Wisdom

As we become more mature, we gain greater wisdom and self-control. If we have negative addictive habits, eventually we feel motivated to clean up our life. We start reaching out to get support from others who are also putting their lives in order.

By attending various support groups, you have an opportunity to experience the chemistry that comes from shared maturity. There are all kinds of support groups. There are church-sponsored groups, "parents without partners" groups, Alcoholics Anonymous groups, and so on. All of these places are excellent for making new friends who will open many new doors to find your soul mate.

By attending support groups we can find people with similar maturity.

If you are not making the changes you feel you should be making, then you will be less attractive to others. A potential soul mate may just feel something is missing. What is missing is another attempt to put your life in order.

Putting Our Lives in Order

When Justin heard this, he realized that he had been afraid once again to try to quit smoking. He thought that if he tried he would just fail. When he heard that with maturity the power to change increases, he decided once again to give up smoking. He was thirty-eight and decided that he could do it.

At a party he told some of his friends that he had quit smoking. They were very proud of him. That evening, Christina, a former girlfriend, approached him and they started talking. She was very impressed with his change. She realized that when she had felt so attracted to him, his smoking had been the main reason that she held back from fully embracing him. Justin and Christina were soul mates, but they didn't know it until Justin reached a certain level of maturity.

It was not that smoking made Justin unattractive. What

made him unattractive was not living up to his potential. By holding on to habits that he was strong enough and mature enough to release, he had made himself less attractive. Because he made the commitment to change, they were both eventually able to make the commitment to get married.

The More We Know, the More We Don't Know

The more we know, the more we don't know. With the wisdom of greater maturity, we naturally seek out additional information on subjects that are dear to us. Another way to find someone with your level of maturity is to take a class in a subject that is important to your well-being.

Carol, an insurance salesperson, said, "I met my husband in a Mars/Venus workshop. I was so impressed by his interest in learning more about women and relationships. I thought if there was anybody that I would want to marry it would be someone who knew these things about men and women or at least was interested in learning more. I guess I wanted insurance.

"Right away I knew I could trust him. I felt it was fate that brought us together. I helped out a little, however. I only took seven workshops before I met him. The odds were in my favor that I would meet a man interested in a quality relationship."

Letting Go of the Past

Sometimes as we get older we just assume things will be the same. We don't realize that patterns can and do change. Both men and women hold back from getting involved when they assume that every relationship has to be the same. When we take time to learn from the mistakes in our past relationships, we can have confidence that our future relationships will be better.

Pauline worked as a manager for the phone company. She said, "I met my husband, Craig, at a dinner party. My friends introduced us, but I wasn't the least bit interested in getting involved again. I had been married twice before. But there was something different about Craig. I wasn't physically attracted to him at all, but he was the most interesting man I had ever met.

"Craig is seven years older than me, but that adds to my attraction to him. I have always been mature for my age. He responds to things in such a thoughtful and considerate manner. I admire his wisdom about the world.

"I realized that I just needed someone who had more maturity to stimulate me. In previous relationships, I had always followed my sexual attractions, but this time, even though there was no sexual chemistry, I felt that he was very interesting. He pursued me. After a while, it finally happened. I was really surprised to experience that I felt a passionate physical attraction for him as well. It took a while to build, but for years now it just keeps on burning."

THE FOURTH ELEMENT OF CHEMISTRY: RESONANCE

The fourth element of chemistry is resonance. Soul mates have similar values that resonate. This element of chemistry inspires us to be the best we can be. When we are with our partner, what is most important to him or her resonates with what is really important to us.

Your partner's values concerning God, family, work, recreation, politics, money, character, sex, and marriage resonate within you and inspire you. You are able to see the good in your soul mate and respect and admire his or her values. To have similar values does not mean that you will necessarily think and feel the same way about issues. You will be able to respect your partner's viewpoint and admire where he or she is coming from.

One person could be a Democrat and the other a Republican. Even though they have different approaches, they both value a fair government for the people. But if one valued the tyranny of dictatorship and the other valued democracy, there would not be enough resonance to create soul chemistry.

The most common place people find their soul mate is at their church, their synagogue, or some other place of worship. This is because people of similar values will be drawn to a particular spiritual institution. They are able to meet people whose spiritual values resonate with their own.

Roberto felt chemistry with Lucia because their values resonated. Roberto, an engineer, said, "I met my wife, Lucia, at church. We attended several classes together and eventually went out. I noticed her right away, but as I got to know her I fell in love with her. I think sharing the same faith made it easier for us to accept and trust each other. We have so many differences, but we do share the same beliefs about life and family. I respected her values and I wanted her to be the mother of my children. I feel so fortunate to have met her. I think it was meant to be."

Sharing values makes us compatible with someone. It helps us to overcome the challenges that come with any relationship. When we experience the inevitable ups and downs, we can always get back up when deep in our souls we resonate with the highest values of our partner. This compatibility allows us to make compromises without giving up who we are or what is important to us. By going to places where our values are supported, we are also sure to meet our soul mate.

HAVING FUN TOGETHER

Another place to find a soul mate is on vacation. If you like to dance, party, and have fun, then a vacation where eveyone eats together and shares recreational activities is ideal for meeting your soul mate. Cruises and resorts like Club Med are excellent places to meet a soul mate.

Crystal, a schoolteacher, shared, "I met my husband, Charlie, at a Club Med resort. We were both recreational instructors. We both loved water sports and enjoyed having lots of fun. Charlie is a great dancer and I just fell in love with him. I think it was fate that brought us together at that particular location. There were so many other locations to pick from and this was not even the one I wanted to work at. It was the only one that had a job opening.

"Charlie now works in the publishing business. We still love going on vacations together and we live by the water. When we fight about things we take time out to go dancing or sailing and then it is so much easier to make up."

21

101 Places to Meet Your Soul Mate

By combining the four elements of chemistry—different interests, complementary needs, maturity, and resonant values—we achieve the possibility of lasting and passionate love. To find a partner and create a relationship with this kind of potential, we need to look in the right places. We don't have to wait for a chance or accidental meeting. We can begin looking for our soul mate by putting ourselves in places where the odds are in our favor. Let's review all of the different ways and places to find a soul mate and explore a few more. As you read the list, see if you can recognize which of the different elements of chemistry you are sure to find.

101 WAYS TO MEET YOUR SOUL MATE

1. Attend a friend's party, give a party yourself, go dancing with friends. There is still no better way to meet someone than being introduced by a friend.

2. Call up a friend's date if and when they stop seeing each other. Be certain your friend is no longer seeing the person.

3. Get involved with an old friend whose spouse has died or who is now divorced. Even if there was no attraction in the past, it may spring up now that your friend is available.

4. Join the Adopt-a-Single program. Ask a couple to adopt you for a three-month period and introduce you to their friends. Ask them how they met and then try going to similar places. Spend time with couples who are happily married; whatever it is they have will start to rub off on you. Having a positive picture in your mind of what a relationship can be like will also help you pick the right person for you. If you are negative about the opposite sex, then you will keep getting negative relationships.

5. Join a community cause or participate in a service activity like feeding the poor or helping children without parents. In the process, you will not only feel good but you will meet people who admire you and appreciate your goodwill. This will lead to meeting your soul mate.

6. Go to places where you have a lot of expertise and people feel comfortable coming up to you for support or advice. Do not hesitate to meet someone by offering your help or assistance.

7. Take a class that is particularly popular because the professor or teacher is so interesting and stimulating.

Then, when you meet someone, you will also seem very interesting. Ask a potential partner to help you with your homework for a class or do a class project together.

8. Go to school reunions. So many people meet again and fall in love. Sometimes we're just not ready for our soul mate, but the chemistry can remain.

9. Go to places where you don't have any expertise so that you feel comfortable going up to someone and getting to know him or her by asking for help. A man can also charm a woman when he is open to getting advice from her.

10. Become friends with the friends of someone you would really like to meet. Be up-front in your friendship by asking questions about their friend.

11. Go to places where the numbers work in your favor. Women should go to places where many men are present and vice versa.

12. Go to a town meeting. You can easily meet people and talk about their views on what is being discussed. To hear and support a person's beliefs and convictions when that person is feeling challenged can make him or her a friend for life.

13. Go to places where people are interested in things that you are not interested in. If you are not interested in museums, then go to a museum and ask questions of people who are art lovers.

14. In a restaurant, a woman should get up several times and walk to the rest room so that a man has a chance to see her and be interested. He should take the risk and get up to meet her if he is interested. He can simply give her a card if he is shy.

15. Make eye contact with the person you are interested in. A woman can look away, talk to a friend, ask her to look, then talk a little bit, look back, and smile. This gives a man a clear message that she is interested.

16. Go to places where you like the way you look. If you like wearing a bathing suit, then go to the beach. If you don't, don't bother. Go where you feel most beautiful or handsome.

17. Wear a uniform occasionally, even when you are off duty. It makes you more accessible to others. They feel they can ask you a question or ask for your help in some manner.

18. Create opportunities to meet apart from the group you are with. It can be very intimidating for a man to approach a woman in a group of six women. If he is rejected, he knows all six will be discussing him.

19. At a party, when a woman continues to move around, a man has an easier time approaching her. Avoid getting stuck on the couch.

20. People are always most comfortable talking and meeting in kitchens. Hang out where the food is.

21. Participate in church or school fund-raisers, gatherings, events, and celebrations.

22. Even better, help put on church, school, and community events.

23. Join the support team at your church. It is always easiest to get to know people when they are in the mode of service. They can offer to help and they can ask for help.

24. Go to places where you are not very competent and need the assistance of others.

25. If you are a single parent, get to know all your children's friends' parents. Become friends by sharing the baby-sitting. Ask them to take your child sometimes; then they will feel comfortable asking you. Then ask them to adopt you as their single friend and help you to meet someone.

26. Volunteer to handle the seating or name tags at a school, church, or community celebration. This way you get to make contact with everyone single.

27. Help out or learn to facilitate a Mars/Venus workshop or any other singles program and meet people with similar values.

28. If you are a Democrat, visit a gathering or rally of Republicans. Let them try to convince you of their point of view. This makes for great conversation and connection.

29. If you are not interested in gardening, then take a class in gardening, go to a public garden, or buy vegetables from a market where people who enjoy gardening shop.

30. If you are not into history, go on a town walking tour. Ask lots of questions and meet the people in your community.

31. If you can't operate a VCR, spend time in an electronic equipment store and ask questions. Or go to the yearly conventions that showcase the latest gadgets.

32. If you are not interested in therapy and have never done it, take a personal growth workshop and meet people who are interested in and benefit from therapy.

33. If you don't watch *Monday Night Football,* then start going to local sporting events at all levels, from kids' soccer, baseball, basketball, and football games all the way up to professional sports. Ask lots of questions to learn all the rules and who the players are.

34. Bring food to community events.

35. If you are not religious, begin visiting your local church, or synagogue, or some other place of worship. Ask your friends which one to visit. Participate in their classes.

36. If you always buy books, try hanging out in the library, where people read but don't buy.

37. If you don't read a lot, try hanging out in a bookstore and ask people who their favorite authors are. Strike

up a conversation and get to know someone by asking more questions about favorite books.

38. Go to book signings of authors you really like.

39. If you don't eat out, try dining out more often.

40. If you have a favorite restaurant, try a new one occasionally.

41. If you are not a morning person, get up earlier and go for a walk or jog and meet all the morning people.

42. If you rarely walk, try walking around your neighborhood at the same time for a week. Then change the time the next week. Continue to change the time, and eventually you will meet more people. Repetition of contact creates a familiarity that can stimulate chemistry.

43. If you always go to movies, try hanging out at the video store. Direct your questions about movies to people whom you feel some chemistry with.

44. If you rarely go to the theater, try hanging out at the bars and restaurants people visit after the theater.

45. If you love the theater but don't go to movies, then go to a new movie and wait in line. Lines are great for getting to meet people.

46. If you don't go to openings or big events because you don't like crowds, then your soul mate is probably there missing you.

47. If you like opera but don't like pop concerts, then try going to a concert with friends. You may meet your soul mate.

48. If you don't like to dance, then definitely get out there and dance. Take dance lessons and go to dance competitions.

49. If you like to eat out, then take cooking lessons and learn to cook.

50. If you love to cook, never miss an opportunity to cook for your friends. Let it be known to all what a good cook you are.

51. If you drink and generally hang out at a bar, then try hanging out in a coffee shop where no alcohol is served. Your soul mate may not drink.

52. If you don't like loud music, get some friends together and go to where the music is loud. Wear earplugs and dance a lot. If you meet someone, then let him or her know you would like to talk sometime when you can hear each other.

53. If you are not drawn to water sports, then go on a vacation where most of the people love water sports.

54. If you've never been on a cruise, or you are not even interested in one, that's all the more reason to go on a cruise and meet someone who loves cruises.

55. If you hate standing in lines, then your soul mate may be the patient one waiting in a line somewhere. If you

just can't bear the line, at least go to openings and popular events to walk up and down the line as if you are looking for someone.

56. If you bring a bag lunch to work, try eating out sometimes.

57. If you don't take breaks at work, take one for tea or coffee—you may meet someone new.

58. If you eat out a lot, spend a lot of time in your local market. Your soul mate may just love to make dinners.

59. If you prefer heath foods, your soul mate may be waiting for you to inspire him or her. Try eating at fast-food restaurants sometimes.

60. If you generally like very formal and fancy entertainment and food, try going out with friends to a more simple, relaxed, and less expensive establishment.

61. If a woman always wears a lot of makeup or jewelry, she should try wearing less and sometimes none. Her soul mate will love her just the way she is, and it may take some time for him to also like her in makeup.

62. If a woman always dresses in a sexy manner and attracts the attention of many men, she should try dressing in a less provocative manner and attract the attention of more discerning guys who are also interested in getting to know her.

63. If you don't like getting dressed up, then pick an event each month where dressing up is required. Cruises are great for this. There are many formal events. Every man looks great in a tux, even if he doesn't like getting all dressed up. Women get a chance to shine when they dress up.

64. If you like to sit by the ocean and not at the pool on vacations, then try a change. Sit by the pool each day to meet the people there as well.

65. If you don't like the sand and prefer sitting around the pool, try going for long walks by the ocean. Your soul mate probably loves the sand.

66. If you don't like sunbathing or you don't have a tan, then head for the resorts of sun worshipers. Your soul mate probably loves sunbathing.

67. If you don't like camping, start doing it. Hang out at wilderness stores and ask lots of questions. Get with some friends and go camping in a place where you will also meet other campers and hikers.

68. If you don't like to bike, then start building up those muscles and go on a group biking adventure. If you make new friends, even when none of them is the one, they may connect you to the right person.

69. If you don't like to ski, then go skiing with friends and hang out in the common areas where people eat and drink or spend time in hot tubs or spas.

70. Men can meet so many women by going to aerobics classes, while women can meet men in the workout room. They can easily meet by spending some time at the gym.

71. Go on an adventure tour with others and make new friends.

72. If you like to work out or play inside, then try exercising or playing outside. There is generally a lot of chemistry between inside and outside people.

73. If you are a morning person, make the effort to go out and stay up late. The person for you may be a night owl or a party person who needs your stability.

74. Participate in school projects like plays, celebrations, fund-raisers, and sports activities. You will have the opportunity to meet all the single parents. Even if you don't have children, help a friend out with his or her children and take them to their events. When you get involved with a person who has children, you will get the extra benefit of his or her gratitude to you for being there for the kids as well.

75. Baby-sit for friends and stroll with their child through the park, or borrow a friend's dog for a walk. Women are particularly attracted to a man who can care for a child or a pet. When a man or a woman is walking a dog, it is easy for someone to strike up a conversation about the pet. Everyone is attracted to a baby and feels free to strike up a conversation.

76. If you like to dress up in a formal manner, then try wearing more casual clothes.

77. If you are always very organized and plan out your free time, make no plans and just follow your instincts. Sometimes we are so much in our heads, figuring out what to do, that our gut instincts don't have the opportunity to move us toward our soul mate.

78. If you always go to places with friends, try going alone. When we are alone, we tend to feel our need for support more and are more receptive to meeting someone. Others are more inclined to offer help and assistance when you are alone.

79. If you have never ridden a horse or you don't like horses, it's time to go for a ride.

80. If you don't like to drive fast, go to a racetrack or an amateur racing day. Quite often, when one soul mate likes to drive fast, the other likes it slow and safe.

81. If you like to live in the lap of luxury, try going for a backpacking trip in the wilderness and you may meet your soul mate. You don't have to go alone; there are all kinds of groups that will support you. Go to a store that sells camping equipment, and the staff will be able to give you the help you need.

82. If you have never been to a garage sale, then this is the time to start shopping. If you don't go to sales, then your perfect partner might wait until there is a sale before going shopping. You may need a little more frugality in

your life and you will find him or her at a sale trying to save money.

83. If you have a definite routine, try changing it to create the opportunity for change to happen. Try changing the route you take to work. Eventually take all possible routes.

84. If you always park in a garage at work, try parking down the street and walking a distance to work. It is good exercise and you may meet new people.

85. Go alone on a river-rafting adventure with a group. When you don't know anyone and you're having an exciting adventure, a new part of you will come out.

86. If you like going to rock and roll concerts, try going to the symphony or the opera. During intermission, you may find your partner by going to food and drink counters and by checking out the bathroom lines.

87. Go out to find a partner on weeknights. Don't wait for the weekend. During the week, people are much less likely to be on a date and therefore much more available and interested in getting to know someone.

88. Quite often soul mates have a different temperature preference. If you generally go to warm climates, try going to a cooler climate. Go skiing or ice-skating. If you like the cold, then try going to the beach on a hot day to find your partner.

89. If you are not interested in computers or high-tech equipment, then go to a computer fair and ask a lot of

questions. People will love to help you. Men particularly love to be experts.

90. If you are not interested in having a great view, then your soul mate will always prefer a view. Go to places that promise a commanding and spectacular view to meet your soul mate.

91. Be a tourist in your own town. Pretend that you are alone and from out of town. You will meet all kinds of people who want to share your town with them. You will discover things that you never knew existed and in the process could meet the right person for you. Get help from the office of tourism. Visit all the sights, parks, museums, colleges, and universities. Take guided tours. Your soul mate may be a tourist who is being guided to come to your town to find you.

92. If you don't like weddings, this is the time to start going. People are most inspired at weddings. If you are not drawn, then your partner probably is. You may need him or her to inspire you.

93. Visit comedy clubs with friends. When you are laughing and having a good time, it brings out the best in you. Sometimes when you are feeling your best, you will attract the best person for you.

94. When you are in a bad mood, do something that you really don't like doing. This way it can't make you feel worse. Sometimes when we are in a bad mood, deep inside we are feeling our deep need to be loved and to be loving. This vulnerability can attract the right per-

son who has what we need. Sometimes it is when we are down and out, when we really need help, that God's angels bring us a miracle.

95. Meet your soul mate through placing or answering a singles ad. When writing your ad, remember to express your most positive self and clearly maintain the appropriate role. A woman's role should be similar to that of a shopper or the role of someone offering a job. She should not say anything to win a man's interest; instead, she writes what she wants in a man and what she enjoys most. A man, however, needs to maintain the role of applying for the job. He needs to talk about himself in glowing terms and describe what he has to offer and is hoping to offer. In short, a man describes what he has to give and a woman describes what she would like to receive.

96. Dating services are a great way to meet the right person for you. They make it so much easier to get to know a person before actually meeting. It is similar to having a friend introduce you to someone. You get to feel as if you know something about a person before you meet. If you would never consider a dating service, then your soul mate probably would.

97. If you have finished going to school, try continuing your education. Take classes in things that you have never studied, particularly when they involve labs, projects, or discussions.

98. Join a chorus and sing—particularly if you don't like to sing, you can't sing, or you are too serious. Singing

frees the soul and will connect you to your feelings of joy and inspiration.

99. Go on a vacation where people pay one price and then share everything. Some people go to Club Med or other similar resorts.

100. Your grocery store is a great place to meet someone by comparing recipes and asking for advice. Make it a practice to always ask people questions or offer advice while shopping.

101. On an airplane, hang out near the rest rooms and strike up a conversation while waiting in line. It is also easy to start a conversation by asking where someone is from and where he or she is going. Be sure to walk up and down the aisles to be seen and to see if your soul mate is there.

By referring to this list again and again, you will not only be inspired and motivated to keep dating but you will more quickly find your soul mate. By visiting places where you have a better chance to find chemistry, you will awaken the elements of chemistry in yourself. As a result, you will be a more fulfilled person capable of enjoying the adventures of being single.

22

And They Lived Happily Ever After

Some people do live happily ever after. They haven't studied the five stages of dating, nor did they take a workshop to discover how to pick the right person for them. They just did it. They either gracefully went through the five stages without even knowing it or they just lucked out and picked the right person anyway. After getting married they gradually learned the skills of making a marriage work on their own.

For most of us, finding the right person and being able to make a relationship work are important skills we need to learn, develop, and practice. It is easy to become discouraged in our journey to find the right person if we don't understand that there are many different roads to reach the same destination.

THREE STYLES OF LEARNING

Finding a partner is like any other skill in life; it takes talent, education, and practice. The more information, education, and experience you have, the better you will be. Through gaining all three, your chances of mastering a skill are the highest. Shakespeare alluded to these three styles of learning when he said, "Some are born great, some achieve greatness, and some have greatness thrust upon them." Another way of putting it is that there are runners, walkers, and jumpers. Let's explore these styles in greater detail.

Style One: Runners

Some people are just gifted. They are born with an enormous talent. For example, they can sit down at a piano and practically start playing right away. They can just hear a song and then play it. They don't need to read music. These gifted students or prodigies are the runners. They quickly find success and achievement in a particular endeavor. In relationships, runners are those few who just meet someone, fall in love, and live happily ever after. They are the minority. Most of us are not runners.

Style Two: Walkers

Most people are walkers. They learn from a teacher and through trial and error. These people do not have greatness given to them. Instead they earn it, they attain it, they seek it out and find it, they do something to make it happen. These people discover their talent through education and a series of life experiences. In learning to play the piano, for example, they gradually learn to play with the expert guidance of a teacher and by learning to read music.

In relationships, this can be likened to learning from each relationship how to understand and "read" the opposite sex correctly. By steadily moving ahead, walkers eventually find the right person for them. Every relationship assists them in moving on to finding the right person for them. Through taking the time to move through the different stages of dating and ending relationships with a positive note, they are able to hit the target and find their soul mate.

Style Three: Jumpers

Jumpers are late bloomers. They have greatness thrust upon them. For many years they may appear not to be moving forward or progressing. They may even seem to be going backward. They may practice and practice but to no avail. Although it may seem that they are not learning, they are. What goes in eventually comes out. With enough observation of others playing the piano, with enough listening to music and enough practice, they just start playing one day.

Einstein was a jumper when it came to learning to speak. As a child, he said nothing for years. He just listened to others speak. He observed and took it all in. Then, at five years old, he began to speak in full sentences. He jumped from saying nothing to complete sentences and skipped the stages in between.

In relationships, jumpers meet the right person for them long after all their friends are married. To their great surprise, they find someone, fall in love, and live happily ever after. There are many people who are forty or fifty years old who have not gotten married or have not experienced a deeply intimate relationship. As a result of reaching a certain level of maturity, their innate talent and wisdom for having a loving and intimate relationship suddenly emerges and they meet their soul mate. Even if you are a jumper and your time is yet to come, the wisdom of the five stages will assist you in having more fulfilling relationships until the time is right for you.

By understanding these three different styles of learning, we can more easily appreciate the importance of the five stages of dating. As we continue to get closer to finding true love, it is easy to be thrown off track if we lack an understanding of our differences.

DIFFERENCES ARE NOT OBSTACLES

Even when we feel chemistry with someone, we can easily make the mistake of assuming that we are just too different to make a relationship work. This is why the insights of *Men Are from Mars, Women Are from Venus* have helped so many relationships. Couples commonly make the mistake of assuming that they are just too different ever to get their needs met.

In many cases they were able to begin getting what they needed by understanding their differences, and they discovered that differences were a source of fulfillment and support rather than an obstacle. In a similar manner, when you meet someone who has different interests, it does not mean that a relationship is hopeless.

With good communication skills, different interests don't have to be a source of conflict. When a woman complains that her husband plays too much golf or is too involved in sports, his interest in sports is not really the problem. The problem is their inability to nurture each other's needs.

RESENTMENT CREATES POLARIZATION

When men and women misunderstand each other, misinterpret each other's actions, and miscommunicate their feelings, they are unable to successfully nurture each other and get what they need. The result of this is resentment.

When resentment builds, our different interests become more extreme. We begin to polarize. These are some examples of how resentment and polarization affect a relationship:

How Resentment Creates Polarization

She wants to go out; he becomes very tired.

He wants to go to a movie; she wants to go to a concert.

She wants to have Chinese food; he wants Italian.

He wants sex; she is not in the mood.

She wants to go for a walk; he wants to watch TV.

He is late for work; she wants to talk.

In each of these examples their interests and desires are polarized. When one person wants something, the other wants something else.

> When resentment builds, then our different interests become more extreme.

The more we are polarized, the more interested we become in the things our partners are not interested in. When resentment is released with better communication, understanding, and forgiveness, our differences do not show up as obstacles.

> As we love our partners, over time we actually start becoming more interested in their interests.

We are attracted to people with different interests because in some way they make us feel whole; they balance out our lives. By means of their different interests, they express some aspect of themselves that we have not yet developed within ourselves. Over time, as our love unites us, we begin to share more and more interests. Their presence stimulates our growth and keeps us more interested in all the different aspects of living.

SOUL MATES HARMONIZE THEIR DIFFERENCES

It is very important not to expect our partners to resonate so much with our values that they think and feel the way we do. We must be careful not to conclude that resonating values means having the same interests or even the same needs.

As we have already explored, soul mates have different interests and they have different emotional needs as well. Resonance of values creates a basis from which we can work through our differences and find fair compromises. Resonance helps soul mates harmonize their differences.

> Resonance of values creates a basis
> from which we can work through our
> differences and find fair compromises.

Resonance helps us to understand and support our partner's point of view or needs, even when our perspective is different. Although it is sometimes difficult to find a win-win solution, with good communication, love, and shared values, it is possible.

While our differences are definitely inconvenient, they stretch us to be more whole, loving, and considerate. We are attracted to someone who is different in order to satisfy the deep yearning of our soul to expand and embrace that which is beyond ourselves. In this way, we expand to more of what we can be. In this sense, a relationship assists and supports us in being all that we can be.

> **We are attracted to someone who is different
> in order to satisfy the deep yearning
> of our soul to expand and embrace that
> which is beyond ourselves.**

To maintain a realistic expectation of how soul mates harmonize their differences, let's explore a few examples of how we can be very different but have the same values.

- Vincent and Angela vote very differently, but their values resonate. They both care about and are committed to the well-being of the community.

- Coleman likes to buy things on impulse and Robin likes to take a lot of time researching a purchase. They both care about having nice things around them. When they buy something together, Coleman now takes much longer than he would on his own. Many times what they get ends up being much nicer. At other times when they buy something for him, they just get it right away.

- Leann likes therapy and Jack likes football. They both do what is important for them to relax and get in touch with their feelings. They respect each other's different approach to finding some peace of mind.

- Jerry likes to not talk much about his problems, while Barbara likes to get it all out. They cope with their issues differently, but they perfectly complement each other. He likes to watch the news and she likes to give it. When she needs to talk, he has learned to be a great listener. Sometimes he then talks about his day too.

- Lucy is really sensitive about certain things and Roger isn't. She gets upset when there is a change of plans and he just goes with the flow. Roger is still able to respect this difference because they share similar values. They both make their love more important than their differences.

  As he takes the time to listen to what bothers her, he is respectful even though he doesn't feel as strongly bothered as she does. He can be supportive even though he doesn't necessarily agree with her point of view. They agree to disagree sometimes.

- Claudia is really involved with parenting and Clarence isn't. Clarence is a hard worker who wants to provide the very best for his family. They could experience a lot of conflict, but they don't. They are aware that they share the same good intent—for their children to have the best they can provide. They just show that intent differently.

- Keith wants sex more than Theresa. They both value intimacy. He likes physical intimacy more, while she likes sharing her life and feelings. This understanding that they really share the same intent—to get close—makes it easy to make compromises at times without feeling they have to give up what is important to them. Theresa is also able to recognize that his desire for sex does not mean he doesn't care about her. It is his way of feeling intimate with her. It helps him to feel connected to her.

- Bob likes high-tech equipment, while Ava likes things simple and old-fashioned. They both care a good deal about beauty in their home. Shopping and remodeling for them can be quite a challenge, but they end up with something much more interesting.

- David is interested in new cars and Doris likes keeping things for a long time. They both value getting the full benefit out of something. He wants to make use of the latest cars being developed and she wants to use what she has, so he gets new cars and she keeps hers.

- Thelma is into the environmental movement and Jacob is into his business. They both care about the world. He focuses more on helping people in his work, while she helps people by being an activist and writing letters to the government.

- Paul likes parties and gatherings; Anna likes to spend time with a few friends at most. They both care about quality interactions. It is just that a party brings out the best in Paul, while an intimate gathering brings out the best in Anna. They simply alternate so both get what they need. Over time, she begins to like parties more and he grows to enjoy quieter social activities as well.

- Jackson likes to travel and Martha likes to stay put in her garden. They both value quality relaxation time. She wishes sometimes that he would be more interested in

364 • JOHN GRAY

the garden, while he sometimes wishes she would enjoy traveling more. Yet the most important thing is that they love each other very much.

Over the years, Jackson has grown to appreciate and enjoy the garden much more, while Martha enjoys traveling more. Through respecting their differences and making some sacrifices, they eventually grew closer. What was an annoyance in the beginning is now a source of greater fulfillment.

With this understanding, we can clearly see our different interests as a source of stimulation and growth, not as an obstacle. Because of the differences, there will always be room to grow together. When we feel chemistry, it is a sign that this growth is possible.

LOOKING IN THE RIGHT PLACE BUT FINDING THE WRONG PERSON TO LOVE

By looking in the right places you will eventually find the right person, but sometimes you may find the wrong partner even in the right places. You may feel strong chemistry, but it is with a person who turns out to be way off the mark. This is all part of the learning process. By clearly learning from our mistakes, we will gain the ability to distinguish between healthy and unhealthy chemistry.

By learning to recognize unhealthy chemistry and not act on it, you increase your ability to feel healthy chemistry. If you keep getting intimately involved in relationships based on unhealthy chemistry, your ability to feel healthy chemistry with the right person is minimized. To live happily ever after and find your soul mate, it is very important to distinguish between these two kinds of chemistry.

UNHEALTHY EMOTIONAL CHEMISTRY

When a man feels needed, the chemistry he experiences tends to be healthy, but when a man is primarily motivated by the possibility of getting his needs and wants satisfied, then the chemistry he feels is not necessarily very healthy. If he is just thinking about what he can get, then it is unhealthy. He may be a little unhealthy, like having a cold or the flu, or he may be really sick and need the help of a professional.

When chemistry is unhealthy, it doesn't mean anything about the ultimate potential of a relationship. When the problem is corrected, there may or may not be a potential for healthy chemistry between two particular people.

When chemistry is unhealthy, if you are careful to follow the stages of dating and don't rush into intimacy, the unhealthy chemistry will dissipate. During the five stages of getting to know a partner, the unhealthy chemistry will lessen. If you are in the right relationship, chemistry will return in a healthy way. These are some warning signals of unhealthy chemistry for men.

Warning Signals of Unhealthy Chemistry in Men

- He is attracted to wealthy women because he needs the money or doesn't want to work.

- He falls in love with his nurse: His attraction needs to be tested after he gets well. Only then can he know if he has something to offer her other than his appreciation for taking such good care of him.

- He feels he needs a very attractive woman to prove to others that he is a success.

- He feels the need for sexual gratification from a sexually assertive or suggestive woman but clearly knows that he would not like to pursue a relationship with her.

- He wants to move in with a woman because he wants to share the rent. Instead of moving in with her, he can easily find a buddy to share a place with.

- He wants to get intimately involved right after ending a relationship. He is like a hungry person, starved for love and companionship. His discernment is low. After he gets back on his feet, he may easily lose his feeling of attraction to the woman.

- He feels a woman loves him so much that he doesn't want to end a good thing, but he clearly has no intention of marrying her one day.

- He is attracted to a woman because she says, "You are the only man I have ever really liked. You are not like other men." This may sound like a compliment, but it is a sign that she still has big issues about men. When she finds out that he is from Mars like other men, there will be a big disappointment.

- He is involved with one woman and he feels chemistry for another. Certainly this will happen, but if he encourages it by pursuing or flirting with the other woman, he will experience even more chemistry with other women. In his primary relationship, the chemistry will not have a chance to grow.

- He feels chemistry for a woman who is not available or not available to him.

- He gets involved because a woman puts pressure on him, but he doesn't feel a sexual attraction. She may even assure him that it will develop over time. While a woman's sexual feelings do develop over time, a man tends to feel it from the start or not at all.

- A woman says she loves him, but what he does is never enough to satisfy her. He will have a love-hate relationship. Certainly every woman continues to want more, but he should be getting a clear message that who he is and what he provides are enough.

Warning Signals of Unhealthy Chemistry in Women

When a woman feels needed more than she feels she is getting her needs met, she begins to feel unhealthy chemistry. These are some examples:

- She feels sorry for a man and worries about how he will survive without her.

- She feels that she just wants to love him and she doesn't care about what she gets in return. Although this sounds noble, it will weaken him and she will eventually feel resentful.

- A man says he needs her desperately and she is so flattered that she gets involved.

- A man is also seeing other women, but when he is with her he says she is the most special. If a man is seeing other women, then she is just fooling herself. There is no such thing as being the most special woman if he is dating other women. It means that she clearly isn't the most special even if he says she is.

- She sees a man's potential and feels that with her help he could be great. When a woman takes credit for a man's success, it is very likely that he will leave her one day to find a woman that he can take credit for making happy.

- A man has a destructive habit and she feels she can help him. This chemistry occurs because a woman with low self-esteem feels better about herself when she feels that her problems are not her fault. By having someone to blame for her problems, she can hide from the truth that she is responsible for her life.

- She feels sexually attracted to a man right away. This is a sign that she is reacting to her expectation of who this man is, not the man himself. Before acting on this chemistry, she needs to make sure they have moved through the first three stages.

- She feels eager to accommodate and please a man. This is clearly a sign that she feels a man can give her what she needs, but she has not yet gotten what she needs. She should be careful to hold back until she actually gets what she needs.

- She feels strong chemistry but clearly feels a man will have to make changes before she will get what she needs.

She hopes that her love will change him. It is not fair to her or him if she gives of herself now, and then expects more from him later. This tendency will backfire.

- She doesn't feel respected by a man, but she is understanding of why he can't do the right things. When he is disrespectful, he will justify it by either blaming his past or her.

- She feels sexual chemistry, but she clearly doesn't trust that she will ever get her other needs satisfied.

By not understanding the signs of unhealthy chemistry, we can easily make the mistake of getting involved with someone who is clearly not right for us.

IT IS NORMAL TO MAKE MISTAKES

It is normal to make mistakes in finding the right person for you. The difference between success and failure is being able to learn from our mistakes to become more discerning. If you want to hit a home run, the chances of striking out go up dramatically. Babe Ruth, who held the record for the most home runs, also held the record for the most strikeouts.

If you want your relationship to be more than what previous generations have experienced, then new skills must be learned. If you want to run fast, then your chances of falling also increase. The secret of success is to get up and keep going. You can do it. Once it happens, you will look back and realize that it happened at the right time for you.

To find a soul mate, not just a secure partner, takes new insight, education, and lots of practice. With this kind of support, you can develop your ability to navigate through the five stages of dating to experience true and lasting love.

By weathering the storms and droughts of love that inevitably arise from time to time, by repeatedly overcoming the challenge of harmonizing differences, and by coming back to your commitment to having a quality relationship, you will find your soul mate and live happily ever after.